Peter M. Bitsilli

CHEKHOV'S ART

A Stylistic Analysis

Translated by
Toby W. Clyman & Edwina Jannie Cruise

Ardis / Ann Arbor

Ardis Publishers
2901 Heatherway
Ann Arbor, Michigan 48104

Library of Congress Cataloging in Publication Data

Bitsilli, P. M. (Petr Mikhailovich), 1879-1953.
Chekhov's art, a stylistic analysis.

Translation of: Tvorchestvo Chekhova, opty stili-
sticheskogo analiza.
Includes index.
1. Chekhov, Anton Pavlovich, 1960-1904—Technique.
I. Clyman, Toby W. II. Cruise, Edwina. III. Title.
PG 3458.28B513 1983   891.72'3   83-2493
ISBN 0-88233-489-1

CONTENTS

Preface

Peter Mikhailovich Bitsilli (1879-1953) served a long and distinguished career as Professor of Modern History at the University of Sophia. A prolific scholar with diverse interests, he wrote both in Russian and in Bulgarian on topics ranging from Greek and Roman history to verbs in the Russian language. In the west, however, his reputation is based largely on his studies in nineteenth-century Russian literature. Most of his articles originally appeared in journals with limited circulation; his work written during the war years (which includes some of his best criticism) was published at the University of Sophia and has, until recently, been especially difficult to obtain.[1]

Chekhov's Art: A Stylistic Analysis, the work by which he is best known, is a case in point. It was originally published in 1942 in the journal of the history and philological faculty of the University of Sophia. Never reprinted in the Soviet Union, it was considered a bibliographic rarity until 1966. In that year Bitsilli's study of Chekhov appeared in a German translation by Vincent Sieveking (Forum Slavicum); a year later University Microfilms (Ann Arbor, Michigan) issued a microfilm-xerography facsimile of the original Russian text.

Chekhov's Art reveals the trademarks of Bitsilli's approach to literature. Although he has benefited from the critical insights emanating from the Formalist movement, he acknowledges no authority higher than his own ability to read a literary text. He is eclectic, sometimes unpredictable and in the context of the period in which he wrote, controversial. His analysis is unencumbered by the narrow historical bias which informed much of literary criticism published in Soviet Russia at the time. (For example, he steers clear of the familiar linkage of life and works [*zhizn' i tvorchestvo*];

references to Chekhov's biography are few.) His rejection of Marxist esthetics may well explain his relative obscurity as a literary critic in the Soviet Union today. Bitsilli's work is not included in K.D. Muratova's 1962 Academy bibliography of nineteenth-century Russian literature.

At the very outset of his study, Bitsilli pointedly denies a historically determined view of Chekhov. Contemporary readers, he writes, "saw the heroes as typical 'victims of stagnation' and 'superfluous people.'" The modern reader, however, "now interprets a Chekhov character independent of and without reference to cultural traits of a bygone era. . . .

> If now we react to Chekhov's works more intensely than did readers of an earlier period, this response is directly linked to their formal excellence. In other words, what is usually taken to be the content of a work (which now least of all commands our attention) is subordinate to another underlying content of quite a different nature, one inseparable from form. (3)

"To interpret Chekhov," Bitsilli emphatically states, "means to elucidate the elements of his formal excellence and at the same time the underlying content of Chekhov's work" (3). In his approach here Bitsilli comes closest in spirit to structuralist poetics. Only after he establishes concrete evidence of a system at work—the complex linguistic conventions and the patterns of internal organization characteristic of Chekhov's stories—does he examine the stories as organic entities, with an eye to the worldview they reveal.[2]

Initially Bitsilli relies on comparative evidence to identify Chekhov's "creative individuality." "Every artist has, figuratively speaking, his stereotypes, clichés, recurrent words, images and set phrases which testify to his view of life, his 'obsessions' and his creative 'complex'" (23). To define this creative complex, Bitsilli first isolates elements in Chekhov that belong to a "common pool of knowledge" among writers and considers how Chekhov dealt with these communal resources. He then establishes links to major writers such as Lermontov, Gogol, Tolstoy and especially Turgenev, and examines how Chekhov reworked what he assimilated from them. Having determined the extent and character of this indebtedness, Bitsilli then turns to the distinguishing features in Chekhov's art.

The body of Bitsilli's study divides into three topics which provide a framework to describe style and structure in Chekhov: impressionism, laconicism and musicality. Bitsilli uses the term "impressionism" to characterize one of the most essential components in Chekhov's artistic system: the method by which he structures empirical reality for the reader's apprehension. Here Bitsilli distinguishes between prose or analytic style and poetry or synthetic style. The prose writer tends toward a comprehensive, sequential and mimetic reproduction of life; he examines empirical data from a multitude of viewpoints. The poet—and Bitsilli places Chekhov in this category—conveys reality symbolically and impressionistically. He presents the reader with a vision of reality limited to a specific moment in time and confined within the responses of a single viewer. This circumscribed perspective controls perception. Whereas observable reality is organic and indivisible, the poet isolates a limited number of details to convey the sense of an object, situation or emotion. He thus renders the world as a series of powerful "partial" images from which the whole may be inferred.

Bitsilli finds evidence for this impressionistic tendency in Chekhov in his abundant use of impersonal constructions such as "to seem" [*kazat'sya*]. Expressions of this type prompt the reader to apprehend isolated images collectively despite their sequential presentation: "'to seem' renders the perception of separate objects and separate phenomena as an indivisible whole" (57). Moreover such impersonal constructions suggest that man is not in control of the logical order of his perceptions. He glimpses reality in a set of images to which he is a passive observer; he becomes the object rather than the subject of his impressions.[3] A prose or "analytic" style denies the possibility of structuring reality in this way:

> Fidelity to logic and a hierarchical principle—the "analytic" tendency—hinders the fusion of images; ... it impedes the merging of sensory perceptions as well as the emotions evoked by them in the process of verbalization, into a single whole, into a poetic image. (61)

Impressionism in Chekhov connects closely with laconicism. As Bitsilli defines the concept, laconicism of style implies that words, details and images are strictly motivated by their contribution to the perception of the whole.

Chekhov's statement on the fundamentals of his poetics are very well-known: if there is a gun mentioned in a story then ultimately it must go off. In his view every work of literature should theoretically be a *system* of interconnected elements in which nothing can be replaced by anything else; otherwise the entire system collapses. This, in fact, is the essence of laconicism. (35)

Laconicism is, therefore, a vital component in the impressionistic depiction of reality; it fuses with impressionism and "implies the avoidance of anything which influences us in and of itself, therefore hindering the perception of all images as a single image" (69).

Having established the importance of impressionism and laconicism, Bitsilli describes the characteristically Chekhovian devices which prompt the reader to apprehend a work as a harmonious poetic image. He uses the analogy of music to define the unifying rhythm-forming elements in Chekhov's prose. In its narrowest sense, architectonic harmony is attained by alternating rhythmically concise and protracted sentences or by dividing complex sentences into a tripartite articulation of: "a) a statement, b) spontaneous reflection and c) a conclusion which expresses the particular dialectic in the development of the poetic image" (79).

In a larger sense Chekhov creates a sense of rhythm and harmony by the use of recurrent images and themes which link separate moments of a story to each other and thereby comprise "a major factor in our perception of the story as a unit" (97). "The Steppe" provides an especially vivid example of symbolic repetition. In this story "contrasting themes are expressed in a series of highly varied image-symbols,... the alternation of which creates the rhythmic structure of Chekhov's poem" (87). Repetition structured in this fashion approximates a musical development of themes; literal and varied repetition induces the reader to collate what he perceives in such a way that each separate image is reflected in the total image or impression. "The work can be perceived as a whole only when one makes the connection between these details and catches those hints which suggest the whole; each moment in the present connects to a past, as well as a future, moment" (93).

Thus, three concepts—impressionism, laconicism and

musicality—form the core of Bitsilli's analysis of style and structure and provide the basis from which to interpret Chekhov's stories. His reading of the mature stories, most notably "The Bishop," where "Chekhov fully reveals himself, applying his stylistic manner with maximum consistency" (148), amply documents the extraordinary achievement of Bitsilli's inquiry into Chekhov. "The Bishop," Bitsilli argues, represents "the epitome of Chekhov's art" (149); we might also say the same of Bitsilli's analysis of this story: it represents the epitome of his art as a literary critic.

Bitsilli's investigation of Chekhov's artistic quests ultimately leads him to a formulation of the worldview which the stories suggest. Bitsilli is well aware that Chekhov's apparent lack of an ideological program has long confounded and disgruntled critics. He responds to this confusion with an almost evasive simplicity, yet his formulation of Chekhov's philosophic credo is firmly rooted in the elaborately detailed analysis he has undertaken:

> [Chekhov's] worldview cannot be expressed in a system of concepts. It is contained in his symbolism. Something flashes by, enters our field of vision, image after image, and then slides away; these flashes and disappearances arouse our anxiety, a spiritual tension, which is followed by a catharsis—a resolution through the fusion "of all this" into something whole which points to ("it seemed") an inexpressible truth, to a fulfillment and completion in another plane of reality. (162)

Bitsilli's study of Chekhov includes a puzzling chapter on the drama. His remarks on the plays—centered on the premise that Chekhov could not write for the theater—are inductive rather than deductive and seem petulant and unfounded. But the failure of this chapter in terms of its critical method reinforces by negative example the elaborately structured and amply documented argument in the chapters on prose.

Occasional philosophical digressions further detract from the focus of Bitsilli's efforts, but in the context of the whole, they represent only a minor distraction. When Bitsilli brings to bear on the stories his subtle understanding of the nuances of language and his thorough familiarity with the whole of Chekhov's corpus, he is unexcelled. Bitsilli has immeasurably enriched our understanding of Chekhov's art; his insights find echoes throughout Chekhov criticism to this day.

T.C.
E.J.C.

NOTES

1. See "Verzeichnis der philologischen Schriften Bicillis," in Petr M. Bicilli, *Anton P. Čechov, Das Werk und sein Stil,* trans. Vincent Sieveking, *Forum Slavicum,* vol. 7, Munich, 1966, pp. 239-43.

2. The structure of his argument suggests a logical separation into themes and topics, but Bitsilli himself did not divide his study into chapters. The translators have followed the chapter divisions used by Vincent Sieveking in his German translation (*Anton P. Čechov; Das Werk und sein Stil*).

3. Bitsilli expands on this notion of lack of control and passive perception, as well as the motif of misunderstanding and reversal of expectation, in Chapter Six, "Anecdotal Structure."

Acknowledgments

We are grateful to Melinda Stanojevic for her contributions during the initial phases of this translation project. We are indebted to State University of New York at Albany and to Williams College for financial support which has enabled us to complete the translation.

Chapter One

Chekhov and Russian Literature of His Time

Literary works are traditionally divided into two categories: poetry and prose. Whereas works in the first category are evaluated primarily from the perspective of their formal excellence, works in the second category typically are evaluated by two criteria: "richness of content" and "artistic merit." Thus, it is important not only how an author writes, but also what he writes about. Interestingly, even now the following opinions about Tolstoy still prevail: "He is a very great novelist, but his use of language is often incorrect and careless; in this regard he is inferior to Turgenev and Goncharov." Clearly there is some kind of misunderstanding here since, in fact, everything that a writer shows is communicated through the medium of language. If what he shows is well shown, then his means of showing it are also well chosen. The impression created by a work of literature is the sole and absolute criterion of its artistic, i.e., literary excellence.

It is not by mere chance, however, that the misunderstanding mentioned above has prevailed almost from the time that the study of literature, and literature itself, has existed; it reflects certain natural tendencies in life itself. Works of fiction, for the most part, belong to the narrative or "story" genre. "Story" (or historical narrative), i.e., narration about what happens in people's lives, can arouse our interest, excite us and command our attention independent of the manner in which it is related by the author. Hence the success of the so-called "roman-feuilleton," however uninspired or ungrammatical (as it often was), not only among the common reading public but among an erudite audience as well. In any given instance the subject of interest is an event which, albeit

1

invented—a fiction—might nevertheless happen, and happen not only to the heroes of the narrative, but to the reader himself. Naturally, once our attention is drawn to the substance of the narrative, to a particular "slice of life," and once we become involved in the destinies of the characters (I reiterate that because we unconsciously and imperceptibly put ourselves and our close friends in their place), then the more thoroughly the lives of the heroes are developed, the more we are satisfied by the narrative. Hence, the traditional hierarchy of prose fiction forms is based upon quantitative rather than qualitative criteria; first the novel, with its large narrative form, followed by the novella [*povest'*], and finally the short story [*rasskaz*].

Interestingly enough, when friends of the young Chekhov discerned his talent, they tried to persuade him to abandon the short story in favor of the novel. Indeed, Chekhov himself was tempted to do so, even after he had achieved artistic maturity. He wrote nothing similar, however, to the Tolstoyan *roman-fleuve,* or to the "novel-tragedy" of Dostoevsky. His novellas, in fact, scarcely differ from his short stories. There is no plot *per se;* the conflicts which arise among the characters are outwardly quite uncomplicated, and the *dramatis personae* are very limited. Most important, there is no denouement, no conclusion or solution to the drama. From the reader's viewpoint, the substance of the narrative is nothing more than a casual and insignificant episode.

There is, however, another aspect to narrative prose: the people depicted and what happens to them are of interest insofar as they are characteristic of a particular moment and a particular time. Chekhov's contemporaries did, in fact, evaluate his characters in this light. They saw the heroes as typical "victims of stagnation" and "superfluous people"; the intelligentsia of the time recognized the characters as friends and kindred spirits. But this attitude has long since been discarded. Now even a Russian reader interprets a Chekhov character independent of and without reference to cultural traits of a bygone era. As a character in the abstract, the Chekhov figure is only vaguely perceived because he is shown, as it were, only in passing. Unlike the heroes of Tolstoy, Dostoevsky, Flaubert or Dickens, Chekhovian heroes do not make an indelible impression on the reader's mind. Like pale, transparent shadows, they merely cast a feeble glimmer before us, and they are easily transposed from

2

one story to another in our memory, or simply forgotten—like people in real life whom we have chanced to meet only casually and briefly. This is all the more true because the setting in which the characters are shown is alien and unfamiliar to the modern reader; it elicits no associations which might facilitate recognition of the characters depicted therein.

It is, nonetheless, precisely at the present time that Chekhov finally seems to have received due recognition; it is only now that no one hesitates to call him a great writer. What is most significant in this regard is that Chekhov was first honored not in his own country,[1] but in England, where, needless to say, his stories were least of all seen as historical narrative. And this is the most convincing proof of how insubstantial or conventional is the differentiation of literature into prose and poetry. If now we react to Chekhov's works more intensely than did readers of an earlier period, this response is directly linked to their formal excellence. In other words, what is usually taken to be the content of a work (which now least of all commands our attention) is subordinate to another underlying content of quite a different nature, one inseparable from form. Thus, to interpret Chekhov means to elucidate the elements of his formal excellence, and, at the same time, that underlying content in his works.

To explain the mystery of an artist's excellence one must discover his creative individuality, and the only way to approach this problem is through a comparative approach. First, of course, it is necessary to "localize" the artist, to consider him in his historical context. It is important to isolate in Chekhov's art that which is not uniquely his, but belongs, rather, to a general pool of knowledge; then one must identify the particular manner in which he deals with these communal resources. This alone provides the impetus for the discovery of other parallels.

Chekhov is the younger contemporary of the great Russian "Realists" (one must place that term as well as many others in quotes, so conventional has it become) Tolstoy, Turgenev, Dostoevsky, and likewise of the *bytoviki,* who wrote of everyday life, and of the populists (contemporary from the perspective of historical, if not always formal chronology). Chekhov is also the older contemporary of the early Symbolists, the so-called Decadents. Although he remained outside the movement associated

3

with these latter writers, he had, as we shall see, some contact with its practitioners.

It is natural to assume that Tolstoy ought to have had the greatest influence on Chekhov, not only because for him, as indeed for all of us, Tolstoy was the greatest master of narrative literature, but also because they were contemporaries in the literal sense of the word; furthermore, Chekhov knew him personally. As we shall see later, this influence is manifest in numerous aspects of Chekhov's art.

The more profound the influence of one artist on another, the more hidden this influence is and the less does the "pupil" make use of the "teacher's" works as material. There is only one instance, if I am not mistaken, where Chekhov makes use of Tolstoy in this way. This discovery was made by Pleshcheev in "Name-Day"[2] ["Imeniny"], and he pointed it out to Chekhov in a letter.

> Olga Mikhailovna's conversation with the peasant women about childbirth and the detail in which she is suddenly struck by the sight of the back of her husband's head suggests an imitation of *Anna Karenina,* where, in a similar situation, Dolly talks with peasant women, and elsewhere, when Anna suddenly notices her husband's misshapen ears. (October 6, 1888)[3]

Pleshcheev evidently considered this a shortcoming in Chekhov's story; this misunderstanding is attributable to a very widespread and persistent conception of the essence of a work of art. If writers did not allow themselves this kind of plagiarism, literature could not exist. Moreover, it would be simply inconceivable to avoid such plagiarisms. What we are dealing with here, no doubt, is not a case of intentional borrowing but the result of unconscious recollection.

Generally speaking, in analyzing one writer's influence on another, and indeed, the sources of any work of art, one must distinguish between kinds of borrowing; to wit, what comprises the narrative structure [*syuzhet*] and fable or story material [*fabula*], and what pertains to the means of expression. The *syuzhet* aspect by itself is, in many instances, *res nullius,* and coincidences in the *syuzhet* may very often be explained precisely in this way. Even if the *syuzhet* is new and original, the author who has borrowed it from its inventor can be considered, on the strength of that alone, only circumstantially under the influence of the latter. The important point, after all, is how the *syuzhet* is worked out. There is little doubt that Chekhov's "The Death of a Government Clerk" ["Smert' chinovnika"] was suggested by the ending of "The Overcoat" ["Shinel'"]. Yet it would be the height of naiveté to see in this a confirmation of the famous formula that all Russian literature after Gogol emerged from his "Overcoat." Furthermore, as regards the means of literary expression, one must necessarily distinguish well established stereotypes and clichés, which belong to "the common pool," from that which is unique to each writer.

Proceeding from this assumption, it is evident that, for the most part, the determination of the sources of a writer's art becomes a very complex problem. In Chekhov's case, this problem is further compounded. First of all, his work appeared at a time when, on the one hand, literary production had grown to an extraordinary degree, while, on the other hand, the most varied criteria were employed in evaluating these works—"elegance," "refined style," "the social thrust," "richness of content"—for example. It is difficult, therefore, to state a priori precisely who among the writers could or should have been the "authority" in the eyes of an author. Secondly, although many valuable comments about literature are scattered throughout Chekhov's letters, we rarely find in them an indication of precisely what he read and how he evaluated what he read. Frequently, therefore, one is limited to speculation, and great caution is required in indicating any of Chekhov's possible sources. Nevertheless, to facilitate the task, I think it is first necessary to consider the problem of influence: aside from Tolstoy, who among the most prominent Russian writers contemporary with Chekhov might have had an influence on him?

Significantly Chekhov wrote not a single word about Dostoevsky; with the possible exception of one oblique criticism, it is as if Dostoevsky did not exist for him.[4] This is understandable when one considers the profound differences in their artistic temperaments. The same could be said of Saltykov. Chekhov respected him as a man who was able, as no one else, to "condemn openly" and to condemn above all "that mean spirit which dwells in the ordinary kind of small-minded, spiritually warped Russian intellectual" (letter to Pleshcheev, May 14, 1889), but there is no indication that he valued Saltykov as the great literary master that he was. In another letter to Pleshcheev from the same period (September 15, 1888) he seems to put Saltykov on a par with Shcheglov.[5]

In his youth, in a letter to his brother Mikhail Pavlovich, Chekhov offers this advice: "If you want to read a travel book that won't bore you, read Goncharov's *The Frigate Pallada*" [*Fregat Pallada*] (July 1, 1876). But in 1889 he wrote to Suvorin about Goncharov:

> By the way, I am reading Goncharov, and I am amazed. I am amazed at myself! How could I have considered Goncharov a first-rate writer all these years.... I am crossing Goncharov off my list of demi-gods. (early May, 1889)

We may assume that the marvelous story "A Daughter of Albion" ["Doch' Al'biona"] was inspired by a passage from *The Frigate Pallada* which concerns English mores in Singapore:

> There is only one thing I cannot understand: how is it that a prim and proper Englishwoman, whose own brother does not dare enter her bedroom, and in whose presence one cannot mention the word "pants," can live among this population which goes without pants altogether? Are such women really so full of aristocratic disdain for everything that is beneath them, like Roman matrons, who, knowing no shame before their slaves, bathed in their presence and did not even deign to notice them?

In Chekhov's story the Englishwoman shows her disdain of the "slave," the landowner, by paying no attention when he undresses before her and enters the water naked.

A passage from "The Steppe" ["Step' "] is reminiscent of a corresponding passage from Chapter Three, Volume One, of *The Frigate Pallada,* written in the form of a letter to Benediktov, wherein Chekhov depicts the steppe, languishing at night, aware that "its wealth and inspiration *perish in vain* to the world, glorified by none," and he "hears it call: Bard, bard!" Compare in *The Frigate Pallada:*

> After the scorching day, the long, stifling sweet night descends, with a twinkling in the sky, with a fiery stream under one's feet, with a tremor

6

of sweet bliss in the air. My God! these nights *are lost in vain* here. There are no serenades, no sighs, no whispering of love, no singing of the nightingale. (Italics mine.)[6]

The author then suggests to Benediktov that he take up "his lyre" and set out on the ocean to sing of the steppe in the "language of the gods."

In this same chapter Goncharov's description of the sunset over the ocean suggests a parallel to a similar description at the end of "Gusev," in which Chekhov describes the colors and forms which the clouds assume at sunset. This may be, however, only a coincidental similarity, for Chekhov had also traveled by sea (on his return from Sakhalin).

Borrowings, citations and plagiarisms do not in themselves offer evidence of one writer's influence on another; they only permit conjecture. Genuine influence is revealed in style, tone and outlook on life. From this point of view Chekhov has nothing in common with Goncharov. The portrayer of "superfluous men" crossed off "his list of demi-gods" the author of *Oblomov* precisely when the "superfluous man" (not in the ironic sense of the term as it is used in the title of Chekhov's story) becomes a central figure in his own work. Chekhov's "superfluous man" is a far cry from Oblomov's hero, whom he characterized in the letter to Suvorin mentioned above: "a flabby sluggard . . . , a simple, commonplace, petty nature." He is much closer to the superfluous man of Turgenev, in his many incarnations. Chekhov correctly understood the "chief misfortune" not only of Goncharov's most famous work, but of all his works as well: "cold, cold, cold" (in the same letter). Goncharov could only be foreign to Chekhov, an "artist of life beyond compare," as Tolstoy so aptly called him.

Of the prestigious classical writers after Tolstoy, we have yet to consider Turgenev. The influence of Turgenev on Chekhov was extraordinarily significant and manifested itself in an extremely complex manner. It is difficult to assess Turgenev's influence precisely because it is so complex and heterogeneous. Turgenev, on the one hand, is an accomplished painter with words, a gifted landscape artist; one can readily see in this fact alone Chekhov's affinity to him. Thus, it seems to me, insofar as one can make an a priori assertion, that the painterly aspect of Turgenev's art could not help but be reflected in Chekhov. On the other hand, Turgenev is also a "realist," a writer of everyday life; moreover, it is particularly characteristic of him to use a medium-length or short narrative form to depict reality. Even the novels of the author of *A Sportsman's Sketches* [*Zapiski okhotnika*] approach the novella or the short story in their form. They are limited in scope, contain few characters, and the narration encompasses a relatively brief time segment.

In this regard Turgenev differs from Tolstoy, Dostoevsky and Goncharov, and is similar to the sketch writers, to the short story writers of the 1860s and to those of Chekhov's time. Chekhov belonged to the same social sphere as did these latter and depicts mainly the same social milieu they did: government clerks, *raznochintsy* [members of the non-gentry intelligentsia], *petite bourgeoisie,* clergy and peasants. Turgenev, on the contrary, knew almost exclusively noblemen and peasants. Naturally, in order to better understand Turgenev's influence on Chekhov, it is first necessary to "clear the air," so to speak, by verifying how Chekhov could be and was indebted to other short story writers. Only a collective effort might fully accomplish this task. The material is too extensive, and in too many instances it would be necessary to check precisely what is on each page of G. Uspensky, Ertel, Sleptsov, Garshin and many others, and to isolate their individual features from common clichés. This procedure is complicated by the fact that we cannot establish in an exhaustive manner exactly what Chekhov happened to read. I will therefore confine myself to certain more or less random observations in an attempt to resolve the immediate problem.

In one of his early letters (1883) to his brother Aleksandr Pavlovich, Chekhov speaks about Leskov as "my favorite hack." Is not the first episode in the story "In the Steam Bath"["V bane" 1885] a variation of "A Journey with a Nihilist" ["Puteshestviya s nigilistom"]? In Chekhov the one who is suspected of having "ideas in his head" is the deacon; in Leskov it is the deacon who suspects the court prosecutor of nihilism. Quite possibly both these stories derive from some popular anecdote. Yet the same sympathetic attitude towards the clergy is found in both Chekhov and Leskov. Clergymen are the most likable among the characters of each writer. But, again, it would be risky to assert on this basis that Leskov exerted an influence on Chekhov. Chekhov's regard for the clergy might be the result of childhood and early adolescent impressions, particularly his family's close relationship to the church. It might also be explained by the fact that of all the teachers at the Taganrog High School Chekhov's religious instructor made the best impression on him. [7]

Chekhov loved Leskov for his wit, his inventive use of language and his knowledge of the Russian milieu. Yet how far apart they were in spirit! Leskov was least of all an artist of life, if one takes that to mean life as composed of concrete personalities. For example, no matter how sympathetically he sketches his cathedral folk, they nonetheless do not live in our consciousness. They are anecdotal types rather than living people. As far as I can determine, his "favorite hack" did not exert any artistic influence on Chekhov.

In a letter to Pleshcheev Chekhov writes:

> I have ... a certain topic [in mind]: a young man in the Garshin mold, uncommon and deeply sensitive, chances for the first time in his life to visit a brothel. (Sept. 15, 1888)

He had in mind here Garshin's stories "An Incident" ["Proisshestvie"] and "Nadezhda Nikolaevna." This example confirms what we said earlier about the difficulty of resolving in each separate instance the problem of one author's influence on another. Indeed, not only were both Garshin stories indebted to "Nevsky Prospect," but "An Incident" is a direct reworking of Gogol's story. Did Chekhov really not notice this? Chekhov knew Gogol's work very well and was profoundly influenced by him; I suspect he could have come upon the theme of "A Nervous Breakdown" ["Pripadok"] without Garshin as an intermediary. It is true, however, that the general tone of "A Nervous Breakdown" seems closer in spirit to Garshin than to Gogol.

There is a tragically touching mood suggestive of Garshin in two Chekhov works quite different in theme, "Volodya" and "Sleepy" ["Spat' khochetsya"]. But in these stories it appears that Chekhov is even closer in spirit to de Maupassant, whose works he came to admire very early in life. The ironically grotesque depiction of daily routine in "Volodya" is reminiscent of de Maupassant— something that does not happen in Garshin. [8]

9

Among the banal feuilletons of "Antosha Chekhonte" one frequently encounters works such as "Words, Words and Words" ["Slova, slova, i slova"] which is remarkable for its subtlety and laconic style. This early Chekhov piece deals with the theme of the fallen woman and is very much like an ironic rephrasing of *Notes from Underground* [*Zapiski iz podpol'ya*]. One difference, exceptionally important for an understanding of Chekhov, is that Dostoevsky's hero, at the last moment, renounces his intention of saving the fallen woman because he believes that he does not have the moral right to perform this noble act. Indeed, he would have saved her not for her own sake, but for his personal satisfaction. The hero of Chekhov's story, however, has no such intention. He has limited concern for Katya, and he misleads her with this expression of superficial pity, which does not commit him to anything. He merely gives in to his inherent kindness, worth little more than the impulse which prompts Gogol's Ivan Ivanovich Pererepenko (in "The Tale of How Ivan Ivanovich Quarreled with Ivan Nikiforovich" ["Kak Ivan Ivanovich possorilsya c Ivanon Nikiforovichem"]) to talk to beggars. It is as though Chekhov were giving a Gogolian answer (Gogolian, of course, only figuratively speaking) to Dostoevsky in this story. Here, as in all his art, Chekhov does not caricature the "good man." His hero gets off with "words, words and words," but good words nevertheless, not like those with which Ivan Ivanovich ends his chat with the old beggar woman: "What are you standing around for? Am I beating you?"

The nature of such effortless kindness is revealed even more subtly in the story, "The Beggar" ["Nishchii"]. Here the "good man" really tries to help the "fallen man," gives him work and looks after him. Only afterwards does the man saved by Skvortsov disclose to him that it was, in fact, Skvortsov's own cook who was his salvation. She chopped wood for him, cried over him and, as a result, he reformed, and stopped drinking and begging.

Here Dostoevsky and Gogol are at polar opposites. Dostoevsky's characters suffer from an excess of spirituality, thereby destroying the soul's essence; Gogol's creations wholly lack both qualities. Actually neither type is a real human being; they are either fallen angels or automatons. But in Chekhov we find only people.

Herein lies the fundamental difference between Chekhov and the *bytoviki,* who place in the foreground not man, but a social milieu in which people serve merely as illustrations. Among the rare exceptions to this last point are two experiments in the "psychological novel" by Pomyalovsky, *Bourgeois Happiness* [*Meshchanskoe schast'e*] and *Molotov*. As it happens, there is some evidence that these two works had an influence on Chekhov. He mentions *Bourgeois Happiness* in a letter to Leikin:

> In your place I would write a short story about the merchant milieu, in the manner of Ostrovsky. I would describe ordinary love and family life without villains, and angels, without lawyers and demons. I would take as my *syuzhet* the uninterrupted, ordinary flow of life as it really is, and I would depict "merchant happiness" just as Pomyalovsky has depicted the happiness of the bourgeoisie. (May 11, 1888)

Chekhov evidently borrowed the theme for two of his short stories, "A Naughty Boy" ["Zloi mal'chik"] and "Zinochka," from *Bourgeois Happiness* and *Molotov* (which in certain respects is a re-working of the former). Interestingly, in "Zinochka," the later work, the narrative is closer to the original source than in "A Naughty Boy." In "Zinochka," the girl who kisses the child's brother occupies a position analogous to that of Molotov in *Bourgeois Happiness;* she is the governess of the boy who secretly watches her kiss his brother. In *Bourgeois Happiness,* Molotov performs various duties for the landowner Obrosimov (at whose estate his beloved Lenochka is staying), including giving lessons to his son. As in *Molotov* the boy in "Zinochka" (as opposed to the "naughty boy" who simply blackmails the lovers) is confused by his discovery:[9]

> Fedya overheard the conversation at the door and told the other [children] that Nadya had been kissing, and that her father had severely reprimanded her for this (...). The children began whispering among themselves.
> "Why can't people kiss? asked... Fedya. "After all, we kiss."
> "That's entirely different...," answered Katya.
> "Why?"
> "People who are engaged kiss," said Masha.
> "And that's no good."
> "And what's a 'libertine'?" asked Fedya.
> "You shouldn't speak about that..." he was told.
> "Why?"
> "It's improper...."

Compare with "Zinochka": "From all I had seen I understood only that Sasha was kissing Zinochka. That was improper. If *maman* heard of it, they would both catch it. Feeling for some reason ashamed, I went back to the nursery." In both Chekhov stories, as in *Bourgeois Happiness,* each boy reveals to the enamored couple what he has learned (but in entirely different ways).[10] In *Molotov* there is one other episode which evidently served as material for Chekhov as well—the quarrel which Dorogov starts with his children with no cause other than that he is in a bad mood:

> Perhaps he hadn't had enough sleep, or things weren't going well at the office; maybe his pet canary was sulking, or there were too many onions in the soup; or perhaps the cloudy day simply had a bad effect on him; all this expressed itself at once in words and action. He loved venting his anger on someone. . . .

Compare this to the beginning of Chekhov's "The Head of the Family" ["Otets semeistva"]: "It usually happens after losing heavily at cards or after a drinking bout, when his sinuses start to act up." In keeping with Chekhov's manner, what "it" is is not explained, but simply shown through action and dialogue. It is not mere coincidence that in both writers the "drama" is played out at the dinner table, that the boy in Chekhov and one of Dorogov's sons are both named Fedya, that the nagging of each father assumes an almost identical form, and that the whole affair ends when the father becomes ashamed and tries to make up with the person whom he has offended. The image of the father venting his anger on the other members of the family persists in Chekhov. It is repeated in "Out of Sorts" ["Ne v dukhe"], where the police chief, chagrined by his gambling losses, decides to whip his son because he "broke a window the day before" in order to vent his anger on something. It occurs again—this time without the burlesque effect—in "Difficult People" ["Tyazhelye lyudi"]. Chekhov's own childhood impressions probably play a role here; his father was a "difficult person" of this type. But everyday impressions are one thing; converting them into a work of art is something else altogether. The thematic similarity of "Difficult People" and "The Head of the Family" to the passage mentioned above from Pomyalovsky is too obvious to be ignored. The strength of the evidence is at issue here: the larger the body of evidence, the greater the likelihood of one artist's dependence on

12

another. I shall cite one other piece of evidence. The hero of both Pomyalovsky stories is a commoner who has been educated, and has risen somewhat in the world, but nonetheless is not recognized as an equal by the landowning class in which he now finds himself. He is acutely aware of this and, as a result, he is ashamed of himself; he has no self-confidence and is reserved in all his dealings. It is therefore difficult for him to establish a relationship with Lenochka; she, not he, takes the initiative in declaring love. He generally finds it difficult to speak about such things as "poetry" and "love," not because he despises them, but because of "some inexplicable shyness, timidity and bashfulness," and the awareness of his common origins. Of course, it is also true that he has as yet known neither life nor love, but basically we are dealing here with a case of what is traditionally referred to as an inferiority complex.

Pomyalovsky does not explore the indivisibility of the spiritual make-up of his commoner. In this respect Chekhov went further than he, and fully realized what is given merely in raw, unpolished form in Pomyalovsky. We should mention how often one encounters in Chekhov a similar type of *raznochinets* "who has risen in the world" or a "voluntary déclassé" (Misail Poloznev in "My Life"["Moya zhizn'"], who is shown from different perspectives and in different variations; among these are the Laptev brothers in "Three Years" ["Tri goda"], Lopakhin in *The Cherry Orchard* [Vishnevyi sad], Ognev in "Verochka," and many others. Anna Akimovna in "A Woman's Kingdom" [Bab'e tsarstvo] also fits this category. The element of indecision inherent in the personal relationships of all these Chekhov characters is shown with great subtlety, and without explanation or self-analysis; nevertheless, we feel it to be one of the factors contributing to their overall personalities. Pomyalovsky's hero renounces the "bourgeois happiness" which his romance with Lenochka promises, not because he is uncertain of his love for her or his ability to love in general, but rather because of pure circumstance. He cannot tolerate his position at Obrosimov's and decides to leave. We may compare this to Lopakhin's behavior toward Vera or Ognev's toward Verochka. Significantly, the external situation in all three works is also analogous: in *Bourgeois Happiness* and "Verochka" *he* leaves, and in *The Cherry Orchard* *she* does, and each of these works ends with such a departure.

It would be imprudent, however, to assert that Chekhov relied solely on Pomyalovsky here. The theme of "departure" and the "missed moment" is also present in Turgenev, whose influence on Chekhov was undoubtedly more significant. In this respect "Asya" comes closest to certain Chekhov works. The ending of "Verochka," when Ognev returns to her house after a tête-à-tête with her, is reminiscent of a parallel episode in "Asya" (cf. yet another analogous episode in "The House with an Attic" ["Dom s mezoninom"]. The figure of the commoner in the previously mentioned works by Chekhov obviously invites comparison with *Fathers and Sons* [*Otsy i deti*].[11] Nevertheless, one should not lose sight of the fact that, in one respect, Turgenev's commoner is farther from Chekhov's than is the commoner in Pomyalovsky. Bazarov is certain of his superiority to people of higher social standing, and he has no doubt of his right to personal happiness. Bazarov is a "hero." He does not acknowledge in himself the "slave" whom he would have to "squeeze out, drop by drop" (Chekhov's words partly about himself in a letter to Suvorin)[12] like Chekhov's heroes or Molotov in Pomyalovsky's work (although in Pomyalovsky this is not as deliberate as it is in Chekhov). A. Derman[13] is correct in regarding this "squeezing the slave out of oneself" as a dominant theme in Chekhov's art. From this viewpoint, the characters mentioned above, like the "young man" in the letter to Suvorin, are autobiographical,[14] just as Egor Ivanovich Molotov is in Pomyalovsky. We may add here, incidentally, one other bit of indirect evidence: Molotov's first name is Egor—in childhood, Egorushka. Egorushka is also the name of the Chekhov boy in "The Steppe," who is sent to the city to study in order "to rise up in the world."

At first glance, the likelihood that Pomyalovsky, a sketch writer, could influence such an artist as Chekhov might appear amazing and even improbable, especially if one considers that these two works of Pomyalovsky are nothing more than studies for an unfinished novel and are distinguished by the same formlessness which, in general, characterizes almost all the populist-sketch writers, including even the very gifted Gleb Uspensky. Pomyalovsky, however, like Gleb Uspensky and Nikolai Uspensky, was a "lost talent."[15] But there are certain unexpectedly striking passages scattered throughout his clumsy, unpolished works, weighed down

14

by esthetic slovenliness. Evidently Chekhov sensed in him a potentially great artist, and assimilated from Pomyalovsky what the former was unable to develop in himself.

To account for Turgenev's importance in the genesis of Chekhov's art, it is first necessary to dwell on direct evidence. There are two such pieces of evidence. "The Gamekeeper" ["Eger'"] is undoubtedly a variation of Turgenev's "Meeting" ["Svidanie"] (from *A Sportsman's Sketches*). Turgenev describes a meeting between a valet and a peasant girl who is infatuated with him; he is shortly to depart for the capital with his master. In Chekhov there is a chance meeting of a hunter with his wife, a peasant woman, with whom he does not live. The parallel passages follow:

"The Gamekeeper":

"Meeting":

A small, white *cap* with a straight jockey peak, *evidently* a gift from some generous *young gentleman,* perched jauntily on his handsome flaxen head.

...He was wearing...a coat... *probably* from the shoulders of some *gentleman,* and a black velvet cap with gold lace.

[The hunter explains to his wife why he can't live with her in the village.] Once the spirit of freedom has taken hold of a man you will never root it out of him. In the same way, if a gentleman goes in for being an actor or for any other art, he will never make an official or a landowner. *"You are a woman,* and *you do not understand, but you must understand that."*
"I understand, Egor Vlasych."
"You don't understand, if you are going to cry..."

[Akulina's lover explains to her why he is drawn to Petersburg.] There are simply such marvelous things there, that you, stupid girl, could not begin to imagine.... "Anyway," he added, "why am I telling you all this? *You can't possibly understand it."*
"Why do you say that, Viktor Aleksandrych? I understood, I understood everything."

[The hunter]: *"Well now,* I've chattered long enough...I must be at Boltovo by evening...."

[Viktor]: *"Well,* it's time for me to go...."

15

Egor puts his cap on ... and ... continues on his way, Pelageya stands still and gazes after him ... She sees his moving shoulder blades, the youthful back of his head, ... and her eyes are full of sadness and tender affection....

[Viktor prepares to leave.]
Akulina looked at him ... In her sad gaze was so much tender devotion, venerating submission and love.

A second piece of evidence is contained in the ending of "An Anonymous Story" ["Rasskaz neizvestnogo cheloveka"]. It is very close to the ending of *On the Eve* [*Nakanune*] which Chekhov liked very much.[16] In both works the hero and heroine journey to Italy and stay in Venice; in both the hero is ill with tuberculosis; both stories convey the contrast in the way the heroes experience the charm of Venice, the *joie de vivre* which emanates from everything they see there, the tragedy of their circumstances, and an awareness that they are not meant to enjoy the happiness that seems to unfold before them.

Evidently "The Wolf" ["Volk"] (1886) is also inspired by a Turgenev story, "The Dog" ["Sobaka"].[17] True, the mysterious and the "miraculous" element, *per se,* is absent in Chekhov, but a mysterious timbre is retained. In both stories the attack on the man (for the second time, in Turgenev) by the terrible, mad animal, which no one can catch, occurs at night. In Turgenev the narrator goes to sleep in a hayloft to escape the heat; in Chekhov, Nilov goes outside the miller's hut. Both gaze into the distance in the moonlight and suddenly notice something which attracts their attention.

"The Dog":

And suddenly it seemed to me just as though something were moving about, far, far away ... as if I were imagining it. Some time elapsed; again the shadow rushed by, a little nearer now; then again, still nearer, What is it, I wondered. Can it be a hare? No, I thought, it's too big to be a hare and it doesn't move like a hare. I looked and again the shadow appeared, was moving across the pasture ... like a *huge blur:* an animal, a fox or a wolf? My heart skipped a beat ... but what was I afraid of, after all? Aren't there plenty of wild animals running about the fields by night? But curiosity is stronger than fear. I got up, strained my eyes and suddenly *turned cold* all over. I froze on the spot *as though I had been buried in ice up to my ears;*

God only knows why. And I saw the shadow growing bigger and bigger, which meant that it was *rolling* straight for the hayloft. . . . And then I could tell clearly that it really was an animal, large, with a big head. . . . It dashed onward like a whirlwind, like a bullet. . . . Good heavens! What was it? Suddenly it stopped short, as though it smelled something. . . . Why . . . it was the mad dog I had encountered that day! I couldn't shout . . . ! It ran to the gate, eyes glaring—and dashed straight at me over the hay!

"The Wolf":

Suddenly it seemed to Nilov, that on the opposite bank . . . something like a shadow *rolled* by like a black *ball*. He squinted. The shadow disappeared but soon appeared again and *rolled on* zigzag toward the dam.

"The wolf!" Nilov remembered. [NB He has been forewarned; they had just been talking about the mad wolf at the mill.] But before it occurred to him that he should run back to the mill, the black ball already was rolling along the dam. . . .

"If I start running, he'll attack me from behind," conjectured Nilov, feeling how the scalp under his hair *was turning to ice.*

With this type of parallelism in mind, one might occasionally find in Chekhov other citations from Turgenev (which, of course are most likely the result of unconscious, involuntary recollection).

"On the Road" ["Na puti"]:

Fathers and Sons:

There extended a row of gaudy prints . . . next to the icon. In the dim light of the candle and the icon lamp these pictures seemed to form a continuous belt covered with black patches; but when the tiled stove . . . drew in a blast of air with a howl, and the logs . . . burst into bright flames . . . then . . . one could see above the head of the sleeping man first the faces of Seraphim, then the Shah Nasr Edin, and finally a fat, dark-skinned boy . . . , whispering something to a girl with a singularly vacant and indifferent face. . . .

There too hung a rather unflattering photograph of Fenichka herself, an eyeless face with a forced smile, in a dark frame, and nothing else could be made out; and above Fenichka hung General Ermolov, in a cloak, scowling menacingly into the far-off Caucasian mountains, from beneath a little silk shoe for pins which fell right onto his brows.

17

"The Steppe":	"Bezhin Meadow" ["Bezhin lug"]
The light from the fire lay like a great flickering patch on the earth; though the moon was bright, everything seemed impenetrably black beyond that red patch. The light struck the waggoners' eyes and they saw only part of the great road; almost unseen in the darkness the horses and the wagons loaded with bales looked like a mountain of undefined shape.	From the circle of light it was hard to make out what was going on in the darkness; everything close at hand seemed shut off by an almost black curtain; but farther away on the horizon hills and forests were dimly visible in long patches.

While there is, of course, almost no literal correspondence in these cases, we find, nonetheless, a very obvious similarity in the speech pattern and method of presentation. Here is another example of a similar recollection:

Bluish smoke curled up from the censer and bathed in the broad, slanting patch of sunshine which cut across the gloomy, lifeless emptiness of the church. ("The Requiem") ["Panikhida"]

Compare in Turgenev:

In the golden dust of the sun's rays the peasants . . . quickly lowered and raised their heads . . . ; the smoke ran in a thin blue stream from the opening of the censer. ("Hamlet of the Shchigrov District") ["Gamlet Shchigrovskogo uezda"]

In the early Chekhov story, "Holy Simplicity" ["Svyataya prostota"] (1885), the genuine Chekhov breaks through Antosha Chekhonte. In this story a Moscow lawyer visits his father, a church prior in a provincial town. Father Savva is both proud and disconcerted that he has such a "gallant and grown-up son" and tries "to sound learned" when talking to him. From the conversation it becomes clear that the son enjoys life and squanders his money; the father discloses that he intends to leave 1,500 rubles—his life savings—to his son. The son replies that this money should be left to his father's nieces. He does not need it: "1,500—phooey!" The father has not expected this.

18

He was somewhat offended.... His son's callous, indifferent attitude towards his life savings upset him. But the insult and confusion soon passed.... The old man was again eager to chat with his son, to engage in another "learned" conversation with him, and to recall the past, but he didn't dare disturb the prominent lawyer. He kept walking back and forth through the dark rooms, continually thinking, and finally he went into the hall to have a look at his son's fur coat. In an excess of paternal rapture he clasped the coat in both arms, and all at once he was hugging it, kissing it and blessing it, as though it were not a coat but the son himself, the university man.... Sleep was out of the question.

We find described here in a somewhat "lowered" form a relationship reminiscent of the one between Bazarov and his parents (in Turgenev the father tries not to discredit himself before his educated son); in Chekhov the features of both Bazarov's father and mother are combined in Father Savva. Father Savva is overcome by a feeling of maternal, undiscriminating, venerating love for his son. The image of the [Turgenev] mother, who is timid in her son's presence, yet venerates him, is repeated in Chekhov's most perfect work, the apex of his art, "The Bishop" ["Arkhierei"]. Thus at the beginning of his artistic career, the best in Chekhov was inspired by the best in Turgenev.

Footnotes to Chapter One

1. I have in mind the then popular attitude toward Chekhov. Tolstoy, Pleshcheev, Grigorovich and Suvorin, of course, were quick to recognize his talent.

2. All stories and plays have been translated in accord with the bibliographical index in David Magarshack, *Chekhov: A Life,* Westport, Ct., 1970 [tr.].

3. *Slovo, sbor. 2-oi k desiatiletiiu smerti Chekhova,* 256.

4. The only mention of Dostoevsky is reported by V.I Nemirovich-Danchenko in his memoirs: "He (Chekhov) once told me that he hadn't read *Crime and Punishment* [*Prestuplenie i nakazanie*]. 'I am saving this pleasure until I am forty,' he said. I asked him again when he was past forty. 'Yes, I have read it, but was not terribly impressed' " (*Iz proshlogo,* Moskva, 1938, 81).

5. In this letter he explains why he writes so little and so slowly, and finishes: "Praise be to the prolific Shchedrin and Shcheglov...."

6. Here and throughout the text the emphases are Bitsilli's.

7. Incidentally, it was he who gave Chekhov the humorous nickname "Chekhonte" which the latter used as a pseudonym for the journal *Fragments* [*Oskolki*].

8. The *syuzhet* of "Volodya" was suggested by Grigorovich: "Were I somewhat younger and somewhat more gifted," he wrote to Chekhov on December 30, 1888 (*Slovo,* I, 1914, 207), "I would certainly describe a family and their seventeen-year-old boy who goes to the attic and

19

shoots himself." But, as is evident from the context, Grigorovich understood this theme as "social" in character, one which would provide a basis for expressing a "social thought," "to touch upon a sore social wound." There is nothing of that in the Chekhov piece. He reworked the theme suggested by Grigorovich, in the de Maupassant style. De Maupassant's influence on Chekhov is revealed mainly in some early works which, although of considerable artistic value, Chekhov subsequently rejected. He did not include in the collected works published during his life-time (included in *Complete Works* [*Polnoe sobranie sochinenii Chekhova*], Marks, 1911) such stories as "A Retired Slave" [*"Otstavnoi rab"*], "The Incident at the Dacha" [*"Dachnyi kazus"*], and "The Cynic" [*"Tsinik"*]. These stories contain elements of de Maupassant's sarcasm, burlesque and grotesque, and a depiction of the tragic or the ugly which is concealed in everyday life. True, these elements are somewhat Gogolian in spirit, particularly, since, like Gogol, both Chekhov and de Maupassant are possessed of the same crude simplicity, but they lack Gogol's hyperbole, and his violation of the boundary between reality and fantasy. Subsequently, de Maupassant's influence on Chekhov decreases as humor comes to prevail over the former's sarcasm.

9. The difference is that in *Molotov* the boy does not watch the lovers, but overhears a conversation between the father and his daughter, who had kissed Molotov.

10. The boy in the other Chekhov story is also "malicious"; he teases Zinochka and enjoys the awareness of his power over her. The boy in Pomyalovsky is "good."

11. Chekhov thought very highly (and quite justifiably so) of Turgenev's novel: "My God! How magnificent *Fathers and Sons* is! It defies description. Bazarov's illness is so powerfully rendered that I grew weak and felt as though I had caught the infection from him. And Bazarov's death? And the old folk? And Kukshina? The devil only knows how he did it. It's simply a work of genius" (to Suvorin, Feb. 24, 1893).

12. "Write a story about how a young man, the son of a serf, who has worked as a shopkeeper, has sung in the choir, has attended high school and university, who has been brought up to respect everyone of higher rank and position, to kiss priests' hands, to revere the ideas of others, and to be thankful for every morsel of bread, who has been whipped many times; who has trudged to lessons without galoshes; who has been used to fighting and to teasing animals [All these features, as is well known, are completely autobiographical; the last incidentally is applied to Misail Poloznev in "My Life."]: Cherpakov and I used to catch goldfinches and linnets in the fall and sell them at the market.... We would ambush flocks of migrating starlings by firing small shot at them; then we would pick up the wounded, some of which died in terrible agony.... When any recovered, we would sell them."

13. *Chekhov,* 1936, 45, 66 and *passim.*

14. I would only say potentially, not actually. There is no evidence, for example, that Chekhov was ever a "hypocrite before God and men." Chekhov depicts himself not as he *had been* in his youth, but as he *might have become* in those circumstances in which he had spent his childhood and youth.

15. Turgenev understood this, despite his distance from the *raznochinets* writers of his time: "Read," he wrote to Fet on Jan. 7, 1861, "Pomyalovsky's novella *Molotov* in *The Contemporary* [*Sovremennik*]; you will detect a fresh scent of something like talent." Also in a letter of February 4, 1862: "You have sent me a whole diatribe on *Molotov.* Instead of immediately understanding that *Molotov* was written by a very young man who still does not know what tune to dance to, you have taken him for some worldly Panaev. You did not notice two or three beautiful and naive pages depicting how this Nadya or that Nastya developed and grew. You were so preoccupied with needless trivia that you did not notice other signs of a young talent." Fet, *Moi vospominaniia,* Moskva, 1890, I, 383, 391.

16. "I don't like anything in *On the Eve* except Elena's father and the ending. There is a great deal of tragedy in the ending" (to Suvorin, Feb. 24, 1893).

17. Chekhov thought very highly of this story. Later (1893) he wrote to Suvorin: " 'The Dog' is very good, the language is wonderful. Please read it, if you have forgotten it" (Feb. 24, 1893).

Chapter Two

Chekhov and the Russian Classics

The preceding discussion is sufficient to understand the influence Turgenev exerted on Chekhov's art; however, it is not sufficient for an understanding of Chekhov the artist. Having established links between Chekhov and Turgenev, as well as other writers, we should investigate how he reworked what he assimilated. Chekhov himself indicates where to start. Nina Zarechnaya gives an engraved medallion to Trigorin *(The Seagull)* [*Chaika*]. The engraving refers to his [Trigorin's] story: "'Days and Nights,' p. 190, lines 11 and 12," where Trigorin finds these words: "If you ever need my life, come and take it." Even in Chekhov's time it was noted that these are Vlasich's words addressed to Ivashin in Chekhov's "Neighbors" ["Sosedi"]. Elsewhere in *The Seagull* Treplev speaks about those "devices" which Trigorin has worked out and which Treplev himself is unable to use:

> He mentions *the neck of a broken bottle, glittering against a dam and the black shadow of a mill-wheel;* and there's your moonlit night all cut and dried. But I have a quivering light and the silent twinkling of the stars and the distant sound of a piano dying on the calm, scented air. This is agony. (*The Seagull,* Act IV)

Chekhov quotes himself here, since Treplev's words echo a passage from "The Wolf":

> There wasn't a speck of shadow on the moonlight-bathed dam. In the middle of it the *neck of a broken bottle* shone like a star. Two *water wheels* at the mill, *half-hidden in the shadow,* looked angry and dejected.

22

Obviously Chekhov especially valued his find. In 1886 (the year he worked on "The Wolf") he wrote to his brother Aleksandr:

> You will get the effect of a moonlit night if you write that on the mill-dam a fragment of broken bottle flashed like a bright star . . . and the black shadow of a dog or a wolf rolled by like a ball.[1] (May 10, 1886)

And in a later story, "Ionych," he used a variation of this image:

> No one in the town remembered her [the singer Demetti], but the lamp at the entrance [to her grave in the cemetery] reflected the moonlight, and looked as though it were burning.

Trigorin is clearly Chekhov "in code."[2] Significantly, Trigorin-Chekhov composes this ironic "epitaph" for himself: " 'Here lies Trigorin,' people will say, looking at his grave. 'A good writer, but not as good as Turgenev.' " This type of qualified praise was made about Chekhov more than once, both during his lifetime and after. I shall not consider whether his comment in *The Seagull* is an indication of resentment or an attempt at objective self-evaluation. To do so would lead to pointless psychologizing. I consider it important solely as a means of orientation with regard to the problem posed above. The fact remains that there are few Russian writers to whom Chekhov was more indebted than Turgenev; in one respect, Chekhov was his whole life dependent on Turgenev and, consciously or unconsciously, he struggled with Turgenev and tried to surpass him.

We can determine Chekhov's debt to Turgenev from certain, apparently insignificant, but, in fact, very characteristic features in Chekhov's work—his "birth marks," so to speak. Every artist has, figuratively speaking, his stereotypes, clichés, recurrent words, images and set phrases which testify to his view of life, his "obsessions" and his creative "complex." We see such a "constant" in Chekhov's image of the evening, less often of the morning, sun reflected on a cross (or the windows) of a church:

> A view of a courtyard, a large pond . . . a village on the opposite bank, with a high, narrow belfry on which there burned a cross reflecting the setting sun. ("The House with an Attic")

Here was the train; the windows, like crosses on a church, were flooded in bright light.... ("In the Cart") ["Na podvode"]

Nikolai and Olga watched the sunset, and saw how the gold and crimson sky was reflected in the river, in the church windows, and all through the air.... ("Peasants") ["Muzhiki"]

But on the opposite shore a streak of light already stretched across the hill; the church was shining.... ("Peasants")

And then the copse was left behind. The tops of the factory chimneys came into view. The cross on the belfry glittered....[3] ("In the Ravine") ["V ovrage"]

Because I was ascending, everything seemed to have disappeared into a hole in the earth. The cross on the church, bathed in red from the rays of the setting sun, gleamed brightly in the abyss and disappeared. ("The Rolling Stone") ["Perekati-pole"]

This image recurs throughout Chekhov works; it can already be found in his early stories:

A large shadow already lay across the village, the huts darkened; the church, diffuse in the twilight, grew in width and, it seemed, was descending into the earth. A weak red light, which must have been a reflection of the evening sunset, caressingly twinkled on its cross. ("The Meeting") ["Vstrecha"] (1887)

They look ahead... and see a spot which is growing white. The raft again rushes toward the same white church. The Lord's temple tenderly winks at them with the sun which is reflected on its cross and the glossy green cupola.... ("On the River") ["Na reke"] (1886)

The sun had already set, but not completely.... Here and there chimneys were still golden and church crosses sparkled.... ("A Clever Fellow") ["Khitrets"] (1883)

Significantly, there is a similar image in Turgenev:

About twenty courtyards clung around the old, wooden, single-domed church with a green cupola and tiny little windows, which

24

glowed bright red in the evening sunset. ("A Trip to Poles'e")
["Poezdka v Poles'e"]

From the same story:

> The entire horizon was covered with a pine forest; *nowhere did a white church glisten,* the fields were not shining, there were just trees and trees. . . .

It is possible that this Chekhov "constant" was suggested by Turgenev.[4] This is an example of creative assimilation, and not imitation, the result of influence in the literal, strict sense of the word. A further example supports this claim—the frequently encountered endings on the theme of "departure."[5] There is a great similarity here between Chekhov's and Turgenev's technique of composition, as these selections from *A Sportsman's Sketches* illustrate:

> Half an hour later we parted. ("Raspberry Water") ["Malinovaya voda"]

> The next day I left the hospitable roof of Mr. Polutykin. ("Khor and Kalinych") ["Khor i Kalinych"]

> Trifon Ivanych won two and a half rubles from me and left later, completely satisfied with his victory. ("The District Doctor") ["Uezdnyi lekar' "]

> We set out hunting. ("The Steward") ["Burmistr"]

In another connection, I shall dwell in more detail on variations of Chekhov's reworking of this motif and explain the different functions which it fulfills both in Chekhov and Turgenev. For the time being I shall note only that if one takes the trouble to read the endings of all the stories indicated above and compare them with Turgenev's, it is impossible to overlook their rhythmic and lexical similarities.

Chekhov's attitude toward both Turgenev and himself (it is difficult to separate the two because Chekhov was so taken with Turgenev) is extremely complicated, and all the more difficult to clarify because Chekhov only speaks of it indirectly. His author's confession, which, as we have seen, is delivered by Trigorin (and by Treplev about Trigorin), is extremely important in this respect, especially the following passage (Trigorin's conversation with Nina in Act Two):

> I'm never satisfied with myself. I dislike my own work. I drift around in a trance and often can't make sense of what I write; that's what's so awful. I love this lake here, the trees and the sky, and I have a feeling for nature; it inspires me, gives me a violent urge to write. But then, I'm more than an artist, aren't I? I'm a citizen too. I love my country and its people. As a writer, I feel I must discuss ordinary people, their sufferings, their future—science, human rights, all that stuff. So I do discuss it, all in great haste, with everyone furiously hounding me in all directions.... I seem to see life and learning vanishing into the distance, while I lag more and more behind...and end up believing that I can only write nature descriptions, and that everything else I write is bogus through and through. *(The Seagull)*

If we assume here that Trigorin is Chekhov's *alter ego,* then we must admit that Chekhov gives an evaluation of himself which is too severe and one-sided but, to some extent, justified. No sooner do the "intellectuals" in his stories (not to mention those in his plays) begin a conversation, then they almost always embark on discussions about how pale, bleak and boring life is. They consider themselves unable and unwilling to work, and were this not so, life might be beautiful and happy, and so forth (cf. for example, "Three Years," "My Life," "The Duel," "The Princess" ["Knyaginya"], "On the Road," "Neighbors," "The Betrothed" ["Nevesta"] and numerous other works). In such cases, moreover, they switch from conversational speech to a more literary language. It is true that in the short stories, if not in his dramas (of which more will be said later), Chekhov usually exercises restraint, limiting his editorializing and moralizing; gradually he frees himself from it altogether. But the mere presence of these elements, particularly in some of his more significant works, violates, to some extent, the overall impression. We find other indications that Chekhov was disturbed by his penchant for editorializing. Gorky's reminiscences of Chekhov contain a particularly interesting episode: Chekhov was telling Gorky of the plight of village schoolteachers. He got carried away, spoke long and heatedly, and then "he looked around and jested at his own expense: 'Well, I have drummed up a whole editorial for you from a liberal newspaper'."[6]

Chekhov is quoting himself here. In one of Chekhov's early stories the hero, from whose viewpoint the story is told, recalls:

> After dinner I approached Zina and, to show her that there were people who understood her, I began to talk about the oppressive surroundings: about justice, work and women's liberation. From the topic of women's liberation I merrily went on to a discussion of passports, . . . sincerely and logically, as though I were reading aloud an editorial. ("A Daughter of a Councillor of Commerce") ["Doch' kommertsii sovetnika"]

But even in later stories, likable, mature people about whom Chekhov does not mean to be ironic, talk in a similar fashion. In other examples, one feels that the story, with its *syuzhet,* and its "intrigue," is only a pretext for a sermon, as it almost always is in "civil" and "exposé" literature; but, in fact, when one finishes any of these stories, it becomes clear that the main point relates not to the sermon, but to something else which is "symbolized" by the *syuzhet.* Here Chekhov shares a quality in common with Turgenev. Indeed, in Turgenev such instances of editorializing and philosophical dialogue are so inserted that they could easily be removed intact from the narrative and used for a student composition on "superfluous men," "idealists of the 1840s," and so forth. By contrast, there is nothing of this in Tolstoy. In his works, personal and intimate conversations, as well as abstract subjects, are organically connected to each other and to the exposition of the *syuzhet;* a consistent tone of everyday speech is maintained throughout.

It would be imprudent, however, to assert that this is a shortcoming in Turgenev. Turgenev was a "man of the 1840s" and, evidently, these people spoke to one another in this manner. The correspondence of the Bakunins or of Herzen with his friends would testify to that. But what is completely "realistic" in Turgenev is more often an anachronism in Chekhov. In his works such passages hinder the perception of the whole as a "landscape." Perhaps Chekhov-Trigorin is not even fully aware of what he means when he calls himself mainly a "landscape painter." The important point is not the category of an artist's material (whether it be "genre" or "landscape"), but its treatment by the artist. In this regard, Chekhov is as similar to Turgenev as he is different from him. Turgenev is an accomplished painter with words, but it is precisely this mastery which frequently betrayed him: he was aware of this but unable to avoid it. In a letter to P.V. Annenkov he says:

> I have been reading Avdeev's novel in *Contemporary Survey,* [*Sovremennoe obozrenie*]. Poorly done, very poor. Perhaps it made such an unpleasant impression on me because I recognized in it a certain imitation of my own style, and the limitations of my style became all the more annoying to me. I believe that if I had to read a lot of Avdeev, I would surely throw away my pen in disgust. *Oh, literature that smacks of literature!* Tolstoy's main virtue is that his works smack of life. (Feb. 21, 1886)[7]

This is profoundly true. Turgenev often misused his mastery, often succumbed to the temptation to "speak beautifully" (notwithstanding the demands of his own Bazarov), without regard for the overall design. Even the marvelous chapter from *Fathers and Sons* describing the illness and death of Bazarov—among the very best of Turgenev's writing—contains such a passage (Bazarov's sudden change for the worse):

> The whole house seemed suddenly to be plunged into gloom; everyone went about with long faces and a strange hush fell. A particularly raucous cock was removed from the backyard down to the village *and long remained mystified as to why he should have been thus dealt with.*

This last "Gogolian" phrase jars with the general tone and style of narration. It stands out conspicuously and disrupts the perception of the whole. This is not the only example in Turgenev. In this he differs from the classics (in the strict sense of the word): from Gogol in *Dead Souls,* Part I, "The Overcoat," and "The Carriage," ["Kolyaska"]; Pushkin in "The Queen of Spades" ["Pikovaya dama"] and "The Captain's Daughter" ["Kapitanskaya dochka"]; and Lermontov in "Taman'". Chekhov's best works, such as "The Steppe," "Verochka," "The Darling" ["Dushechka"], "The Bishop" and "In the Ravine," also differ from Turgenev's works.

The question automatically arises: how much did these true classics help Chekhov? What was the extent of their influence? To answer these questions we should begin with the writers most contemporary to Chekhov: first Gogol, then Lermontov, and then Pushkin. I shall begin, as before, with "direct evidence." As far as Gogol is concerned, I have elsewhere pointed out[8] the obvious citations from *Dead Souls,* as well as from *Taras Bulba* in Chekhov's "The Steppe." I will cite one more parallel:

"The Steppe:"

[A description of evening] As if because the grass cannot see in the dark that it has grown old, a gay youthful twitter rises up from it, such as is not heard by day; chirruping, twittering, whistling, scratching, the basses, tenors, and sopranos of the steppe all mingle in an incessant, monotonous roar of sound in which it is sweet to brood on memories and sorrows.

"Ivan Fedorovich Shponka and his Aunt"
["Ivan Fedorovich Shponka i ego tetushka"]

And what an evening! How free and fresh was the air! How everything has come alive then: the steppe becomes red and is ablaze with flowers; quail, bustards, gulls, grasshoppers, thousands of insects; they fill the air with whistling, chirping, buzzing, droning and, suddenly, merge into one harmonious chorus; and not for a moment is there silence. And the sun gradually sets and disappears.

Chekhov describes another evening in the steppe which also suggests a rephrasing from Gogol: "The sun went to sleep, covering itself with a brocade of gold and crimson" ("In the Ravine"). Compare: "The weary sun was leaving the world, having calmly blazed all through the morning and noon ... " ("The Sorochintsy Fair") ["Sorochinskaya yarmarka"].

We should recall again the common formula that modern Russian literature emerged from "The Overcoat." This is usually taken to mean a humanitarian tone, which has prevailed in our literature. Compassion for man, and an awareness of human brotherhood is its dominant idea. Evidently Chekhov was the first to see another dimension in "The Overcoat." Akaky Akakievich is pitiful and at the same time frightening; he is frightening in his love for a dead object—an overcoat[9]—frightening in the vulgarity he thus reveals. We find in Chekhov a second reincarnation, so to speak, of Akaky Akakievich. The petty clerk in the story "Gooseberries" ["Kryzhovnik"] has dreamt all his life of his own summer home, where he will retire and grow gooseberries; he finally realizes his dream. He is in love, so to speak, with his gooseberries, just as Akaky Akakievich is in love with his overcoat. Both of them abide in a dimension of "negative infinity" [*durnaya beskonechnost'*].

Afanasy Ivanovich in "The Old World Landowners" ["Starosvetskie pomeshchiki"] also abides in a plane of "negative infinity" insofar as his love for Pulkheriya Ivanovna bears the imprint of automatism; he is not frightening, however, but pitiful and touching. His fidelity to daily ritual is established while his wife is still alive; after her death it is conditioned by fidelity to her memory. Chekhov also writes of another character who lives in the same dimension of "negative infinity," the old woman Chikamasova in "The Trousseau" ["Pridanoe"], an early story (1883) which is artistically perfect nonetheless. The old woman, who for many years sewed a trousseau for her daughter, continues to sew even after her daughter's death, now mechanically and automatically; in the same fashion, Afanasy Ivanovich continues to eat those foods which his deceased wife especially liked.

After Gogol we move on to Lermontov. I shall cite a passage from "The Duel" which describes the beginning of the actual duel. Neither the principals nor the seconds, it turns out, are familiar with the established procedure:

> "Gentlemen, do any of you remember Lermontov's description?" Von Koren asked with a laugh. "Turgenev's Bazarov also dueled with somebody."

As a matter of fact, there are passages in "The Duel" which closely correspond to passages in "Princess Mary" ["Knyazhna Meri"], particularly when the dueling episode is recounted.

"The Duel":

[Von Koren's arrival at the dueling site] *"I've never seen anything like it*—how fabulous!" said Von Koren, appearing in the glade and holding out both hands to the east. "Look—green light!"

In the east two green beams stretched *from behind the mountains,* and they were indeed beautiful. The sun was rising.

"Oh, hurry up and shoot," thought Laevsky, sensing that his white, trembling, pathetic face must make Von Koren hate him even more.

"Princess Mary":

[Pechorin and Verner ride to the dueling site.] *I do not remember a bluer and fresher morning.* The sun had just appeared *from behind the green summits,* and the merging of the first warmth of its rays with the waning coolness of the night pervaded all one's senses with a kind of delicious languor.

The captain winked at Grushnitsky, and he, thinking that I was scared, assumed a proud air, although up to then a dull pallor had been spread over his cheeks.

"Princess Mary," however, is not the only source for "The Duel." The end of the duel between Laevsky and Von Koren is so like the end of the duel in "The Captain's Daughter" that one cannot help but assume a borrowing from Pushkin's story. The deacon in "The Duel," who shouts from behind the bush, "He'll kill him!" plays an analogous role to Savelich in Pushkin. With regard to borrowings from Lermontov, we should mention that another Chekhov story, "Horse Thieves" ["Vory"], is an obvious reworking of "Taman'." In both stories a girl, a member of the thieves' gang, entices a traveler who chances to stay the night with them; she gives her accomplices time to finish what they had begun.[10]

Aside from this parallel between "The Duel" and "The Captain's Daughter," I find no other correspondences between Chekhov and Pushkin. This does not mean that Pushkin's prose had no influence on Chekhov. Chekhov's prose has one extremely important and especially characteristic feature which harks back to Pushkin and to no one else. But I shall speak about this in another context.

Footnotes to Chapter Two

1. It is hardly coincidental that the dog and the wolf are mentioned together. It is indirect evidence in support of Chekhov's debt to the Turgenev story.

2. The degree to which Trigorin, generally, may be "autobiographical" is not at issue. I think that V.I. Nemirovich-Danchenko, who knew Chekhov well, is correct when he asserts that Trigorin is more like Potapenko than Chekhov, and then qualifies it: "He is, of course, not one or the other, but both one and the other and a third and a tenth" (*Iz proshlogo*, Moskva, 1938, 48ff.).

3. Compare in the same work: "The hospital, new and recently built, with large windows, stood high on a hill; it was all in light from the setting sun and seemed to burn from within."

4. There is, incidentally, a similar image in Gogol in Part II of *Dead Souls* [*Mertvye dushi*]; this has been pointed out by V.A. Desnitsky, in an article, "Zadachi izucheniia zhizni i tvorchestva Gogolia" (sb. *N.V. Gogol',* pod red. V.V. Gippiusa, izd. Akad. nauk SSSR, 1936): "These were remote villages; the human eye could no longer make them out. Only the golden church cupola, blazing like a spark, revealed that it was a large populated settlement." V.A. Desnitsky is correct in his observation that in this excerpt (I am only quoting a part of it) there is "...a landscape, which provides a direct link to the landscape painting of Turgenev" (104).

5. See the stories: "The Tutor" ["Repetitor"], "A Chameleon" ["Khameleon"], "Surgery" ["Khirurgiya"], "Choristers" ["Pevchie"], "A Captain's Uniform" ["Kapitanskii mundir"], "Murder Will Out" ["Shilo v meshke"], "The Privy Councillor" ["Tainyi sovetnik"], "Slime" ["Tina"], "Cold Blood" ["Kholodnaya krov' "],"A Nervous Breakdown," "A Boring Story" ["Skuchnaya istoriya"], "Difficult People," "The Duel" ["Duel' "], "The Peasant Wives" ["Baby"], "Terror" ["Strakh"].

6. Sb. *Pamiati A.P. Chekhova,* 1906, 84.

7. Quoted in *Russkie pisateli o literature* (1939), 328.

8. In the excursus to "K voprosu o kharaktere russkogo iazykovogo i literaturnogo razvitiia v novoe vremia," *God. na Sof. Univ.,* 1936. "The Steppe" has something in common with the first two chapters of *Boyhood* which leads me to believe that aside from the Gogol pieces, this work might also have served as a source for Chekhov's story. About this see below.

9. See Professor Chizhevsky's wonderful article on "The Overcoat" in *Sovremennye zapiski,* v. 67.

10. This has already been pointed out by M.A. Osorgin in his article in *Recent News* [*Poslednie novosti*]. Unfortunately, I am unable to give the title of the article and the date of its publication.

Chapter Three

Laconicism

Classical art is perfect art. The perfection of an artistic work consists in its wholeness, its harmony and the absence of anything superfluous. The road to this end is extremely difficult and treacherous. In striving for perfection, in resisting the weaknesses which hinder him in this, the artist is frequently unfair to himself; he does not sufficiently value his achievement. He sacrifices much that should be preserved and used. His attempt to free himself from everything superfluous and his struggle with all kinds of stereotypes and external beauty lead him in the direction of self-imposed restraint and creative asceticism. In a letter to Gorky, Chekhov writes:

> Your descriptions of nature are artistic; you are a real landscape painter. Only your frequent personification (anthropomorphism)—when the sea breathes, the sky gazes, the steppe basks, nature whispers, speaks, mourns, and so on—makes your descriptions somewhat monotonous, sometimes sugary, sometimes obscure; color and expressiveness in nature are attained only by simplicity, by such simple phrases as "The sun set," "It grew dark," "It began to rain," and so on. (January 3, 1899)

But what would remain of Chekhov were he to eliminate similar personification from his own works? What, for example, would remain of his masterpiece "The Steppe?" And how is it possible to achieve "color" and "expressiveness" relying solely on those "simple phrases" which he gives as examples to Gorky? This misunderstanding is probably best explained by the fact that when an artist recognizes in someone else an exaggerated form of something which is peculiar to himself, he considers it annoyingly conventional. Let us return to the comparison cited above concerning the artistic manner of Treplev and Trigorin: "... but I have a quivering light and the silent twinkling of the stars and the distant sound of a piano..." Might this be an oblique criticism of a passage from Turgenev's "Yakov Pasynkov?"

> He [Pasynkov] always insisted that whenever they played Schubert's "Constellations" in his presence, it seemed as if, along with the sound, bluish light poured down on him from above, straight into his heart. To this day when I see a cloudless night sky with softly twinkling stars, I always recall Schubert's melody.... [1]

In Chekhov, however, the description of the moonlit night is by no means always reduced to mention of a glittering bottle fragment. It is a question of the *extent* and *frequency* of comparisons as well as of other means of expression, and principally of their *motivation* [*motivirovannost'*]—the correspondence of "form" and "content," i.e., the general impression one gets from the work in its entirety. With this in mind we might compare Chekhov's "The Gamekeeper" to its model in Turgenev. Turgenev's story begins with a description of the "scene" where the "action" is to take place; it occupies a page and a half. The birch grove is shown from the author's perspective; he comments on his description; "I confess I don't like this tree very much—an aspen—with a pale lilac trunk..." and so on. Once again the story ends with a description of approaching evening. These descriptions are delightful in themselves, but they have no relation to the *syuzhet* of the story. "Landscape" and "genre" are not merged into one whole, into a unified picture; the landscape is merely a "framework" to the story. This is not the case in Chekhov. Although this story also begins with a landscape description, this introductory passage is limited to four lines:

> A sultry, stifling midday. Not a wisp of cloud in the sky.... The sun-scorched grass had a *disconsolate, hopeless* look; even if there were rain, *it could never be green again....* The forest stood silent, motionless, as though it were looking at something with its treetops *or expecting something.*

34

These images evoke the emotional state of a woman in love with her husband, constantly and vainly awaiting his return. Hence, the theme of the story is already embodied in the initial landscape description. Once the landscape has fulfilled its function, it is no longer needed. The story ends with a description of Egor's departure, as seen by his wife:

> He walked down a long road, straight as a taut strap [the symbol of Pelageya's emotional tension]. . . . She stood pale and motionless, like a statue, her eyes seizing upon every step he took. But the red of his shirt merged with the dark color of his trousers, his step could not be seen, and the dog could not be distinguished from the boots. Nothing could be seen but the cap, and . . . suddenly Egor made a sudden turn to the right into the clearing, and the cap vanished in the greenness.
>
> "Good-bye, Egor Vlasych," whispered Pelageya, and she stood on tiptoe to see the white cap once more.

Chekhov's statements on the fundamentals of his poetics are very well known: if there is a gun mentioned in a story, then ultimately it must go off.[2] In his view every work of literature should theoretically be a *system* of interconnected elements, in which nothing can be replaced by anything else; otherwise, the entire system collapses. This, in fact, is the essence of *laconicism*. Such economy of language, of course, is partially related to brevity and terseness; the shorter the perception of a work of art in time, (poetry and music, for example) the easier it may be assimilated as a whole. Laconicism, however, is not the same as brevity; consider, for example, the divine prolixity of Schubert. The elimination from his quartets or from the "Unfinished Symphony" of even a single measure would destroy the whole. This is an important distinction because literary critics occasionally confuse these two concepts.

Chekhov considered "The Student" his best work. In support of this opinion A. Derman cites the compressed content and utmost brevity of the story.[3] Perhaps Chekhov himself was of the same opinion.[4]

In critical remarks scattered throughout his letters, Chekhov constantly stresses the need for maximal brevity in a writer's work. Some of his own works, however, are in no way inferior to "The Student," yet they come closer in length to the "large" narrative form. These works contain many details which, at first glance, may appear superfluous; they require careful analysis to clarify their function within the "system." I shall cite an example from one of his best works, "In the Ravine," in which Lipa brings her child, who has been scalded to death, home from the hospital:

> Lipa went down the road, and before reaching the village, sat down by a pond. A woman led a horse to water, but the horse would not drink.
> "What more do you want?" the woman said to it quietly, perplexed. "What more do you want?"
> A boy in a red shirt, sitting at the water's edge, was washing his father's boots. Not another soul was in sight, either in the village, or on the hill.
> "It's not drinking," said Lipa, looking at the horse.
> Then the woman with the horse and the boy with the boots walked away, and there was no one left at all.

Why is this passage necessary? It becomes clear from what follows:

> Oh, how lovely it is in the open country at night, in the midst of the singing [of birds] when you yourself cannot sing; in the midst of the incessant cries of joy when you yourself cannot be joyful, when the moon, which cares not whether it is spring or winter, whether men are alive or dead, looks down, lonely, too. . . . When the heart grieves, it is hard to be without people. If only her mother, Praskovya, had been with her, or Kostyl, or the cook, or some peasant!

Lipa's difficult situation is emphasized by the fact that at a time when she seeks the company of somebody, anyone at all, the people she meets are concerned with their own insignificant affairs. Lipa makes an effort to take an interest in the horse who will not drink and in the woman leading the horse. But she does not really care about the woman, nor the woman about her. Later, I shall try to show that other details—both the boots which the boy is washing and the red shirt he is wearing—also have an important function in the story. This requires an examination of "In the Ravine" in its entirety. Before proceeding to an analysis of this story, as well as several other outstanding examples of Chekhov's work, we must first become acquainted with various recurring features of his style, or in other words, his laconicism.

Laconicism assumes, first of all, a very carefully motivated use of words; secondly, unity in the system of symbols; and finally, unity in structure [*kompozitsionnyi plan*]. With respect to the first condition, the avoidance of synonyms becomes a criterion of laconicism. There are few writers who do not succumb to the strong temptation to use the wealth of a language, which the wise Fonvizin called "a fool's wealth." That is to say, there are words available in certain categories which, through frequent use, have lost the richness of their original meaning, and their uniqueness; as a result, they have become "synonyms" for other words in ordinary speech. In poetic language one frequently uses synonymous expressions for the sake of variety and stylistic adornment. Precisely the opposite is the standard of artistic perfection—namely, the absence of any *à peu près,* the use of every lexeme, every phrase in a single, specific meaning that can be only approximated by another lexeme, or set phrase. The artist returns meaning to the word, introducing it into a context, or he endows it with *new* meaning previously contained only *in potentia.*

The extent to which Chekhov satisfied this condition may be determined if we compare his use of one category of lexemes with its use by other writers. The particular category of lexemes I have in mind denotes acts of speaking in a narrative context. I have chosen precisely this category because the words it contains, by reason of their common function, have a natural tendency towards synonymity (Indeed, they fulfill, so to speak, an auxiliary role: they indicate the speaker and nothing more.). My choice is further dictated by the fact that, in Russian, unlike many other languages, the number of synonymous lexemes in one of the subcategories of this category is vast—hence, the temptation to spend that "fool's wealth" haphazardly.

This category of lexemes breaks down into two subcategories: words which express the act of speaking in general, and words which express the act of answering questions. The first subcategory includes many words which express nuances of intonation in the act of speaking. I shall cite examples which show Chekhov's use of this lexical wealth and compare this to other artists, among whom, as we have seen, Turgenev is closest to Chekhov in many respects. In the context of the present study I have decided to limit myself to two stories, Turgenev's "The Singers" ["Pevtsy"], considered one of the best examples of his work, and Chekhov's "The Witch" ["Ved'ma"].

"The Singers":

"Begin, begin," chimed in Nikolai Ivanych, approvingly.
"Let's begin, by all means," said [*promolvil*] the boothkeeper,
coolly, "I'm ready."
"And I'm ready," Yakov *pronounced* [*proiznes*] with excitement.
"Well, begin,..." *whined* [*propishchal*] Morgach....
"Begin!" said [*progovoril*] Diky-Barin sharply and sullenly.

Clearly Turgenev does not distinguish shades of meaning
(emotional, intonational) in *said* [*promolvil*], *pronounced*
[*proiznes*], and *said* [*progovoril*]; otherwise he would not add the
modifiers ("coolly," "with excitement," "sharply and sullenly"). If
these verbs alternate in his work, then obviously it is for variety and
stylistic adornment. Compare in "The Witch":

"I know," he [Sexton Savely] muttered [*bormotal*], shaking his finger
menacingly under the bed clothes.
"Come to bed!" *growled* [*provorchal*] the sexton.
"It's the mail," growled [*provorchal*] Savely....
"It has driven by," said [*skazal*] Savely, getting into bed.... The bell
went on ringing awhile, then died away again.
"I don't hear it," *muttered* [*probormotal*] the sexton....
"The postman is lost in the storm," he *wheezed* [prokhripel],
glancing menacingly at his wife.

[The postman, snowbound at Savely's, goes to bed.]

"It's a dog life,"... he *muttered* [*probormotal*], putting his hands
behind his head and closing his eyes.

Savely's suspicions about the witch—his wife—are strengthened,
and he heaps abuse on her. His wife does not leave this unanswered:

"Ah, you long-skirted devil!" *hissed* [*proshipela*] his wife....
"Though I am a long-skirted devil," Savely *said* [*progovoril*] after a
brief interval, "they've no business sleeping here...."

Savely wakes the postman and hurries him off.

"But when are you going?" Savely *prattled on* [*zabarabanil*].

"Your witchery was all in vain: he's gone off," he *said* [*skazal*], grinning with malignant joy....

Savely undressed slowly, clambered over his wife and lay down next to the wall.

"Tomorrow I'll let Father Nikodim know what sort of wife you are!" he *muttered* [*probormotal*], curling himself up.

We would have to quote the entire story to show with absolute clarity how all these individual variations of "to say" [*skazat'*] are motivated. The sexton "mutters" [*bormochet*] when he is half-asleep; still not fully awake, he "growls" [*vorchit*] when he becomes convinced, as he had suspected, that the travelers are "under the witch's spell"; he "mutters" [*bormochet*] again when he begins to think that the danger of anyone arriving has passed, and so forth. Significantly, no direct adverbial attribute is used with any of these verbs: each use of the verb is motivated by a context in which the mood of the speaker is shown through facial expressions and actions. We should also note how Chekhov adheres to the principle of laconicism: when Savely calms down, his speech is rendered by a "neutral" verb, "said" [*skazal*]. When this neutral verb is used a second time, Chekhov conveys the mood of the speaker by indicating his facial expression. This indication suffices, and any equivalent of "said" [*skazal*] would be superfluous here.

Let me add one incidental remark: in prose prior to Chekhov three neutral verbs were used with the meaning of "to say": *skazat'*, *promolvit'*, and *progovorit'*. Turgenev, for example, uses *promolvit'* and *progovorit'* as exact synonyms for *skazat'* in contexts where Pushkin uses only the latter verb. Chekhov uses two neutral verbs of this class: *skazat'* and *progovorit'*, but not without a distinction. The meaning of *progovorit'* is qualified in Chekhov by some attribute which gives slight emphasis to intonation, whereas *skazat'* fulfills an absolutely neutral function. Here are several examples taken at random:

Aunt Dasha came into the room and said [*skazala*]: "Alena upset you, darling. I have sent her home to the village...."

"Auntie," *said* [*progovorila*] Vera *quickly,* "I am going to marry Dr. Neshchapov." ("At Home") ["V rodnom uglu"]

The horses were white as snow (. . .). "Pure swans," *said* [*progovoril*]
Rodion, *looking at them with reverence....*

"Yes, they're white, but what of it?" he [Kozov] *said* [*skazal*]. ("The
New Country House") ["Novaya dacha"]

Zhenya shook her head, and *tears came to her eyes.* "That's
incomprehensible!" she said [*progovorila*]. ("The House with an
Attic")

Compare in the same story:

"Oh, Mama," Zhenya said [*skazala*], "It's not good for you to sleep
during the day."

The verb *progovorit'* by itself is neutral in Chekhov; therefore
he allows for different kinds of modifiers[5] and never uses it without
such modifiers, which justifies its use side by side with the verb
skazat'. These verbs are not synonyms in Chekhov. The fact that of
these two verbs, Chekhov invariably chose to use *progovorit'* rather
than *skazat'* with a modifier, is fully justified from a lexical point of
view: *progovorit'* does not appear in everyday, conversational
speech and is, therefore, felt to be a more weighty and expressive
lexeme than *skazat'.*
   The second subcategory consists of two lexemes, *otvechat'* and
otvetit', both meaning "to answer." They have a very complicated
history which would take too long to treat in any depth here. At the
same time, however, it is essential to consider some examples which
will establish Chekhov's place in the history of the Russian literary
language in general. I shall, therefore, devote time to these lexemes,
but confine myself to the larger aspects of their evolution.
   Old Russian knew only *otvechat'.* According to I.I. Dmitriev,
otvetit' appeared in everyday language during the latter half of his
life: "Only peasant men and women from Kashira and other upriver
cities used to speak that way before."[6]
   I have nowhere encountered *otvetit'* in the Russian classics of
the first half of the nineteenth century, nor in Tolstoy, whose
language is lexically the same as that of Pushkin and Lermontov.
Otvetit' appears for the first time in Herzen, Turgenev, and also
among the *raznochintsy* writers; both in the latter and in Turgenev
otvetit' and *otvechat'* are synonyms. We find the following examples

from *Fathers and Sons:* " 'We'll see, (...)?' 'As you command,' answered [*otvetil*] Bazarov." Compare: " 'Take a look and see if my tongue is yellow.' 'It is,' answered [*otvechal*] Arkady." These verbs with their attributive words and phrases are not at all differentiated here:

> "Evgeny Vasilevich," answered [*otvechal*] Bazarov in a lazy, but masculine voice....
> "Hello," she answered [*otvetila*] in a soft, but sonorous voice.

In another dialogue Bazarov "answered [otvetil] with a brief yawn," and in the same place "carelessly answered" [otvechal].[7]

In Chekhov *otvechat'* and *otvetit'* are differentiated. In the first place he understands *otvechat'* to be an imperfective or iterative verb. This explains its use, for example, in the following context:

> As a rule I went in unannounced....
> "Who is there?" I would hear...a voice....
> "It is Pavel Konstantinovich," answered [*otvechala*] the maid or the nurse. ("About Love") ["O lyubvi"]

Compare also:

> They sent for the steward to come to the house every now and then. "Tabunov?" they would ask him. "Kopytin? Zherebovsky?"
> "No, not at all," *answered* [*otvechal*] Ivan Evseich and...continued to think aloud. ("A Horsey Name") ["Loshadinnaya familiya"]

Compare also:

> When Ariadne and I fished for gudgeon, Lubkov...poked fun at me or instructed me in the art of living. "Can you live without romance?" he asked. "I am baffled, sir.... I'm nearly ten years older than you, but which of us is the younger? You tell us, Ariadne." "You, of course," Ariadne *answered* [*otvechala*]. ("Ariadne") ["Ariadna"]

Only once do we find *otvechal* used without an iterative nuance:

> "Why should we accept that?" shouted [*krichal*] von Shtenberg....
> "Whose cauldrons are these?" "Nikitin's...." a bass *answered* [*otvechal*] sullenly. ("Lights") ["Ogni"]

41

Here *otvechal* corresponds to *krichal* [*shouted*]. Instead of an iterative nuance, duration is implied; from the context, obviously, it is a long drawn out argument, leading nowhere.

Secondly, and in connection with this underlying meaning of *otvechat'*, the verb is used (rarely, by the way) to express a hint of indecision and langour in a speaker who is responding to a question:

> "I believe it is time for you to have your milk," Tanya said to her husband.
> "No, it is not time yet ... " he *answered* [*otvechal*], sitting down on the bottom step. ("The Black Monk") ["Chernyi monakh"]

I have found *otvechat'* as a synonym for *otvetit'* only in one early work: "'Who is this Nikolashka?' 'The master's valet,' *answered* [*otvechal*] Efrem" ("The Phosphorous Match"). ["Shvedskaya spichka"]

Footnotes to Chapter Three

1. Compare another example:

> This is what I imagined. Night. A moon, the moonlight, white and soft ... a wide expanse of water, a flat island ...; on the island ... a small marble house with open windows; music is heard, coming from I know not where. ... ("Faust")

Chekhov intentionally deflates this poetic image of night in his story, "Lights" ["Ogni"]:

> I remember I was sitting in an easy chair by the wide-open window, and gazing at the trees and the darkening sky. The silhouette of the acacias and lindens was just the same as eight years ago; the same as then ... far away a piano clinked dreadfully. ...

Incidentally, a description of moonlight is rendered in great detail in Turgenev's story, "The Dog," which served as a model for Chekhov's "The Wolf"; there everything is reduced to the sparkling neck of a bottle. This provides added evidence that Chekhov's style evolved, to a significant extent, as an "answer" to Turgenev.

2. S. Shchukin, "Iz vospominanii o Chekhove," *Russkaia mysl'*, 1911, X, 44. Also in a letter to Lazarev-Gruzinsky, 1889: "One can't put a loaded gun on the stage if no one plans to fire it." Nemirovich-Danchenko contends that he suggested this formula to Chekhov as a criticism of the first draft of *The Seagull* (*Iz proshlogo*, 51). But Chekhov began to write *The Seagull* in the 1890s, while the letter to Lazarev-Gruzinsky is dated 1889.

3. *Op. cit.*, 201.

4. Consider what he wrote to Grigorovich about his work on "The Steppe":

> Every single chapter consists of a particular story and all the chapters are closely interrelated, like the five movements of a quadrille. I am trying to give them a unity of feeling and tone; this is not difficult to achieve since one character figures in all the chapters. [Jan. 12, 1888]

We can find no better means to express the idea of unity of content in a literary work. But it is evident from what follows that, theoretically at least, he has a narrow view of how to accomplish this. Brevity is essential to unity and much must be sacrificed: "as a result you end up with a dry, detailed enumeration, more like a conspectus, than a picture." Fortunately Chekhov, the artist, as usual, parted ways with Chekhov, the theoretician, and "The Steppe" in its final form, can scarcely be called a "dry conspectus."

5. For example, in "Peasants":

"He's no breadwinner," said [*progovorila*] the old woman *tearfully*.

"May they burst!" Fekla, who was sleepy, said [*progovorila*] *spitefully*.

"Enjoy your tea!" said [*progovorila*] Fekla *sarcastically*.

"The zemstvo," said [*progovoril*] Osip *dejectedly*.

"About this time they are serving dinner at the Slavyansky Bazaar," said [*progovoril*] Nikolai *dreamily*.

Sometimes, instead of using such direct modifiers with *progovorit'*, Chekhov relies on a more indirect method, by showing facial expression, gesticulation, etc., which gives the impression of intonation in the utterance:

His mother smiled, beamed, but at once she made a grave face and said [*progovorila*]: "Thank you."

"I have a fever....," said [*progovoril*] the bishop and sat down. ("The Bishop")

6. "Vzgliad na moiu zhizn'," quote from V. Vinogradov, *Ocherki po istorii russkogo literaturnogo iazyka XVII-XIX* vv., Moskva, 1938, 302 ff. In works of Russian folklore I have found *otvetit'* only in one religious poem (Bezsonov, *Kaliki perekhozhie*, no. 26): "Aleksei Bozhy answered [*otvetil*] the father: 'Great thou art, Prince Ofimyany...'."

7. Compare also: " 'You smoke, of course?'
'I mostly smoke cigars,' answered [*otvetil*] Arkady."
But: " 'Did you sleep well?'
'Very well,' answered [*otvechal*] Arkady."

Chapter Four

Impressionism

Underlying Chekhov's art is the strictly motivated use of every means of expression, the elimination of any "ornamentation" in the language which would exist solely for the sake of external "beauty," the exclusion of any *à peu près,* and the inclusion of all details into a system. This tendency becomes apparent when we examine the trivial points just cited—trivial, of course, only when superficially understood. From an esthetic point of view the concept of detail, in the meaning of triviality, is nonsensical. Of what, if not trivialities, does "Über allen Gipfeln" or "On the Hills of Georgia" ["Na kholmax Gruzii"] consist? Karenin's ugly ears are as essential to the novel as Anna committing suicide by throwing herself under a train, because her tragedy is predetermined by those ears. Hence, everything which is indispensable to the system and which contributes to the unity of a work of art is important.

What, then, is this unity? Insofar as our subject here is literature, we must distinguish between "prose," i.e., narration or story, and "poetry." Unity in prose is composed of the indispensable interdependence of concrete phenomena, or events, and their reflection in the conscious mind—what Tolstoy has called "linkages." Herein lies unity of the life process; what happens within a closed circle of a few people is necessarily included in the history of the whole society; what happens *hic et nunc* to each of these people is included in his personal history from birth to death. At its extreme the novel is an epic. *War and Peace* [Voina i mir] leans in this direction, and Tolstoy, as we know, considered the framework of his novel too confining. It was only a prologue to the story of the Decembrists which itself was to be preceded by an epic on Peter the Great.

The content of poetry at its extreme is also unlimited, but in a different way. Neither "Über allen Gipfeln" nor "On the Hills of Georgia" have a beginning or end; therefore, the possibility of expanding the framework is no longer relevant. What is shown, by reason of just *how* it is shown, is *already* contained in an infinity, but this is an infinity of a different dimension than the infinity of the life process; it is an existence not bound by time. There are no linkages here, no "knot" which has to be "untied." The unity here lies in the coordination of symbols which are not necessarily images but can simply be phonations, e.g. the repeated *l* and *au* in Goethe. There is a formal perfection here which in and of itself implies realization, completion, i.e., life within another dimension of reality—timeless, and in this sense, eternal.

"Prose" and "poetry" are thus in a polar relationship to each other. Clearly their means of expression must also adhere to the same relationship. Prose tends toward a realistic or mimetic reproduction of life, poetry toward a symbolic or impressionistic one (which are essentially the same). Hence "prose" requires an exhaustive reproduction of concrete details, although each detail need not be shown directly. The exposition of a single characteristic, trivial detail is in some cases sufficient for the reader to perceive the remainder of a given whole. This, as we know, was Tolstoy's method, so superbly noted by Chekhov: "Tolstoy's heroes are taken as 'whole'," he wrote to Suvorin in Oct. 27, 1889. "Their past and present are deduced from hints, but you wouldn't say that these heroes do not satisfy you."

In poetry, however, from every empirically given object one grasps separate features relating it to a universe, the existence of which is inferred and felt, but which is itself empirically absent. In any event, it is clear that insofar as we are dealing with appropriate means of literary expression, prose tends more to an "analytic" style, and poetry to a "synthetic" one.[1] Moreover, these qualities can appear when the poet's attention is directed to the "first" dimension of reality and not to the "second," whereas the attention of the prose writer is focused precisely on the "second" dimension. Of course, the formula proposed above is necessarily schematic; the "prose writer" and the "poet" are present in every great writer and it is all a question of which tendency predominates at a given moment. With this in mind, Turgenev's works provide a particularly vivid example of "analytic" style, because he was in many ways a "prose poet." Let us take as an example the description of the fair in "Lebedyan":

> Endless rows of carts were stretched out in the market place, and behind the carts stood horses of every possible breed: racers, stud-horses, dray horses, carthorses, posting-hacks and simple peasant nags. Some, fat and sleek, assorted by colors, covered with striped horsecloths and tied short to high racks, turned furtive glances backwards at the all too familiar whips of their owners, the horse-dealers; privately owned horses, sent by noblemen of the steppes a hundred or two hundred miles away, in the charge of some decrepit old coachman and two or three headstrong stable boys, shook their long necks, stamped and gnawed at the fences from boredom; grayish horses from Vyatka huddled close to one another; race horses, dapple-gray, raven and sorrel with large hindquarters, flowing tails and shaggy legs stood in majestic immobility like lions. Connoisseurs stopped respectfully before them. People of every class, age and appearance thronged in the street formed by the rows of carts; horse-dealers in long blue coats and high caps, with sly faces, were on the lookout for buyers; gypsies, with staring eyes and curly heads, strolled up and down . . . looking into the horses' mouths, lifting up a hoof or a tail, shouting, swearing. . . .

We find an extreme example of "synthetic" style, once again a description of a fair, in Gogol's "The Sorochintsy Fair":

> You have no doubt heard somewhere a rushing waterfall, when everything is quivering and filled with uproar, and a chaos of strange, vague sounds floats like a whirlwind around you. Are you not instantly overcome by the same feelings in the turmoil of a village fair, *when all the people become one huge monster that moves its massive body* through the square and narrow streets, with shouting, laughing and clatter? Noise, swearing, bellowing, bleating, roaring—*all blend into one jarring uproar.* Oxen, sacks, hay, gypsies, pots, peasant women, cakes, caps—everything is bright, gaudy, discordant, flitting in groups, shifting to and fro before your eyes. The different voices drown one another, and not a single word can be caught or saved from the deluge. . . . Only the clapping of hands after each bargain is heard on all sides. A wagon breaks down, there is the clank of iron, the thud of boards thrown onto the ground, and one's head is so dizzy one does not know which way to turn.

These are extreme cases. The description of the Christmas fair in Chekhov's "In Moscow in Trubnaya Square" ["V Moskve na Trubnoi ploshchadi"] stands midway between these two extremes:

Hundreds of sheepskins, wadded coats, fur caps and stovepipe hats swarm there, like crabs in a sieve. The discordant singing of birds, recalling spring, is heard. If the sun is shining and there are no clouds in the sky, the singing of birds and the smell of hay make a more vivid impression, and this reminder of spring sets one thinking and carries one's fancy far, far away. Along one side of the square there stands a row of wagons. The wagons are loaded, not with hay, not with cabbages, nor with beans, but with goldfinches, siskins, larks, blackbirds and thrushes, bluetits and bullfinches. All of them are hopping about in crude, homemade cages, twittering and looking with envy at the free sparrows.... Splashing through the mud, schoolboys, workmen, young men in stylish overcoats and bird fanciers in incredibly shabby caps, in ragged trousers that are turned up at the ankles and look as though they had been gnawed by mice, crowd around the birds.

The above excerpt is from Chekhov's early period (1883). To understand Chekhov's artistic development we should contrast the excerpt with two variations of crowd scenes from later masterpieces, "Easter Eve" ["Svyatoyu noch'yu"] and "The Rolling Stone":

"Easter Eve":

We floated straight out of the darkness and stillness of the river into an enchanted realm, full of stifling smoke, crackling light and uproar. By now one could distinctly see people moving near the tar barrels. The flickering of the lights gave a strange, almost fantastic, expression to their figures and red faces. From time to time one caught among the heads and faces a glimpse of horses' heads, motionless as though cast in copper.

"The Rolling Stone":

The large courtyard of the monastery... was a living hodgepodge full of movement, sound and the most uncommon confusion. It... was all choked up with carts and old-fashioned coaches... about which stood crowds of horses, dark and white, horned oxen, while people bustled about, and long black-skirted lay brothers threaded their way in and out in all directions. Shadows and streaks of light cast from the windows moved

47

This path led to the dark monastery gates that looked like a cavern, through a cloud of smoke, through a disorderly crowd of people, unharnessed horses, carts and chaises. All this was rattling, sporting and laughing, and the shadows from the smoke flickered over it all. over the carts and the heads of men and horses, and in the dense twilight all this assumed the most monstrous, capricious shapes: here the tilted shafts stretched upward to the sky, here eyes of fire appeared in the face of a horse, there a lay brother grew a pair of black wings. . . . Talk, the snorting and munching of horses, the creaking of carts, the whimpering of children were heard.

The above examples bear a striking similarity to Gogol. But to establish Chekhov's spiritual genealogy, and thereby understand the essentials of his artistry, it is even more important to cite another example of a collective scene, in which Chekhov shows a much closer affinity to Lermontov than to Gogol; moreover, the passage I have in mind is from a work which epitomizes Chekhov's art, "The Bishop":

In the twilight of the church the crowd *heaved like the sea,* and to Bishop Petr . . . it seemed that all the faces . . . were alike, that everyone who came up for the palm had *the same expression in his eyes.*

Compare this to Lermontov's "Vadim":

Somewhat nearer, among the pillars and opposite the altar gates, stood a multicolored crowd. In front of Vadim was *an excited sea of heads.* . . . Vadim *tried to guess the state of mind of each pilgrim from his outer appearance, but he was not successful;* he lost his sense of reality and soon everything merged before his eyes into a multicolored assembly of tatters, into a heap of eyes and beards; and illuminated by a single light, they seemed to belong to one living and perpetually moving creature. . . .

"Analytic" style in a literary work is not the same, of course, as the style of the "protocol statement," or diplomatic reportage, although Stendhal asserts that he took the latter as his model; nor

48

does Stendhal necessarily shun such figurative means of expression as simile, metaphor, etc., but he uses them with greater restraint. The following excerpt, from Turgenev, is an extreme case in the use of "analytic" simile:

> Over the clear sky the high, thin clouds hardly stirred, yellowish-white like late spring snow, flat and drawn out like dropped sails. Their fringed edge, soft and fluffy as cottonwood...changed at every moment. ("Kasyan from Fair Springs") ["Kasyan s Krasivoi Mechi"]

Here, rather than rendering the object as it might be perceived directly, Turgenev breaks it into its characteristic properties, and for each property he finds something which most characterizes it. The cloud is metamorphosed, as it were, into a laboratory specimen. We may contrast this passage to another excerpt, from Chekhov's "The Steppe," an example of impressionistic, "synthetic" style, just as extreme, but poles apart from Turgenev:

> But at last, thank God, a wagon, loaded with sheaves, came to meet them; a peasant wench was lying on the very top. Sleepy, exhausted by the heat, she lifted her head and looked at the travelers. Deniska gaped, looking at her; the horses stretched out their muzzles toward the sheaves; the chaise, squeaking, kissed the wagon, and the pointed ears of grain passed over Father Khristophor's hat like a brush.

One is immediately struck by the bold use of humor here, which surpasses even Gogol. Not only are the carriage and the wagon personified, but they are assigned a role which we would expect to be performed only by Deniska and the peasant girl. Verisimilitude, moreover, is not violated, notwithstanding the violation in the hierarchy of objects and logic. Of course, the carriage and the wagon, the girl and Deniska, the sheaves and the horses are all elements of one object inasmuch as these elements are unconsciously perceived by Egorushka. Deniska's potential act of kissing the girl is actualized in the image of the chaise bumping into the wagon. The total impression arises from a succession of unconscious hints and suggestions. The image which Chekhov suggests to himself, via his description of the girl and the gaping Deniska, and which in turn he suggests to the reader, supplants both the girl and Deniska as independent objects and includes them in a whole.[2]

Suggestion of this sort, generally speaking, is one of the most characteristic features of "synthetic" style; this is commonly acknowledged insofar as it concerns poetry in the conventional sense of the word, i.e., verse. Critics usually ignore this synthetic element in prose. Yet its presence or absence is a criterion for deciding whether a work, without meter or rhyme, may be considered poetry or prose. We must analyze such a work from this viewpoint in order to understand it. The language of "The Student" ["Student"], a story which, as we have indicated, Chekhov held in high regard, is significant to an understanding of his prose:

[Introduction]: At first the weather was fine and still. . . . A snipe *flew by* [*protyanul*]. And the shot aimed at it rang out [*prozvuchal*] with a gay, resounding note in the spring air. But when it began to get dark in the forest, a cold, penetrating [*pronizyvayuschii*] wind blew unexpectedly from the east, and everything sank into silence. Needles of ice *stretched* [*protyanulis'*] across the pools. There was a whiff of winter. [And further on]: At just such a fire the Apostle Peter warmed himself, said the student, *stretching out* [*protyagivaya*] his hands to the fire.

The italicized verb [different forms of *protyagivat'*] is repeated three times, and attention is further drawn to it by two other instances of alliteration [*prozvuchal, pronizyvayushchii*].[3] This suggests what will happen to the student later on:

"The past," he thought, "is linked to the present by an *unbroken chain* of events, one flowing out of another." And it seemed to him that he had just seen both ends of that chain, that when he touched *one end the other* quivered.

Likewise the ferry crossing at the end of the story is symbolically connected with this.

In "The Murder" ["Ubiistvo"] we find a particularly extensive and subtle use of symbolic imagery and verbal suggestion. The entire action takes place against one background. All the episodes occur at night during the "howl of a snow storm." This is the basic motif of the story, which recurs in a series of elaborations; moreover, the frequent verbal correspondences in separate passages are significant:

50

[Matvei is returning from the station, where the evening service has been celebrated.] There was no frost, and the snow was already melting on the roofs, though it was still falling in big flakes; they were whirling rapidly round and round in the air and white clouds chased them along the railway lines. [He approaches the house.] The barrier was raised, and near it whole mountains had drifted and clouds of snow were whirling round like *witches on broomsticks*.

When used a second time in a new variation, the image vividly reveals its symbolic aspect. It is used in yet another variation in the episode where Yakov leaves home, after the murder of Matvei, when everything has by then been finished:

Lights, red and green, were already gleaming in the station and along the line; the wind had died down, but flakes of snow were still coming down, and the road turned white again.

A similar image appears in the epilogue in the description of a storm, during which Yakov goes to load coal on a ship with a party of other exiles. The story concludes with this symbolic image:

A strong piercing wind was blowing by now; somewhere on the steep cliff overhead, the trees were creaking. Most likely a storm was coming.[4]

This image is strengthened by another, related image, in which voices are heard from somewhere:

[The Terekhovs are at home, celebrating the evening service. Yakov reads in a singsong voice. Aglaya hums along with him.] And upstairs, above the ceiling there was a sound of indistinct voices which seemed like a threat or a foreboding of evil.

This theme of "two voices" is later repeated in a new mode:

[Yakov and Aglaya again are celebrating the service.] But all at once there was the sound of voices. The policeman and Sergei Nikanorych had come to see Matvei. Yakov Ivanych was embarrassed to read aloud and sing while there were strangers in the house, and now, hearing voices, he began reading slowly and in a whisper.... Afterwards the visitors left and silence followed. But Yakov Ivanych had hardly begun reading and singing again when a voice was heard outside the door: "Brother, let me have a horse to drive to Vedenyapino." It was Matvei. And Yakov was troubled again.

What takes place in Yakov's heart and what he relates as having happened earlier in Matvei's heart—something "demoniacal," an obsession—is transferred to nature, and to the surroundings; moreover, it is as if the "demon" is personified in that constantly blowing and howling wind:

> The wind blew straight into his face, flapping his collar, and it seemed as though it were whispering to him all these thoughts, carrying them from the broad white plain. [Further on, Yakov goes out for a walk in the courtyard.] . . . Snow was falling in big flakes at the time. His beard was blown about in the wind. He kept shaking his head as though there were something weighing upon his head and shoulders, as though demons were sitting on them; and it seemed to him that it was not he walking about, but some wild beast. . . .

The senseless murder of Matvei, unexpected by even the participants themselves, is motivated and prepared for, so to speak, by the symbolism of the story, so that it is perceived as something which inevitably *must* happen. The coloring and tone "of demonic possession" is further strengthened by a series of images associated with all that is inherent in the reworking of the themes of cheap pictures [*lyubochnye kartiny*] or religious verse, and of what comprises the element of religion introduced by the people in the story—the *lights* at the station, the *sulfur* which burns with a *blue* light (the match lit by Yakov), the piercing *whistle* of the locomotive, the *"evil,"* heavy *odor* coming from the paper money which Yakov pulls out after the murder in order to silence Sergei Nikanorych, the horses which run out of the yard and *"with their tails raised, wildly* race along the road."

We have seen how repetition of individual, partial images functions in realizing the total image. Having considered this, we are able to interpret definitively the passage cited above from "In the Ravine." Why is mention made of the boy in a red shirt cleaning his father's boots? The boots are connected with a previous episode in which Lipa and her mother return from a pilgrimage, at a time when she is still happy:

> An old woman led a little boy in big boots; the boy was exhausted from the heat and the heavy boots . . . , yet he kept blowing with all his might on a toy trumpet.

The reader unwittingly remembers how Lipa returned home for the first time, and puts himself in her place. The red shirt prepares the reader for the image which follows:

> Then the woman with the horse and the boy with the boots walked away, and there was no one left at all. The sun went to bed, wrapped in cloth of gold and *crimson,* and long clouds, *red* and lilac, stretched across the sky and guarded its slumbers.

The boy, the woman, the sun, etc., all merge into one image, an image of withdrawal and retreat, leaving Lipa alone with her grief. Compare this with a passage from "A Dead Body" ["Mertvoe telo"]:

> A quiet August night. Fog rises slowly from the field and covers everything accessible to the eye with a dull *shroud.* Illuminated by the moon the fog gives the impression now . . . of the sea, now of an enormous *white* wall; . . . not far from . . . the road . . . a light shines. Here . . . lies a dead body, covered from head to foot with new, *white, unbleached linen.*[5]

The analytic writer, the "realist," tries to see and reveal empirical data, so to speak, from all possible viewpoints, or, to restate this in another way, from *no particular* viewpoint; conversely a synthetic, impressionistic view of reality inevitably assumes *one particular* viewpoint. Reality is not shown "empirically," but as it appears to the viewer—the author, or the one for whom the author speaks. Hence authors in whom this tendency is most apparent frequently use expressions like *to seem (it seemed, it seems to me)* [*kazat'sya, (kazalos', mne kazhetsya)*], *something* [chto-to] *as if* [*kak budto*] and the like. True, "realist" writers frequently use *exactly* [*tochno*] and *like* [*slovno*], which introduce developed similes, but most characteristically they use expressions of the first two types. Such expressions are especially common among those writers whom Chekhov most respected: Tolstoy, whose work *The Cossacks* [Kazaki] he particularly admired, and Lermontov, of whose language he wrote:

No one's language is better than Lermontov's. I would do this: I would take one of his stories and analyze it the way they analyze in schools, sentence by sentence, by parts of sentences.... That's how I would learn to write.[6]

We encounter passages in *The Cossacks* where *to seem* appears several times within a single context:

There was a feeling in the air that the sun had risen. The mist was dissolving, but it still enveloped the tops of the trees. The forest *seemed* terribly high. At every step the surroundings changed: what had *seemed like* a tree proved to be a bush, a reed *seemed like* a tree. (end of Ch. VIII)

To seem combined with *all this* [*vse eto*] etc. conveys an integral perception of reality, e.g. in *The Cossacks:*

This *forest*, the *danger*, the *old man* and his mysterious *whispering*, Maryanka with her strong, stately *figure*, and the *mountains—all this seemed* to Olenin like a dream.[7]

It seemed makes possible the combination of even the most logically incompatible components into a single whole, into *all this*. Lermontov's language shares the same characteristics:

It *seemed* the artist had concentrated all of his attention upon the eyes and the smile. The head was larger than life-size, and the hair fell evenly along both sides of the forehead ... which was very prominent, and *it seemed* to have something extraordinary in its structure. The eyes ... shone ... with a strange glitter.... Their probing ... look, *it seemed*, followed one into every corner of the room. ("Princess Ligovskaya") ["Knyaginya Ligovskaya"]

The same thing occurs in "Taman'," about which Chekhov remarked to Bunin: "I don't understand how he, a mere boy, could have done it. If I could write such a work, and also a good vaudeville sketch, then I could die!"[8] *To seem* is used three times in "Taman'" within one passage:

> She sat down facing me (...) her eyes fixed upon me, and I don't know why, but her look *seemed* to be wondrously tender (...). She *seemed* to be waiting for a question (...), now her bosom would rise high, and now she *would seem* to be holding her breath.

Among non-Russian writers, Chekhov especially liked de Maupassant.[9] Significantly, the construction *to seem* is also characteristic of de Maupassant:

> [For example, in "L'Héritage"]: La Seine, lourde, coulait, triste et boueuse des pluies dernières, entre ses berges rongées par les crues de l'hiver; et toute la campagne trempée d'eau, *semblait* sortir d'un bain (...).
> [In "Miss Harriet"]: Le soleil enfin se leva devant nous (...) et, à mesure qu'il montait, plus clair de minute en minute, la campagne *paraissait* s'éveiller, sourire, se secouer, et ôter, comme une fille qui sort du lit, sa chemise de vapeurs blanches.
> [In "Boule de Suif"]: Quand il buvait, *sa grande barbe,* qui avait gardé la nuance de son breuvage aimé, *semblait tressaillir de tendresse:* ses yeux louchaient pour ne point perdre de vue sa chope, et il avait l'air de remplir l'unique fonction pour laquelle il était né.

This passage is especially interesting because of the many stylistic features it has in common with Chekhov. It is difficult to know the extent to which Chekhov's art reflects his enthusiasm for de Maupassant. Evidently Chekhov became acquainted with de Maupassant's works only after he had developed his own style. Despite rather significant differences, their works reveal a common spiritual temperament and artistic direction.

I have already mentioned Gogol's influence on Chekhov. I should like to comment further here on the affinity between their styles. We may observe that *to seem* is also encountered very frequently in Gogol, for example in "The Sorochintsy Fair":

> How luxuriously warm the hours, when midday glitters in stillness and sultry heat, and the blue fathomless ocean ... it seems, has dozed off, bathed in languor....

Already, in the distance, the cool air was felt and *seemed* the more welcome after the exhausting heat.

Mountains of pots...moved slowly along; *it seemed* that they were weary with their imprisonment....

The mountains of musk melons, watermelons and pumpkins *seemed* cast in gold and dark copper.

We also find numerous instances of *to seem* in Turgenev; his work combines "prose" with "poetry," and an "analytic" quality is sometimes displaced by a "synthetic" manner. No writer, however, uses *to seem* more conspicuously than Chekhov. *To seem* occurs on almost every page in Chekhov, not only in his earliest works, but, what is more significant, it is very often seen in his later and more highly polished works. In "The Lady with a Lapdog" ["Dama s sobachkoi"], for example, it appears eighteen times, and in "The Bishop" twenty times; moreover, in the latter work in addition to *it seemed* [*kazalos*] and *it seemed to him* [*emu kazalos*], there are also similar, if not synonymous, words: *it appeared* [*predstavlyalos*], *it was as if* [*pokhozhe bylo chto*], and so forth.

Thus far I have given only a general formulation of the function of *to seem*. Specific examples indicate that, depending on the context, numerous shades of meaning can be differentiated in Chekhov's use of the word.[10] *To seem* is first of all used to render associations linked with an immediate impression,[11] and secondly, to render the distinctive and at times illusory quality of these perceptions. Furthermore, in view of changes in meaning effected by these humorous devices, the perceived "dead" object is sometimes given attributes of a living being; instead of comparing an inanimate object with something living, a character may perceive it directly as though it were alive.[12] Finally, *to seem* renders concrete objective perception when mere simple statement of fact would be too general or colorless. For example, in "The Black Monk":

The glorious bay, reflecting the moon and the lights, was of a color difficult to name. It was a soft and tender mingling of blue and green; in places the water looked like blue copper, and in places the *moonlight seemed to thicken and now filled the bay instead of the water....*

56

Thus, the light in the passage above is made concrete; it is transformed from a concept into an object, as, in fact, it is perceived. There are also many examples in Tolstoy, Gogol and Lermontov, where, as above, *to seem* renders the perception of separate objects and separate phenomena as an indivisible whole, or communicates the subject's general emotional reaction to all these perceptions:

> A March night, cloudy and foggy, envelopes the earth, and *it seems* to the watchman that the earth, the sky and he himself with his thoughts are all *merged together* into something vast and impenetrably black. ("A Bad Business") ["Nedobroe delo"]

> Ilovskaya gazed wonderingly into the darkness, and saw only a spot of red on the icon and the flicker of the light from the stove on Likharev's face. The darkness, the chime of the bells, the roar of the storm, fretful Sasha, unhappy Likharev and his speeches—*all this was mingled together, appearing as one huge impression, and God's world seemed to her fantastic,* full of marvels and magical forces. ("On the Road")

> Vyazove was in sight now, and the school with the green roof, and the church with its crosses flashing in the evening sun; the station windows flashed too, and a pink smoke rose from the engine, ...*and it seemed to her* that *everything* was trembling with cold. ("In the Cart")

> Varvara Nikolaevna had a warm, friendly smile, and *everything* in the house *seemed to smile too.* ("In the Ravine")

> And now the Volga was dingy, all of one even color without a gleam of light, cold-looking. Everything recalled the approach of dreary, gloomy autumn. And *it seemed* as though nature had removed from the Volga the sumptuous green covers from its banks, the brilliant reflections of the sunbeams, the transparent blue distance and *all its smart gala array,* and had packed it away in boxes till the coming spring, and the crows were flying above the Volga crying tauntingly, "Bare, bare!" ("The Grasshopper") ["Poprygun'ya"]

One other lexeme—*for some reason* [*pochemu-to*]—is functionally connected with the use of *to seem*. I will dwell on examples from "The Betrothed," a story in which *for some reason* is very often encountered.

57

And now her mother...*somehow seemed* very young;
And *for some reason one wanted* to cry;
And for some reason it seemed to her that it would be like that all her life...;
For some reason it used to be said about him...;
Now *for some reason* she felt annoyed;
And she felt sorry for him and *for some reason* awkward;
But *for some reason* now...she began to feel dread...;
She remembered *for some reason*...;
And *for some reason* he seemed to Nadya gray and provincial;
And *for some reason* Andrei Andreich arose in her imagination and the naked lady with the vase, and all her past, which now *seemed*...as far away as her childhood;
And *for some reason* it was funny to be lying in this...bed.

The expression *for some reason* conveys the heroine's comprehension of the "unreality" of her surroundings and her experiences. This unreality is the source of her spiritual crisis, a state which she cannot immediately understand or explain to herself. Significantly, we find *for some reason* mainly in impersonal constructions and in conjunction with *it seemed,* thereby further emphasizing her dependence on what she perceives.

The passive attitude of the subject to what is perceived determines the integrity of the perceptions. The practical "active" man reduces what he perceives into parts, then distributes these parts into categories, and thus, guided by practical reason, he defines his attitude to what he has perceived and experienced. The passive or, in other words, "poetic" perception of data is of a totally different character. Certain sentences with *it seemed* cited above help to clarify this point. There this lexeme allows Chekhov to employ devices which are maximally daring and unexpected and, as a rule, are used for attaining humorous effects.

I have in mind instances where perceived objects are enumerated in such a way that something begins "to seem" to the viewer. The established hierarchy of objects, as well as their logical order, is violated. Concrete objects—their attributes and their appearance—are all enumerated as though logically identical in value. (In this respect, Chekhov, as I have said, goes even further than Gogol, who attains humorous effects mostly by violating the hierarchy of objects or qualities.) Incidentally, in similar instances, Chekhov at times dispenses with *to seem:*

The *duty* of smiling and talking incessantly, the *clatter* of crockery, the *stupidity* of the servants, the *long intervals* between the courses and the *corset* she had put on . . . wearied her to exhaustion. ("Name-Day")

Since Nikitin had been in love with Manyusya, everything at the Shelestov's pleased him: the house, the garden, and the evening tea, and the wicker chairs, and the old nurse, and even the word "loutishness," which the old man was fond of using. ("Teacher of Literature") ["Uchitel' slovesnosti"]

And everything about it was uncanny and sinister: the dark *walls* and the *silence,* and the *galoshes,* and the *immobility* of the dead body. ("On Official Duty") ["Po delam sluzhby"]

Compare other variants of this type of passage:

The May twilight, the tender young greenery with its shadows, the scent of the lilac, the buzzing of the insects, the *silence,* the warmth—how marvelous it all was. . . . ("My Life")

The darkness and the two little windows brightly lit by the moon, the *silence* and the creak of the cradle for some reason made them think of nothing but that life was over. . . . ("Peasants")

Compare enumerations in Turgenev:

The former fraülein . . . introduced him . . . to her husband. Everything about him sparkled: his eyes, and his black hair combed into a forelock, and his forehead, and his teeth, and the buttons on his coat, and the chain on his vest, and even his boots. . . . ("Yakov Pasynkov")

Everything is in its proper place here: the "sparkling" parts of the male figure are enumerated in the order in which they are to be viewed, according to their relative significance. The image is broken down into its elements and arranged in a descending line. Compare an analogous instance of enumerations in *Nest of Gentry* [*Dvoryanskoe gnezdo*]:

Marfa Timofeevna was sitting in her room, surrounded by her little court. It consisted of five creatures almost equally dear to her heart: a big-cropped, learned bullfinch..., ...a little dog, Roska, an ill-tempered cat, Matros,...a little girl, nine years old...and an elderly woman..., Nastasya Karlovna Ogarkova by name.

Turgenev obtains a humorous effect here because the "creatures" comprising the "court" of Marfa Timofeevna are enumerated in reverse hierarchial order. How different this is from Gogol or Chekhov where *every* order of enumeration is intentionally violated!

Enumeration, in which the author strives to convey a total impression and a single image composed of separate sensual perceptions, is most characteristic of Turgenev's style:

> I gave myself up entirely to the play of circumstances, of fleeting impressions; in slow succession they flowed through my soul and left on it at last one general sensation, in which all I had seen, felt and heard in those three days was merged.

> Everything—the delicate fragrance of resin in the forest, the call and tap of the woodpeckers, the never-ceasing chatter of the clear brooks, with spotted trout lying on the sandy bottom, the somewhat softened outlines of the mountains, the surly rocks, the little clean villages with respectable old churches and trees, the storks in the meadows, the neat mills with swiftly turning wheels, the beaming faces of the villagers, their blue smocks and gray stockings, the creaking, deliberately-moving wagons drawn by sleek horses and, sometimes, cows, the long haired young vagabonds wandering on the clean roads, planted with apple and pear trees. . . . ("Asya")

First of all, the sensory organs—the nose, the ears, the eyes—determine the order in which the objects are arranged and perceived. Secondly, the background and landscape is given, and then the genre. Thirdly, a hierarchy is observed in the enumeration of everything which relates to the genre: "faces," then "smocks" and "stockings"; people, then "carts"; "settlers" (who are more often encountered), then "vagabonds." The order is also observed in the description of the scenery: the background, which sets the scene, "mountains," then "cliffs" (again a hierarchy), and finally the foreground. The "analytic" tendency is also revealed, for example, in the use of aural impressions, which help to define objects more exactly, i.e., the stream "with its spotted trout."

Fidelity to logic and a hierarchial principle—the "analytic" tendency—hinders the fusion of images in Turgenev; it impedes the merging of sensory perceptions, as well as the emotions evoked by them in the process of verbalization, into a single whole, into a poetic image.[13] By contrast, Chekhov uses sensual perceptions in such a way that the objects which provoke them are wrested from the empirical reality which the Bergsonian *homo faber,* with his practical mind, creates for himself; they are included in another realm, a realm of intuitive comprehension where the concepts of "I" and "not I," subject and object, do not apply. Chekhov, as I have said before, not only follows in the footsteps of Lermontov, Gogol and Tolstoy (and probably also Flaubert and de Maupassant), but goes even further than they do. He owed much of his success to his training. Antosha Chekhonte, after all, served a long apprenticeship in search of comic effects. Already in early Chekhov we find marvelous discoveries in metonymic personification:

The ginger-colored trousers lift their eyes to heaven and begin to think seriously. ("Not Wanted") ["Lishnie lyudi"]

This is still, as it were, an instance of bare metonomy: "the ginger-colored trousers" replace their owner. The humorous quality consists only in the fact that the function performed by the whole is arbitrarily and quite intentionally without motivation assigned to the part. This emphasizes the manner in which the whole is perceived by the presumed spectator. In "To Paris!" ["V Parizh!"] this device becomes more complicated and more subtle. " 'A new grammar by Grotto is recommended,' mumbled Lampadkin, *sobbing* with his *galoshes* full of mud." [" 'Rekomendovana novaya grammatika Grota,' bormotal Lampadkin, *vskhlipyvaya* svoimi polnymi gryazi *kaloshami.*"] Here the part and the whole are in reverse relationship; the whole assumes the function of the part. We see this image developed in another story, "A Night in the Graveyard" ["Noch' na kladbishche"]: "When ... my *galoshes* began *to sob* plaintively, I turned onto the road...." Compare this with yet another instance of the same metonomy in "A Visit to Friends" ["U znakomykh"]: "The field with its flowering rye *which* did not stir in the quiet air and the forest ... were splendid."

Here as well, Chekhov follows the path mapped out by Lermontov and Gogol. Gogol has been sufficiently studied in this

61

respect. To this day, however, Lermontov's prose has not been the subject of careful examination. For the time being we may point out in his early story, "Princess Ligovskaya," a phrase completely analogous to Chekhov's:

> From time to time, he would collide with a pink bonnet, and then apologize in great embarrassment. The perfidious pink bonnet would fly into a rage. Then she would ogle him under the bill of his cap; and having gone on a few steps, she would stop and turn around.

It may be argued that this coincidence between Lermontov and Chekhov is not significant, since this type of metonym is not particularized (I have encountered such personification of trousers, for instance, in the diary of Edmond Goncourt, May 7, 1871: "A la barbe blanche succède un partalon gris perle qui déclare d'une voix rageuse...."). We also find analogies with other predecessors of Chekhov; for example, in Grigorovich, in a conversation between two peasants and a beggar woman: " 'You are lying, auntie...,' noted the *second peasant*. 'Sure he lies,' mumbled the *sheepskin coat*.... 'What a story!'...said the *long-waisted coat*... " ("On Christmas Night") ["Rozhdestvenskaya noch' "]. The similarity, however, is purely external. The humorous metonyms here are gratuitously used; otherwise the "long-waisted coat" would not have alternated with the "second peasant." In addition, they designate the subjects in the act of speaking, and help avoid confusion on the part of the reader: when several people are talking it is necessary to indicate precisely who is speaking in every instance. It is a matter of indifference to the reader whether the person is named directly or metonymically. It is another matter altogether when "the ginger-colored trousers" are provided with "eyes" and with the ability to "meditate," or when a man walking along the street perceives the woman he meets as "a pink bonnet."[14]

Of particular interest is an example of personification in which the development of the poetic image is camouflaged in a joke:

> Suddenly a large block of ice appears on the surface of the river. Behind it, *as behind a goat in a herd,* at a respectable distance, several smaller blocks are strung out. *Against the bridge pier* [o byk] the banging of the block is heard. It breaks and, whirling and pushing in confusion, its pieces rush under the bridge. ("On the River," 1886)

The comparison is probably prompted by the pun on the work *byk* (meaning both ox and pier). We should also note the consistency in tone; in the last sentence, the pieces, if not the block itself, are personified.

Chekhov subsequently developed this device of personification with greater skill and subtlety, (eliminating the punning elements), but with no less boldness. This daring becomes evident in the development of metaphors of personification. A single word, which transfers some animate quality to a dead object, effectively animates all its attributes and surroundings; the personified object, in turn, effects the same change on his surroundings:

> It [the chaise] rattled and *creaked* at every movement; the pail, hanging on behind, *chimed in gruffly,* and from these *wretched* rags of leather hanging loose about its peeling *body* one could judge of its decrepit age and readiness to break apart. ("The Steppe")

Compare in the same story:

> [The rain] and the mat, as though understanding one another, began prattling of something rapidly, gaily and most annoyingly, like two magpies.[15]

Chekhov reveals perhaps even greater continuity when he transfers a perceived object from the plane of everyday reality to the plane of poetic reality; he does not wholly limit himself to "animating" metaphors, but develops the image through other types of metaphors or else dispenses with them altogether. For instance, in "My Life," when Poloznev speaks of houses built by his father, an architect, we find: "The front of the house had a *stubborn, rigid* expression, its lines were *stiff* and *timid.*" And further on: "The roof was *low-pitched* [nizkaya: also meaning "vulgar"] and *squashed down.*" And finally: "And the thin, *flabby* chimneys were inevitably topped by conical lips with rigid, squeaking weather vanes." The metaphors and similes are used economically wherever they are needed. It is enough to say that the roof is "nizkaya" because this epithet applies to an inanimate as well as an animate object. And "flabbyness," combined with the image indicating a spiritual realm, helps create a general impression of the vulgarity which reigns in everything that has relation to his father: "And for some reason all these houses built by his father . . . vaguely reminded me of his top hat and the back of his head, so stiff and stubborn looking."

In its extreme, this device leads to a complete violation of the boundaries between the action of perception and the perceived object; the attributes of the object of perception are transferred to the perception itself, just as in reality:

> His [the doctor's] gray whiskers looked unkempt, and his hair was unbrushed. . . . And his study, with pillows on the sofa, with stacks of papers in the corners, and with a large, dirty poodle lying under the table, created an *impression as unkempt and untidy* as himself. ("Three Years")

From here it is only one step to replace the subject with the objects of perception. Thus, we find in the story "Happiness" ["Schast'e"]:

> An immense crimson sun came into view, surrounded by a faint blaze. Broad streaks of light, still cold, bathing in the dewy grass, lengthening out with a joyous air as though to prove they were not weary of their task, began spreading over the earth. The silvery wormwood, the blue flowers of the pig's onion, the yellow mustard, the cornflowers—all burst into gay colors, *taking the sunlight for their own* smile.

Here the objects which the poet has personified seem to have replaced the poet himself; what he does with them is ascribed to them. As M.P. Stolyarov has so well formulated, the poetic, intuitive perception of observable reality consists in an identification of the perceiving subject with the perceived object; the object of perception is thereby subjectivized, and creates its own poetic reality. Our concepts, based on notions furnished by the practical intelligence of a mere craftsman, are inapplicable to this reality.[16] The metaphors and metonyms are possible because the qualities of a phenomenon they designate in *that* world are not identical with similarly named qualities or phenomena in our prosaic world:

> The melancholy, monotonous chirping of the crickets, the calling of the rail and the whistling of the quail did not break the nocturnal silence, but rather added to it a still greater monotony. It seemed that

it was not the birds nor the insects which were singing softly and charming our ears, but the stars looking down at us from heaven....("Agafya")

I cannot imagine a more effective description of the absurd situation of listening to a nocturnal silence, which thereby reveals the meaning of such images as "the marvelous chorus of heavenly bodies," or "one star talking with another." Can one hear silent conversation? Common sense tells us that *everything* is absurd in that world:

> Her broad, very earnest, anxious *face,* with delicate black eyebrows, the turned-up *collar* of her coat which hindered free movement of her head, and the *whole of her*—thin, graceful, with skirts tucked up because of the dew—touched him. ("The Black Monk")

If we were to eliminate her "face" what then would remain of "her"? In any event, "she" would no longer be "the whole of her." But that is just the point; both her "face," and the "collar" function independently, and yet they are inseparable from "her," no matter how inherently contradictory this may seem. The artist does not transform reality here; he simply conveys the feeling which the man experiences. Indeed, each of us is potentially a poet; otherwise we could not understand poetry. The poet merely actualizes and brings to the surface what the ordinary person unconsciously experiences; if the latter attempted to articulate his experiences and relied on an accepted method of discursive thought, he would distort, destroy and nullify these experiences. Observable reality is indivisible and organic; if we attempt to isolate "the essence" and the "shell," the "center" and the "periphery," then the center, as such, which we perceive directly, will be lost:

> I liked his house, and his park, and his small orchard, and the river, and his philosophy, which was clear, though rather spiritless and rhetorical. I *suppose* I was fond of him for his own sake....("Terror")

By placing the man's "philosophy" on the same level as "his house," etc., it becomes clearly apparent that by liking these things, the narrator, of course, likes the man "for his own sake." But when

65

the narrator tries to separate the man from all these accessories he no longer knows with whom he is dealing; he can no longer say with certainty whether he likes the person himself.

In addition to enumeration of objects or their attributes, which are humorous in origin—that is, which ignore the categorical features of the lexemes—we find another type of humorous word combination in Chekhov. These combinations, which are also based on violation of sentence hierarchy express actions or psychic processes. Let us take as an example a passage from "Three Years," in which we learn that Laptev no longer loves his wife: "She had told him she loved him, and he could only feel as though he had been married to her for ten years, and that he felt like having lunch."

We find the same device elsewhere in the same story: Yulya Sergeevna's spiritual tranquility and equilibrium are revealed through an enumeration of her reactions to a variety of impressions. Here again Chekhov violates the hierarchy of objects of perception and their respective values:

> No matter what was said, it sounded apt and clever; the pines were lovely; the smell of their resin was exquisite, as it had never been before; and the cream was very nice; and Sasha was a good intelligent child. . . .

The same artistic quality which determines Chekhov's violation of lexical logic also controls the violation of syntactic logic. Besides enumerations of separate, categorically (logically or hierarchically) heterogeneous symbols, we also encounter enumerations composed of structurally different sentences, or a combination of both types:

> He (Yartsev) sat half-dozing, swaying from side to side, pondering the play. He suddenly imagined a terrible noise, clanging and shouts in some unknown language . . . , a village wrapped in flames, and the nearby forests . . . , soft pink in the glow of the fire, visible for miles around. . . . ("Three Years")

> Walking was pleasant. Olga and Sasha soon forgot both the village and Marya; they were cheerful, and everything entertained them: an ancient burial mound; a row of telegraph poles marching one after another into the distance and disappearing in the horizon . . . , the

wires humming mysteriously; a farmhouse..., with a scent of dampness and hemp coming from it...seemed for some reason inhabited by happy people; a horse's skeleton making a lonely white spot in the open field. ("Peasants")

And as before there was only the field and the sky with stars, and the birds making noise, preventing one another from sleeping. ("In the Ravine")

The fact that a strange man was asleep and snoring in the drawing room, and the sketches on the walls and the exquisite decoration of the room, and the fact that the lady of the house was dishevelled and untidy—all that aroused not the slightest interest now. ("The Grasshopper")

What constitutes a phrase, a sentence or a syntagma for the practical, reasonable person may be one word for the poet.[17] What is separate for the former is, for the latter, an indivisible whole.[18] The poet may consider each single element of a complex syntactic unit, as well as the entire unit, the equivalent of one word. Often the elements are fused by means of coordinating conjunctions. It is already evident from the examples cited how often Chekhov uses the conjunction *and* [*i*]. Here he is similar to Tolstoy and different from Turgenev, the "analytic writer," for whom such a construction is rare. Consider, for example, *The Cossacks:* "'Perhaps I shall not return from the Caucasus,' he thought, and he felt that he loved his friends and someone else besides. And he felt sorry for himself." And in *Anna Karenina:*

All that he [Vronsky] saw from the window of the coach...was as fresh, gay and strong as he himself: and the roofs of the houses...and the sharp outlines of the fences and corners of the buildings, and figures...of the pedestrians and the carriages, and the motionless greenery of the trees, and the fields..., the oblique shadows falling from the houses, and from the trees and the bushes and the potato furrows—it was all beautiful....

Chekhov, perhaps, is closest to Pomyalovsky in this flexible distribution of what is enumerated and combined with the conjunction *and*. This may seem strange, particularly if we consider

67

that Pomyalovsky was well removed, generally speaking, from the "main line" of Russian literature:

> Tea was being served on the balcony. It was a beautiful evening.... Here and there, peasants were coming out on the streets.... The air was quiet and heavenly, like yesterday. It was all the same, yet different, in the singing of the birds, and in the grumbling of the samovar, and in the slight splashing of the river, and in the air, and in the distant voices; Egor Ivanych felt a new stirring within him, as though something had risen from his soul and together with the evening shadows it also covered the river and the garden and the cemetery. *(Bourgeoise Happiness).*

The similarity with Chekhov is not merely formal; the sentence structure shares the same objective—namely, a merging of internal and external sensory perceptions and emotions into a single whole, a poetic image.

To fully understand the function of *and* in Chekhov we should look at one other example:

> It was a cheerful morning, it was a holiday. At ten o'clock Nina Fedorovna, wearing a brown dress, with her hair neatly combed, was led into the drawing room, supported on each side, and she walked about a little and then stood by the open window, and her smile was broad and naive, and it brought to mind a local artist . . . ,who said she had the face of a saint and wanted her to sit for a picture of the Russian carnival. And all of them—the children, the servants, and even her brother Aleksei Fedorich, and she herself—were suddenly convinced, that she would certainly get well. With shrieks of laughter the children ran after their uncle, chasing him, and filling the house with noise. ("Three Years")

At first glance all these *ands* are out of place, contrary to the content, which consists of trivial facts of daily life, hardly material for a composite, poetic image. But, in fact, this is not true. Nina Fedorovna, after all, is gravely ill, and the certainty of her recovery is illusory. The sudden gaiety in her house emphasizes the tragedy of the situation. Nina Fedorovna is almost at death's door; she is led into the drawing room, and her face is compared to a saint's. This episode from everyday life is given a mysterious coloring. In a similar example, which, at first glance, might also seem unexpected and inappropriate, we find that Chekhov very successfully observes the principle of laconicism by using the conjunction *and:*

> She (Olenka) would fall asleep still thinking of the same thing, how Sasha would grow up, get married and have children, and tears would run down her cheeks from her closed eyes. And the little black cat lay purring beside her: purr ... purr ... purr ... ("The Darling")

Another writer would have probably said: "But the black cat ... " [*A chernaya koshechka*]. Such a construction undoubtedly would seem more suitable to the reader, more satisfying to the demands of common sense. From a prosaic point of view, the cat is contrasted here to Olenka. Olenka cries, thinking of her own problems, and the cat meows, unmoved. But for the "darling," with whom Chekhov would have us identify, there is no distance between herself and what surrounds her (one must read this marvelous story in its entirety to be convinced of this fact.) The cat is identified with "the darling." Her dreams, her crying and the cat's purring are fused into one. The function of the cat image becomes wholly apparent when this passage is contrasted to an earlier moment, a description of the "darling's" feelings of misery and her solitude:

> The little black cat, Bryska, would rub against her and purr softly, but Olenka was not moved by these feline caresses. That was not what she needed. She wanted a love that would absorb her whole being, her whole soul.... And she would shake black Bryska off her skirt and say with vexation:
> "Go away, I don't want you!"

Here Bryska is still detached from "the darling."

I should like to emphasize that laconicism in art implies the avoidance of anything which influences us in and of itself, thereby hindering the perception of all images as a single image. When the specific qualities of this single image which the artist wishes to create cannot be disclosed by any other means, laconicism, therefore, may require an accumulation of images, enumerations and repetitions. We have already seen examples of this in the description of the fair, etc. in Gogol and Chekhov. Let us consider a more complicated example from "Anna on the Neck" ["Anna na shee"]. For all its brevity, this story abounds in detailed allusions to trivia, as well as in lengthy syntactic units. Both these features are determined by the theme of fate which governs the heroine's actions. Anya is an ordinary, practical woman, preoccupied with everyday concerns; at first she is very young, helpless, inexperienced and timid. Having married a man she does not love, she comes to fear him, and is oppressed by the awareness of her dependence on him:

> It seemed to her as though she had long been afraid of him. In her childhood the director of the high school had always seemed a most impressive and terrifying *force, sweeping down like a thunderstorm or a steam engine,* ready to crush her; another similar *force* of which the whole family talked, and of which they were for some reason afraid, was His Excellency; then there were a dozen other less formidable *forces,* and among them were the teachers at the high school, with shaven upper lips, stern, implacable; and now finally, there was Modest Alekseich [her husband], a man of principle, who resembled the school director in every way, including his face. And in Anya's imagination *all these forces blended together into one, and, in the form of a terrible, huge, white bear,* menaced the weak and erring, such as her father. And she was afraid to contradict her husband, and she gave a forced smile, and a show of pleasure when she submitted to his coarse caresses and defiling embraces that terrified her.

The verbal forms in the last phrase merit special attention. Although we are dealing with the caresses of one man, Anya's husband, the fact remains that Modest Alekseich is, to her way of thinking, the incarnation of all those "forces." A sudden crisis subsequently occurs. When she attends a benefit ball for the first time, she is immediately aware of the attention she attracts; this is the first step in her emancipation:

> A *huge* officer in epaulets... *seemed to spring out of the ground* and invited her to waltz, and she flew away from her husband, and it seemed to her that she was sailing away in a boat during a violent storm, while her husband remained far away on shore.

The "*huge* officer" is analogous to the "*huge* bear"; this new incarnation of fate, however, no longer enslaves and oppresses, but

70

liberates her. Anya is totally incapable of reflection; she can see nothing beyond the "everyday" plane of reality and only reacts to partial perceptions of empirical data. Therefore, only this level of reality is shown in detail. It is presented in such a way, however, that a careful reading enables us to consolidate Anya's experiences for her (when we speak of Anya, elements of *irony* are absent; there is no distance between her and ourselves); observing her surroundings through her eyes, we can see what she herself does not see. Anya sees a "bear," and a "huge officer," whereas only we can see one thing in all this: her fate. And we would not see this fate, nor sense its presence, were there fewer details in the story, were the language more pithy, more fragmented. We would not feel drawn into that very life stream in which Anya abides.

Footnotes to Chapter Four

1. Chekhov had long been concerned with the problem of distinguishing prose from poetry, or the "large" form from the "small"—which is the same problem as far as narrative prose is concerned. He cautiously, but successfully, arrived at a solution: "Large, thick works," he wrote to Shcheglov (January 22, 1888), "have their own aims, which require a most careful execution regardless of the total impression. In short stories, however, it is better not to say enough than to say too much, because . . . because . . . I don't know why!" Of course, he actually did know "why." This is evident from his own words about the "total impression" which must be created by a "short story," in contrast to "thick works."

2. A similar sustained metaphor, by the way, also occurs in "The Post" ["Pochta"], when the station clerk bids farewell to his nephew, a student: "Well, God speed! Give my love to your mother, Mikhailo! . . . ." The big bell clanged something to the little bells, the little bells gave a friendly answer. The cart squeaked, and moved. The big bell began to cry, the little bells began to laugh.

3. An analogous instance of "suggestive" harmony appears in "From Siberia" ["Iz Sibiri"]:

> This bank is sloping. . . . It is bare and looks *gullied* [*zgryzen*] and *slippery* [*sklizok*]. Turbid billows . . . lash viciously against it, and promptly recoil, as though they were loath to touch this clumsy, *slimy* [*osklizlomu*] bank, which appears fit only for *toads and the souls of great sinners* [*zhaby i dushi bol'shikh greshnikov*].

By this choice of sounds we seem to hear "the lament and gnashing of teeth."

4. Compare the continuation of the passage previously quoted from the first part of the story—Matvei's return home: "And the oak forest . . . resounded with a prolonged, sullen murmur. When a violent storm shakes the trees, how terrible they are!"

5. We should compare this excerpt to a passage from a letter to Leikin (June 27, 1884), wherein Chekhov describes his presence at a post-mortem of a corpse found near a village, an

71

incident which served as the basis for his story: "Near the silent custodians a fire was dying out.... The corpse, in a *red* shirt and new pants, was covered with a sheet." The coloristic element of the story is not present here.

6. Shchukin, *Iz vospominanii o Chekhove, Russkaia mysl'*, 1911, X, 46. This explains Chekhov's high regard for "Taman'": "Perhaps I am wrong," he wrote to Polonsky in 1888, "but Lermontov's "Taman'" and Pushkin's "The Captain's Daughter," not to mention the prose of other poets, prove the close similarity between Russian poetry and fine prose." I will note, incidentally, that in his evaluation of Lermontov's prose, specifically "Taman'," Chekhov was in complete agreement with Grigorovich: "Take Lermontov's story "Taman'"; you will not find one word which could be omitted or added; it is harmonious from beginning to end...." (*Literaturnye vospominaniia*, soch. izd. Marksa, v. XII, 288). Was it not Grigorovich who made Chekhov aware of Lermontov? It is a well-known fact that we credit Grigorovich with "discovering" Chekhov, and after his famous letter which roused Chekhov's artistic self-awareness, they became close friends. During the early period of their acquaintance, Grigorovich was something of a mentor to Chekhov in his work. He was, of course, only an adviser; his own literary works were quite weak and had no influence whatsoever on Chekhov.

7. Compare in the same work: "The last lights had been put out in the huts. The last sound had died away in the village. The wattle fences and the cattle gleaming white in the yards, the roofs of the houses and the stately poplars *all seemed* to be sleeping the laborers' healthy, peaceful sleep.... In the east the stars were diminishing and, *it seemed*, dissolving in the increasing light."

8. Sb. *Pamiati A.P. Chekhova*, izd. Obshchestva liubitelei rossiiskoi slovesnosti, 1906, 71. See above about the influence of "Taman'" as a source for the story "Horse Thieves."

9. As attested by I.A. Bunin, *ibid.*

10. Concerning the function of *sembler, paraître* in Proust, see Leo Spitzer, *Zum Stil Marsel Proust's, Stilstudien*, v. II (1928), 449.

11. "He [Serezha's father] looked into the boy's big dark eyes and it seemed to him that in these wide pupils he saw his mother and wife looking at him, and everything that he ever loved" ("At Home").

12. "The cable, damp and, *it seemed to me, sleepy*, stretched far across the wide river...." ("Easter Eve")

"To the left a red light still glowed. It winked affably and, *it seemed, smiled.*" ("Agafya")

"And the forest and foggy hummocks and black ditches by the sides of the road, seemed to grow quiet, listening to her [Vera], and something sinister and strange took place in Ognev's soul" ("Verochka").

13. See M.P. Stoliarov's excellent article, "K probleme poeticheskogo obraza," *Ars Poetica,* Moskva, 1927, where we find an unusually profound and convincing analysis of this subject.

14. Incidentally, there is an example of such metonomy in early Tolstoy, in a draft of *Childhood [Detstvo]* describing a crowd on Tverskoi Boulevard: "All the faces of this panorama were exceptionally handsome from a distance, but the closer they came the less attractive they were. Whether a large nose from under a yellow hat, or the indifferent gaze thrown at us by a frock coat or the silly, unattractive laugh of epaulets and frock coats which had stopped to talk—they were immediately disappointing...." (L.N. Tolstoi, *Polnoe Sobranie* pod red. V.G. Chertkova, seriia 1, v. I., Gos. Izd, 1928, 194) Chekhov could not have known these texts. Here, most likely, we see the influence of Lermontov on Tolstoy as well. The prose of *Childhood* and of other early works of Tolstoy, generally, has much in common with Lermontov.

15. Compare in Lermontov, specifically in "Taman'": With an involuntary throbbing of the heart, I looked at the *wretched* boat; but it kept diving like a duck and then, with a wing-

like *upsweep of oars* [it was not in vain that Chekhov demanded that one learn to write from Lermontov], would spring out of the abyss amid a burst of foam.... " As far as vocabulary is concerned, we should not overlook a parallel to a Chekhovian passage in Tolstoy. "The tree shuddered *with its entire body;* it bent and quickly straightened up, swaying at its roots... " ("Three Deaths") ["Tri smerti"]. But in Chekhov, the use of the word *body* is more daring than in Tolstoy. Indeed, a tree is a living being and thus easier to animate than a carriage.

16. In the work of A.N. Tolstoy, a writer of a later period, and strongly influenced by Chekhov, we find analogous devices for creating an organic, poetic image. In enumerations: "The door and that room, the odor of clay, Zyum, and all things were near and dear" ("Sparks") ["Iskry"]. In the development of metonyms and metaphors: "The girl in a gray plaid dress, with a pocketbook over her shoulder, seemed indispensable and terribly important, as if his love for her was also agitated, and thin, in plaid, with a pocketbook, just as severe and clean as Zyum." *(Ibid.)*

17. Here A.N. Tolstoy is also a disciple of Chekhov. For example, in the previously cited story "Sparks": "Have you ever seen a well-travelled road during an October slush? A bare field ... ; a lonely haystack ... ; scraggy telegraph poles ... ; and strung along the well-travelled marshy tracks are carts with people, protected against wind and rain by wet overcoats."

18. Hence, the "substantiation" of infinitive forms and syntagmas. For instance, in "The Island Sakhalin" [Ostrov Sakhalin]: "To *punish* in the performance of one's duty ... , to be *capable* ... of accepting this revulsion and horror, *the remoteness* of the place of work ... —*all this,* taken together, always made work ... exceptionally difficult.... " It is amazing to see how the artist returns the original meaning to the word. Indeed, the infinitives are nothing more than verbal nouns. We should note here the similarity of Chekhov's syntax with Proust's: Sans doute par là voulaient-elles seulement montrer que s'il y avait certaines choses dont elles manquaient—dans l'espèce *certaines prérogatives* de la vieille dame, *et être en relations avec elles*—c'était non pas parce qu'elles ne pouvaient, mais ne voulaient pas les posséder (*A l'ombre des jeunes filles en fleurs,* 35-e éd. v. I, 227). Specific coincidences of this sort are always significant (see below).

Chapter Five

Musicality

We may define as beautiful that which is expressive, that which reveals a sense of its singularity and inimitability; in this revelation we find the disclosure of its idea. The idea is the center where all possible elements are crystallized. All empirical reality is potentially an aspect of cosmic unity—and everything, consequently, is a kind of complex. It is the artist's task to expose with all possible clarity its character, which is a unity in diversity. Hence rhythm [*ritmichnost'*] is basic to the artistic quality of a literary work—the alternation and agreement of light and dark, of accelerated and retarded movement, of the "beautiful" and "ugly," the "good" and the "bad," and the "significant" and "petty," etc. As far as literature is concerned, in works which tend towards prose, i.e., towards the presentation of reality as it unfolds in an empirical plane, the main rhythmic element consists in an alternation of significant and insignificant, attractive and unattractive personalities, and of events, i.e., those moments of tension and stability in interpersonal relationships, that movement from conflict to resolution.

In poetry this rhythmic element plays a comparatively minor role, and most often no role at all. Rhythm [*ritm*] in poetry is created by the alternation of poetic images formed into a single image, i.e., image-symbols, and, concurrent with this, by the flow of speech. We find here a similarity of music and dance to poetry. Here also we can see poetry's dependence on these two "primary" arts of time. Literature, however, has long attempted to free itself from absolute conformity to meter, without which rhythm in music is impossible. The study of literature, however, does not keep pace with reality. Even now literary scholars frequently regard as a sign of beauty and "musicality" the tendency in fiction towards poetic language, that is, towards a language which moves within the confines of classical meter, the iamb and trochee, etc. Russian scholars, for example, consider this one of the major achievements of Turgenev's language.[1] However, this is not true of all Russian prose. In Lermontov, it is rare; it is generally absent in S. Aksakov, Herzen, Dostoevsky and Tolstoy. Pushkin's prose is structurally close to the spoken language; it occasionally slips into metrically ordered language only at the ending of periodic sentences.[2] In such cases it is justified because the emotional coloring of such lengthy sentence units is underscored. Furthermore its own rhythmic movement is not violated because its resumé is located at the end of the period and thus we expect no additional material after the metrically structured phrase. This is not true of Turgenev, as we can see in a passage from "It is Enough" ["Dovol'no"]:

> And this I write to you—to you, my only and unforgettable friend.... Alas! you know what separated us. But I will not refer to that now.... Rising up for the last time, from the mute grave in which I now am lying, I cast a gentle and tender glance over all my past, over all our past.... There is no hope and no return, but neither is there any bitterness in me....

> [I eto ya pishu—tebe, moi edinstvennyi i nezabvennyi drug.... Uvy! ty znaesh', chto nas razluchilo. No ya ne khochu teper' upominat' ob etom.... V poslednii raz pripodnimayas' iz nemoi mogily, v kotoroi ya teper' lezhy, ya probegayu krotkim i umilennym vzorom vse moe proshedshee, vse nashe proshedshee.... Nadezhdy net i net vozvrata,—no i gorechi net vo mne....]

Here "poetry" intrudes into prose and thereby destroys its structure. One would have to be deaf not to expect after "Alas! you know what separated us" ["Uvy: ty znaesh', chto nas razluchilo"], the identical phrase, but without I, instead of "But I will not ... etc." ["No ya ne khochu ... etc."], to obtain the same obligatory metric pair. Furthermore, after "There is no hope and no return" ["Nadezhdy net i net vozvrata"], one would expect "But there is no bitterness in me" ["No net i gorechi vo mne"], instead of "But neither is there any bitterness in me" ["No i gorechi net vo mne"]. The reader's attention is distracted because the rhythm of the passage does not contribute to a perception of the whole.

The rhythm of prose is not only independent of metric elements; on the contrary, it does not permit them (with the exception of cadences, as we have seen). Prose rhythm arises from a harmonious combination of concise and protracted sentences. Every great writer has his own particular pattern of such combinations. Thus, for example, short, compressed sentences prevail in Pushkin; they are only rarely interrupted by lengthy phrases. Chekhov characteristically strings together short, simple sentences, ending in a long sentence of a more complex syntactic structure:

There was the smell of snow in the air,
the snow crunched softly under foot;
the earth, the roofs, the trees, the seats on the boulevards—
everything was soft, white, young,
and this made the houses look quite different from the day
    before;
the street lamps burned more brightly,
the air was more transparent,
the carriages rumbled with a deeper note,
and with the fresh, light, frosty air a feeling stirred
    in the soul akin to the white, young, feathery
    snow. ("A Nervous Breakdown")

This structural scheme is contained in embryo even in the early stories:

We sat and said not a word,// and we felt insulted and ashamed for having been so successfully cheated by that fat, red-nosed old man. ("At the Post Office," 1883) ["V pochtovom otdelenii"]

Ermakov lit up a Havana cigar,// and it began to smell even more of a cultured man in his room. ("The Writer," 1885) ["Pisatel' "]

He acknowledges neither periods nor commas,// and his monotonous reading is akin to the buzzing of bees or the babbling of a brook. ("Deadly Nightshade," 1885) ["Sonnaya odur' "]

In this structural scheme the "thesis" is briefly and generally formulated and then elaborated. Later this scheme often becomes more complex and unites phrases which include enumeration into a structural whole. At times architectonic harmony is attained by stringing together complex sentences, each breaking down into three structurally uniform components:

I. It sometimes happens that the clouds are huddled together in disorder on the horizon, and the sun, hiding behind them, colors them and the sky with tints of every possible hue . . . ;

II. 1. One cloud is like a monk,
    2. another like a fish,
    3. a third like a Turk in a turban.
        The glow of sunset, enveloping a third of the sky,
    1. gleams on the church cross of the manor house,
    2. is reflected in the river and the puddles,
    3. far, far away against the background of the sunset a flock of wild ducks is flying somewhere for the night. . . .
    1. And the boy herding the cows,
    2. and the surveyor driving in his chaise over the dam,
    3. and the gentlemen out walking—
    1. all gaze at the sunset
    2. and every one of them thinks it terribly beautiful,
    3. but no one knows or can say in what its beauty lies.
             ("The Beauties") ["Krasavitsy"]

Just as in architecture and music, prose structure permits great diversity in the combination of its parts, as well as complication of, or digression from, the basic scheme.

   I. I knew
that they would be a good hour getting the samovar;
        that grandfather would be not less than an hour
                drinking tea, and
then would lie down to sleep for two or three hours,
        that I would spend a quarter of the day
waiting, after which there would be again
     the heat,
      the dust,
       the jolting on the road.
I heard the muttering of the two voices,

II. And it began to seem to me that
        the Armenian,
            the cupboard with the crockery,
          the flies,
              the windows with the burning sun
                           beating on them,
    I had been seeing for ages and ages,
and I will cease to see them in the far off future,
and I was seized with hatred
          for the steppe,
             the sun,
                the flies. ("The Beauties")

I. When on a moonlight night you see a broad village street,
        with its cottages,
           haystacks
             and slumbering willows,
a feeling of calm comes over the soul;
II. in this peace, hidden in the night shadows
        from care,
          toil
           and sorrow,
  it is gentle,
      melancholy,
        beautiful.
III. And it seems
    as though the stars look down upon it kindly and with tenderness,
      and as though there were no evil on earth
      and all were well. ("The Man in a Case")

I. To the left the Sakhalin peaks were visible in the mist,
  to the right there were also peaks
    and not a living soul around
      not a bird
      not a fly—
II. and it seemed incomprehensible
    for whom these waves were howling,
      who listens to them at night,
        what do they want,
          and, finally, for whom they will howl when I leave.
III. Here, on the shore, I am filled not with thoughts, but
    with brooding;

I am terrified, and at the same time I feel like standing endlessly
to look at the monotonous movement of the waves
and hear their speech.

(*The Island Sakhalin,* End of Ch. 13)

It is easy to see what these passages have in common. The initial presentation of a statement is followed by "a reflection"; the transition from an objective to a subjective posture is accomplished by means of the verb *to seem* with the conjunction *and.* Alternatively this transition may be effected by "animating" what has been presented; this is equivalent to the use of *to seem,* as in the example from "The Man in a Case" where *to seem* is used, but only in the last part of the periodic sentence. The passages also tend towards a tripartite articulation of separate parts and their components, as well as of the entire unit: a) a statement, b) spontaneous reflection and c) a conclusion which expresses the particular dialectic in the development of the poetic image.

I will cite a few more variations of this pattern of sentence structure, which clearly reveal its formal characteristics, as well as its meaning:

Going almost every day to the nunnery, she wearied Olya,
    complaining to her of her own unbearable misery,
        weeping,
and feeling at the same time that she brought something impure
            with her into the cell,
        pitiful,
            shabby,
and Olya repeated to her mechanically as though a lesson
            learned by rote,
        that all this was of no consequence,
            that it would all pass
            and God would forgive her.
("Volodya the Big and Volodya the Little," the ending)
        ["Volodya Bol'shoi i Volodya Malen'kii"]

The initial statement is followed by her reactions, then another statement, Olya's answer, which is a kind of conclusion.

In the evening and at night she could hear the band playing in the garden, and the crackling and banging of fireworks,

79

and it seemed to her that it was Kukin struggling with his destiny, storming the trenches of his chief foe—the indifferent public;

there was a sweet thrill in her heart, she had no desire to sleep,

and when he returned home at daybreak, she tapped softly at the window from her bedroom, and showing him only her face and one shoulder through the curtain, she gave him a caressing smile.... ("The Darling")

Strict order in the statement, reflection and conclusion is absent here, but the rhythm, based on the alternation of compact and lengthy sentences, is the same as in other passages. The ending in "The Student" provides an example of the free play of all the elements in the basic pattern of the structure:

When he crossed the river by ferry and afterward climbed the hill, looking at his village and towards the west where the cold purple sunset lay like a narrow streak of light, he thought that truth and beauty, which had guided human life there in the garden and in the yard of the high priest, had continued without interruption to this day, and had evidently always been the chief thing in human life and, indeed, in all earthly life; and the feeling of youth, health, vigor—he was only twenty-two—and the inexpressible sweet expectation of happiness took possession of him little by little, and life seemed to him enchanting, marvelous and full of lofty meaning.

First there is the statement, then the reflection, and finally the emotional reaction to what "seemed"; the sequence creates an ever-growing sensation of tranquility derived from the spiritual experience.

We find quite a few passages in Tolstoy similarly structured. I will cite a most characteristic example from *Anna Karenina:*

And what he [Levin] saw then, he never saw again. Especially the children going to school, the bluish doves flying down from the roofs to the pavement, and the little loaves covered with flour, thrust out by an unseen hand, moved him. Those loaves, doves and those two boys were not earthly creatures. It all happened at once: a boy ran toward a dove and gave a smiling glance at Levin; the dove with a whir of her wings darted away, flashing in the sun, amid specks of snow that quivered in the air, while from a little window there came an odor of freshly baked bread put out to cool. All of this together was so extraordinarily nice that Levin laughed and cried with delight.

The first part represents a general exposition; the next part develops this material; and the last part conveys the impression of "all of this." We can see that a tripartite principle is strictly observed. The Tolstoy passage is less effective, perhaps precisely because it is overly schematic. A passage from Lermontov—again from "Taman'"—is closer in structure to Chekhov's elaborations of the general pattern:

> I wrapped myself in my felt cloak and sat
> down on a rock beside the fence. In front of me, the
> sea spread before me, stirred up by last night's storm,
>   and its monotonous sound, like the murmur of a city
> settling down to sleep, reminded me of past years,
>   and carried my thoughts northward,
>   towards our cold capital.

This passage, like so many others in Chekhov, is completely analogous to "On the Hills of Georgia." Nevertheless, a prose work in the narrative genre is not the same as "pure poetry," no matter how concise it is, no matter how much it tends to be perceived as one word, i.e., as an integral poetic image. Its elements of empirical reality cannot simply be symbols; on the contrary, they are distinguished by their self-sufficient role. Herein lies a profound difference between prose and verse. Pushkin was right when, in a letter to Vyazemsky about *Eugene Onegin,* he emphasized that he was writing not simply a novel, but a novel in verse, "a devilish difference." In such a novel everything is subordinate to meter; the external rhythm determines the inner rhythm, and the material, taken from everyday life, from the world of empirical reality, dissolves, so to speak, in the general atmosphere created by meter and strophic division. This explains why Pushkin could so easily toy with Onegin; now he masks him as a Byronic hero, now he hides behind him and forces his hero to speak for him. Only rarely does Onegin become himself—a living person. We may say the same of Tatyana.

This cannot occur in a prose work whose language is close to the langauge of everyday life relationships. The rhythm of the whole, as I have said before, is determined not only by the flow of language and contrasting image-symbols, sounds, etc., but also by an alternation of images, involving the characters and their experiences. As we have seen, this is more easily realized in works of the large form, dealing with rich and varied material. How, then, does one avoid monotony and lack of rhythm in the novella, and especially in the short story, which contain a limited number of characters, who are shown in a short time segment, and where the "weaving" of events is reduced to maximum simplicity?

Chekhov's solution to this problem is his most significant and valuable artistic contribution. It may be described as a blend of the rhythmic elements of prose and poetry—in so subtle a combination that it is only perceived by means of a very careful analysis of his technique—the presentation of real life as it appears on an "everyday" plane, combined with literary suggestions and hints in such a manner which allows him to transpose the material offered by *this* life into the plane of another reality. As far as the material itself is concerned, it consists of his audacious neglect of the categorical distinction between "landscape" and "genre," the world of "nature" and the world of man; thus, he may apply the same methods to both these categories of material and combine their elements, whereas usually material provided by nature is worked out in literature poetically and material provided by the world of human relationships is developed realistically. Of course he was not without predecessors; Lermontov, Gogol and Tolstoy had already paved the way in this area. But as we shall see, Chekhov surpassed them in developing new methods for realizing the rhythmic principle.

With this in mind, let us examine the beginning of "The Betrothed," specifically the first three paragraphs which are, so to speak, an introduction to the narrative:

> It was ten o'clock in the evening, and the full moon was shining over the garden. In the Shumins' house an evening service, celebrated at the request of the grandmother, Marfa Mikhailovna, was just over, and now Nadya—she had gone into the garden for a minute—could see the table being laid for supper in the dining room, and her grandmother bustling about in her gorgeous silk dress; Father Andrei, a chief priest of the cathedral, was talking to Nadya's mother, Nina Ivanovna, and now, by the evening light shining through the window, her mother for some reason seemed very young; Andrei Andreich, Father Andrei's son, was standing by listening attentively.
>
> It was still and cool in the garden, and dark peaceful shadows lay on the ground. There was a sound of frogs croaking far, far away,

apparently beyond the town. There was a feeling of May, sweet May! One drew deep breaths and longed to believe that not here, but far away under the sky, above the trees, far away in the open country, in the fields and woods, the life of spring was now unfolding, mysterious, beautiful, rich and holy beyond the understanding of weak, sinful man. And for some reason one wanted to cry.

She, Nadya, was already twenty-three. Ever since she was sixteen she had been passionately dreaming of marriage and at last she was engaged to Andrei Andreich, the young man who was standing on the other side of the window; she liked him, the wedding was already fixed for July 7, and yet there was no joy in her heart, she was sleeping badly, her spirits were low . . . She could hear from the open windows of the basement near the kitchen the hurrying servants, the clatter of knives, the banging of the swing door; there was a smell of roast turkey and pickled cherries. And for some reason it seemed that it would be like that all her life, without change, without end.

These paragraphs form a kind of prose stanza, each with a nearly identical number of lines. There is an astonishing similarity in the structure of individual sentences; moreover, they occupy the same place in each stanza. The stanzas begin: "It was almost ten o'clock in the evening . . . "; "It was still . . . in the garden . . . "; "She, Nadya, was already twenty three . . . " The second and third stanzas end: "And for some reason one wanted to cry"; "And for some reason it seemed . . . ". The repetition of *for some reason* (see above), as well as the verbal form *to seem,* is significant.

The first paragraph is devoted to the theme of Nadya's day-to-day life. The second treats the theme of the ideal life that she dreams about. The third paragraph returns to the first theme, worked out anew, and emphasizes the vulgarity, baseness and inevitability in life. The similarity in linguistic structure of these paragraph-stanzas forcefully underscores the opposition of their themes. Subsequently, the strophic division is eliminated. This is quite understandable. While appropriate to the introduction, a strophic division would not contribute to the unfolding of the theme or to the development of complex human interrelationships and experiences; in short, it would not enhance the overall impression.

A similar rhythm-forming function is accomplished by a combination of language which tends to be strophic, with final sentences containing "and it seemed." We find this in "Three Years,"

83

where Laptev is overwhelmed by his love for Yuliya Sergeevna and surrenders to it:

> [Supper with Panaurov, who is speaking of love] Laptev, tired, a little drunk, looked at his handsome head, his clipped black beard, and it seemed that he understood why women so loved this pampered, conceited and handsome creature.

> [Panaurov leaves. Laptev accompanies him] After parting with him Laptev slowly returned home. The moon was shining brightly; one could distinguish every bit of straw on the ground, and it seemed to Laptev as though the moonlight were caressing his bare head, as though someone were passing a feather through his hair.

> "I am in love!" he said aloud, and he had a sudden longing to overtake Panaurov, to embrace him, to forgive him, to give him a lot of money, and then to run off into the open country....

> At home he saw Yuliya Sergeevna's parasol lying on a chair.... Laptev opened it and held it over his head, and it seemed to him as though the fragrance of happiness was all about him.

"The Steppe" best illustrates the use of these varied means to create the impression of a rhythmically moving whole in a prose work. We have already mentioned Chekhov's goals with respect to the novella. In a letter to Korolenko he complains of the difficulty of this task:

> From lack of practice in writing long works, and from fear of writing what is superfluous, I go to the opposite extreme; each page turns out compact, the pictures accumulate and crowd together and, obstructing each other, spoil the general impression. As a result one gets not a picture in which all the separate parts, like stars in the sky, merge into one whole, but a conspectus, a dry record of impressions.[3] (Jan. 9, 1888)

Unfortunately Chekhov scholars do not have the wealth of material—preliminary variants of finished texts—available to scholars of Pushkin, Gogol and Tolstoy. Draft versions of "The Steppe" would help to point out those isolated features (not always apparent, even on careful reading) which ultimately enabled

Chekhov to create from "the encyclopedia of the steppe" a picture "in which all the separate parts, like stars in the sky, merge into one whole." Nevertheless, I will point out what I have been able to observe.

Above all, it must be emphasized that "The Steppe" is not a short story and not a novella in the generally accepted sense of these terms, but a *poem* (as Gogol called *Dead Souls*) and, in some respects, a prototype of a poem in prose. It is the analogue of Pushkin's "novel in verse." Its *fabula* is not a primary concern, and in this respect "The Steppe" more closely resembles a "poem" than *Dead Souls* or "Taras Bulba." Just as in Gogol, the road provides the dominant theme. The introduction of the theme of departure corresponds to the conflict; the theme of arrival—the final scene—is equated with the resolution of the conflict; the development of the basic theme—the trip itself—comprises the *syuzhet*. The hero does not act; he is, rather, the recipient of impressions. He is the main character only insofar as he is present in all the episodes, and it is chiefly *his* impressions which are given. Precisely because he is passive and insignificant—he is, after all, only nine years old—he is at times replaced, just like "My Onegin," but with even greater ease. Of course in Chekhov he is replaced by a certain generalized "I" and not by the author, as in Pushkin. This occurs, for example, in Chapter Four, in a description of Egorushka's "sleepy brain" and the fantastic images "conceived in it. And nothing around lent itself to ordinary thought." Later a lyrical description of the steppe at night reproduces impressions and emotions that can in no way be ascribed to Egorushka. Even more significant is a passage from the same chapter where Egorushka and the generalized "I" seem to become fused:

Something extraordinarily broad, sweeping and titanic stretched over the steppe instead of a road.... Its width puzzled Egorushka and brought thoughts of fairy tales to his mind. Who travelled along the road? Who needed so much space? It was strange and unintelligible. One might suppose that giants with immense strides, such as Ilya Muromets and Solovei the Brigand, were still surviving in Russia, and that their gigantic steeds were still alive. Egorushka looked at the road and imagined some half dozen, high chariots racing along side by side, *like those he used to see in pictures in his Scripture history....*

Clearly he is not thinking about Ilya Muromets and Solovei the Brigand; someone else makes these connections for him. Here, as in other similar sections, there is a sharp distinction between "The Steppe" and *Dead Souls*. Gogol does not transform his hero into an authorial "I" or into some other "I"; Chichikov is too vividly characterized for any such conversion. The lyrical digressions in *Dead Souls* are digressions in the true sense of the word; they intrude into the narrative. In "The Steppe" there is no division between such digressions and the narrative proper. In answer to many who asked in bewilderment what Chekhov wanted to say with his study, what was the idea in it, one critic, Obolensky, replied that indeed there was an idea—the contrast between the grandeur of nature and man's pettiness, depravity, baseness and wretchedness. His one regret was that the description of the steppe lacked grandeur; it was too pale and lacked color. [4] The nine-year-old Egorushka understood Chekhov better than his critics; he has good reason to feel equally sorry for the poplar in the steppe and for the grass snake whom Dymov kills, and for the driver Emelyan, and his rain-soaked cookie and his coat, like him, "left to the mercy of fate." In "The Steppe," landscape and genre, "the bosom of nature" as Obolensky has expressed it, and everything that happens in nature, both significant and trivial, has been fused into one. Chekhov uses humorous devices, as we have already seen, to achieve this fusion. Gogol, and at times Turgenev, did the same. However, in Gogol, as in Turgenev, everything relevant to the world of nature is ordinarily personified by comparison to what is "elegant," "noble" and "lofty" in the world of man. In Chekhov, by contrast, the steppe "hid in the fog like Moisei Moiseich's children hiding under the blanket." [5]

We are now in a position to understand the rhythmic components in "The Steppe" and the means by which they are achieved. "The Steppe" belongs entirely to the realm of poetry; one can only master it by reading it at one sitting (all the while paying careful attention to each word), because its total image is formed by the most subtle literary suggestions. [6] The steppe, the road on the steppe and the travelers on it are all one. People are sad or joyful, partially because of the influence of what they see around them in the steppe, but very often it is the steppe itself which is joyful or sad. Egorushka hears singing in the distance, and before he notices a peasant woman singing, "it began to seem to him that it was the grass singing." Once again Egorushka is replaced by a generalized I, allowing for a development of the image of the singing grass:

> In its song, withered and half-dead, it was without words, but plaintively and passionately it attempted to persuade someone that it was not to blame, that the sun was burning it for no fault of its own; it protested that it ardently longed to live, that it was young and might have been beautiful but for the heat and the drought; it was guiltless, but yet it prayed for forgiveness and vowed that it was in anguish, sad and sorry for itself. . . .

Under these conditions rhythm is created not by alternating events of varied import, but by alternating themes—almost in a musical sense of the word—and by alternating tempos and harmonies. A fusion of the background and action into one whole makes possible a very strict parallelism of the processes in the world of nature and the world of men. The general construction is as follows: 1) the slow movement through the uniform, dismal steppe, dry from the heat, the feeling of monotony and boredom; this is a preparation for 2) the crisis: the heat continues to intensify and at the same time a mood builds up, seeking a way out of this melancholy, initially in a collision between Egorushka and Dymov. This prepares us for the second, and tragic part, the approaching storm: Egorushka interferes in the argument between Dymov and his friends and attacks him; the storm bursts right over the wagon train after which Egorushka's illness ensues. There follows, finally, 3) the resolution—the entrance into the city, his recovery, the arrival at the apartment; and 4) the final scene, a variation of the introductory theme of parting with one's former life.[7] Two themes or motifs are interwoven on this canvas: the theme of life-impulse—Bergson's *élan vital,* the thirst for life, the fusion with life in general (because to live, whatever else it means, means to participate in the cosmic life process in its uninterrupted, ceaseless metamorphosis)—and the theme of exclusion from life—loneliness, and at the same time, solidification into immobility and death—the antithesis of the first theme. These two contrasting themes are expressed in a series of highly varied image-symbols, in a series of revelations, the alternation of which creates the rhythmic structure of Chekhov's poem. Figuratively speaking, the *syuzhet* alone determines a certain regularity in the alternating repetition of the two themes and simultaneously the need for diversity in their presentation. The cart (later the wagon) is in motion, but from time to time (and furthermore at definite periods) stops at rest places. This motion would seem to imply a constant change of impressions, yet how often the experiences of the travelers are futile in this respect:

> How suffocating and cheerless! The carriage raced along and Egorushka kept seeing the same sky, plains and hills. . . . The music in the grass grew quiet. . . . Rooks flew over the withered grass; they all looked alike and made the steppe even more monotonous. . . . A white skull or rock could be seen in the tall weeds, breaking the monotony . . . and again the eye was met by the tall weeds, the hills, the rooks. . . .

> Here and there wheat flashed by. And again the scorched plains . . . , again a kite flew overhead. In the distance, as before, a windmill stretched its arms and it again looked like a small person. . . . One grew tired of looking at it. . . .

The motif of loneliness, as I have said before, is organically connected to the motif of monotony, of eternal repetition of one and the same thing: Egorushka's grandmother sleeping alone in the cemetery; the lonely poplar ("Who planted it and why it is here, God only knows. . . . Is this beauty happy? In the summer heat, in the winter cold and snow storms . . . , and above all, alone all its life, alone."); the lonely steppe whose life is spent in vain because of this;[8] the table "almost alone" in Moisei Moiseich's room;[9] and the lonely grave in the steppe. The people are just as lonely; both Egorushka and the drivers, and Moisei Moiseich's brother, Solomon (this astoundingly penetrating incarnation of the "eternal Jew"), who is understood by no one, and does not understand himself. (The pilgrim in "The Rolling Stone" is another version of him.) They all attempt to escape their loneliness, to be close to someone, to be friends, to explain themselves, or—an especially human manifestation of *élan vital,* that social feeling—to quarrel gratuitously and aimlessly (Egorushka's clash with Dymov, for example; actually Dymov is quite drawn to Egorushka). When the drivers encounter a man who has attained this *élan vital* (the Ukrainian who tells of his marriage to the woman he loves, and shares his happiness with them) they "become dejected" because

88

they, too, "would like to be happy." But happiness eludes them. Life's path is like this road. Chance, and not "selective affinity," brings men together and separates them. It is not surprising that attempts "to fuse two beings into one" often result in failure. The suggestion is that Egorushka might have become close to Deniska; but even at the outset of the trip he must abandon the cart. At one of the rest places Egorushka chances to meet a small boy who is obviously attracted by the red of his shirt and approaches him by the stream.

> Perhaps he himself had not noticed how the agreeable red color and curiosity had attracted him from the hamlet below, and now probably he was surprised at his boldness. For a long while Egorushka stared at him, and he at Egorushka. Both were silent and felt a certain awkwardness. After a long silence Egorushka asked:
> "What's your name?"
> The stranger's cheeks puffed out more than ever; he pressed himself against the rock, opened his eyes wide, moved his lips, and answered in a husky bass:
> "Tit!"
> The boys said not another word to each other; after a brief silence, still keeping his eyes fixed on Egorushka, the mysterious Tit kicked up one leg, felt with his heel for a niche in the rock and clambered up it; from that point, staggering backwards and looking intently at Egorushka, as though afraid he might be hit from behind, he ascended the next rock, and so made his way until he disappeared altogether behind the crest of the hill.
> After watching him Egorushka put his arms round his knees and bent his head ... time dragged on endlessly, as though it, too, were stagnant and had come to a standstill. It seemed as though a hundred years had passed since that morning ... Could it be that God wished for Egorushka, the chaise and the horses to come to a standstill in that air, and, like the hills, turn to stone and remain forever in one spot?

At another stop, Egorushka wanders into a church, and recognizes among the worshipers the driver Emelyan, a former choirboy:

> Looking at the back of [his] head and his ears, Egorushka, for some reason, thought that Emelyan was probably very unhappy. He remembered the way he conducted with his hands, his husky voice, his timid air ... and felt intense pity for him. He longed to say something friendly to him.

"I am here too," he said, putting out his hand. People who sing ... in the choir ... are accustomed to look with a stern and unfriendly air at boys. They do not give up this habit, even when they leave off being in a choir. Turning to Egorushka, Emelyan looked at him with a scowl and said: "Don't play in church!"

The third analogous episode describes the travelers' encounter with Varlamov on the wagon train, the "mysterious, elusive Varlamov," "whom everyone sought" and about whom Egorushka had heard so much. Another disillusionment follows and a double one at that. First, this fable-like personality, as Egorushka imagines him, turns out to be a "small, drab man, dressed in big boots, sitting on an ugly nag"; secondly, "driving past Egorushka, he did not look at him; only the horse deigned to look at Egorushka with his large, sad eyes, but with indifference."

Nature, likewise, experiences similar expectation, deception and disillusionment. The sun is rising, and the steppe

> flung off the twilight of early morning, and smiled. . . . The cut rye, the coarse steppe grass, the milkwort, the wild hemp, all withered from the sultry heat, brown and half dead now ... caressed by the sun, revived. . . . But a little time passed, the dew evaporated, the air grew stagnant and the *disillusioned* steppe began to wear its jaded July look.

Consider also:

> The air was more sultry than ever; from the sultry heat and the stillness submissive nature was spellbound in silence. . . . But at last, when the sun was beginning to sink into the west, the steppe, the hills and the air could bear the oppression no longer, and, driven out of all patience, exhausted, tried to fling off the yoke. A fleecy ashen-gray cloud appeared from behind the hills. It *exchanged* glances with the steppe, as though to say, "Here I am," and frowned. [Suddenly there is a violent gust of wind, it is thundering and it seems that it will soon begin to rain.] One effort, one struggle more, and it seemed the steppe would have gotten the upper hand. But the unseen, oppressive force gradually riveted its fetters on the wind, and the air and the dust settled, and the stillness descended again as though nothing had happened.

"Ascents" and "descents," "flights" and "frustrations," tension and resolution into "nothing," meetings and partings, expectation

90

and disillusionment of hopes—all this in its several manifestations imparts a rhythmic movement to "The Steppe." The combination of categorically diverse image-symbols into one whole is lexically reinforced by repetition of such words as *and now* [*no vot*], *suddenly* [*vdrug*], *again* [*opyat'*], *as yesterday* [*po vcherashnemu*], and so forth:

And now . . . a wagon loaded with sheaves came by.

And now the wheat too, had flashed by;

And now, finally, the steppe and the hills could no longer bear it . . . ;

And now someone shouted in front of the wagon train;

And now, finally, the wind tore at the bast matting for the last time and ran off somewhere. About six huge steppe sheep-dogs *suddenly* . . . threw themselves at the cart;

Suddenly Egorushka's boredom returned;

Suddenly something burst in the stagnant air, there was a strong gust of wind which whirled round and round, roaring and whistling over the steppe;

Suddenly the door creaked and the floor shook under someone's footsteps;

Suddenly there was a squall of wind, so violent it almost snatched away Egorushka's bundle and bast matting;

And again [*I opyat'*] the drawn-out song was heard;

And again the coarse steppe grass, the hills and rooks flash before them;

Again the scorched plain stretches on . . . ;

Again Egorushka was lying on the bale. The sun burned as yesterday, the air was motionless and despondent;

As yesterday the air was full of the chattering music of the steppes.

We should note a correspondence between Chekhov's style here and Tolstoy's *Boyhood*. In two very short introductory chapters of *Boyhood* I have counted nine examples using "now" [*vot*] at the beginning of sentences and four instances of "and now" [*no vot*]. The children's journey from Petrovsk to Moscow after Nikolenka's mother dies provides circumstantial evidence that this correspondence is not merely accidental; furthermore, we can observe other analogies between "The Steppe" and this particular section of *Boyhood*. The descriptions of the storm which overtakes the travelers are very similar in both stories: for example, where the onset of a terrible gust of wind is followed by rain:

"The Steppe": But now, finally, the wind tore at the bast matting for the last time, . . . an even, calmer roar was heard, a big, cold drop of rain fell on Egorushka's knee, another slid down his hand.

Boyhood: A raindrop falls heavily on the leather hood of the carriage . . . another, a third, a fourth, and suddenly, it is as if someone had begun drumming over our heads, the whole country resounded with the regular patter of falling rain.

In both works lightning strikes close to the travelers:

Boyhood: The lightning seems to flash right into the carriage, blinding me, and for an instant it lights up the gray cloth, its braiding, and Volodya's figure crouching in the corner.

"The Steppe": Suddenly over his head with a terrible . . . crack the sky burst . . . and he saw how the blinding sharp light flashed . . . on his fingers, his wet sleeves and on the streams running from the bast matting. . . .

"The Steppe" provides a most vivid and telling example of Chekhov's compositional technique, telling because it is the simplest. Here the structure of the *syuzhet* itself determines, as we have seen, its rhythmic unfolding. In other works internal rhythm is not as clearly apparent because it is shown more subtly. I have in mind works of Chekhov's mature period which can be considered short stories only from the standpoint of their external form; in terms of their internal form these works sooner belong to the category of novel or novella. We are aware, however, that these distinctions are conventional and that the boundaries between them are unsubstantial; these stories contain a compact and concise depiction of an entire, large segment of life, revealed in a chain of events.

In the novel each event, each new knot (uniting in links various externally unrelated phenomena) is presented in all its detail. As the reading progresses these details gradually fade from memory, so that after it is finished the work as a whole is perceived in a schematic and simplified form. By contrast, in Chekhov's "novel-short story," separate links of the total process are shown in a few words by illuminating some characteristic detail of each moment. The work can be perceived as a whole only when one makes the connection between these details and catches those hints which suggest the whole; each moment in the present connects to a past, as well as a future, moment. A. Derman, in his incisive remarks on Chekhov's laconicism, [10] has noted that Chekhov sets up landmarks which designate the stages of the descending spiritual odyssey of his "Ionych" by means of such hints and varied repetitions of one and the same theme: at first Ionych walks wherever he goes since "he still does not have his own horses"; then he acquires a pair of horses, and then a troika; and finally we are presented with an "imposing picture" of Ionych driving everywhere in his troika, looking like a "pagan god."

We find an analogous method of uniting the whole in "The Darling," with the major difference that "the darling" does not evolve as a character. She remains the same, in effect, from youth to old age. It is precisely this lack of change which is essential to the story. Chekhov attains the characterization of stasis by means of intentional and almost literal repetition of the basic theme. Olenka's acquaintance and marriage to the entrepreneur Kukin marks the first stage of her life:

> *They got on well together after the wedding.* She *would sit* in his office, look after things in the amusement park and keep the accounts.... And she already said to her acquaintances that the theater was the chief and *most important and necessary* thing in life and that it was only through the drama that one could derive true enjoyment and become cultivated and humane.

93

A second marriage, to the merchant Pustovalov, follows after Kukin's death.

> Pustovalov and Olenka *got on well together after they married.* Usually he sat in the office till dinner time, then he went out on business, while Olenka took his place, and *would sit* in the office till evening, making up accounts and booking orders.... It seemed to her that she had been in the timber trade for ages and ages, and that *the most important and necessary* thing in life was timber; and there was something intimate and touching to her in the very sound of words such as "beam," "post," "boards,"....

Olenka's laments over her two deceased husbands are almost identical. However, such absolute repetition does not happen in life. Olenka does grow older, and her marriage to the merchant is not identical to her marriage with the theatrical entrepreneur; hence, the slight variations in theme. While Olenka was married to Kukin "her rosy cheeks, her sweet, naive and *radiant* smile appeared [mel'kali] now at the office window, now behind the curtains, now at the buffet"; "Olenka grew stouter, and glowed with satisfaction" (because everything was going well at the theater). Olenka's happiness in her second marriage is somewhat different; it is characterized by a certain prosaic and bourgeois solidity. Absent here are the radiance and verbs which express swiftness of psychophysical reactions ("flash," "appear momentarily") [mel'kali]. Their material surroundings emphasize the bourgeois character of this new happiness:

> On Saturdays Pustovalov and she used to go to evening services and on holidays to early mass; they would walk home from church side by side, their faces touched with emotion. There was a pleasant fragrance about them both, and her silk dress rustled agreeably. At home they drank tea, with sweet bread and jams of various kinds, and afterwards they ate pie....

During the first stage of her life Olenka has pink cheeks; during the second phase "once a week the couple would go to the baths and return side by side, both flushed...." The tempo of life slows down correspondingly; Olenka's first marriage lasts only one year—her husband dies suddenly. Her second marriage lasts six years and

Pustovalov is ill the four months prior to his death. The third stage brings the cycle to a close. In the very beginning until her acquaintance with Kukin, Olenka "had loved her father . . . , and still earlier, in school, she had loved her French teacher," now, in her old age, when her last romance—with the veterinary—is a thing of the past, she loves his son, the school boy, Sasha; her "rejuvenated" face is once again "radiant."

Chekhov deliberately uses one and the same image in different variations to attain his aims: laconicism and an impressionistic depiction of reality; moreover, this reality is shown without the authorial comment that would hinder direct perception and thus work against his aims. In this regard he observed to his brother Aleksandr: "In the realm of psychology we must concern ourselves with the particular; God save us from generalizations. It is best to avoid describing the spiritual state of the heroes; one must try to make this understood from their actions" (May 10, 1886). The twice-mentioned image of the cat (initially separate from "the darling" and subsequently identified with her) fulfills this function in "The Darling."

There is an obvious analogy between "The Steppe" and "The Darling." In both stories rhythm is created through a recapitulation of first one, then another theme: in "The Steppe" the themes of travel and stopping; in "The Darling" the themes of happiness and its loss. But there is also a profound difference between these stories. In the former, the *syuzhet* itself obviates the risk of monotony; as we have seen, in the latter, on the contrary, the *syuzhet* presupposes it. Olenka, of course, would like everything to be as it has always been; and she does, after all, behave consistently during the first, second and last stages of her life. She is unaware that she exists in a Heraclitian stream. The artist's task is to show simultaneously both this stream of life and her perception of it. This he accomplishes by combining repeated phrases with elusive (at a superficial reading) stylistic variations that express the nuances of "the darling's" life style and her attitude towards these various love objects. Thus, in describing her life with Pustovalov, for example, Chekhov does not merely confine himself to a repetition of what was said about her life with Kukin ("They lived well . . . ") but notes at the close of this section: "And so for six years the Pustovalovs lived quietly and peacefully in love and complete accord." The language here obviously recalls the oral tale or the old-fashioned "family" novel; it harmonizes with the passages cited above, impressionistically depicting this period of the darling's life.

I will cite one other instance of a recurrent image-symbol, from "The Betrothed." Andrei Andreich takes Nadya to look at the apartment he has rented:

> A big oil painting [a nude lady] in a gold frame hung on the wall, and a purple vase with a broken handle stood next to it.

> "An exquisite picture," said Andrei Andreich, with a respectful sigh. ... Andrei Andreich led Nadya through the rooms, all the while keeping his arm round her waist; and she felt weak and conscience stricken. She hated all the rooms, the beds, the easy chair; she was nauseated by the nude lady. It was clear to her now that she had ceased to love Andrei Andreich. ...

Her escape from home:

> And suddenly she recollected everything: Andrei, and his father and the new apartment and the nude lady with the vase; but none of it frightened or oppressed her any longer; it was, rather, innocent and insignificant and kept retreating further and further away.

She comes home for a vist, a completely different person now:

> And for some reason she imagined the figure of Andrei Andreich, and the naked lady with the vase, and the whole of her past, which now seemed as far distant from her as her childhood. ...

"The lady with the vase" is identified, as it were, with Andrei Andreich; it merges with him into a single image of self-satisfied vulgarity. We should note also how these two recollected images are fused into one; while the impression is still fresh in Nadya's mind, she recalls Andrei and "the lady with the vase" together with Andrei's father and the new apartment. Eventually these "secondary" objects of recollection fade from memory, leaving only Andrei and the "lady," the sight of which so nauseated Nadya. And now, this lady is no longer "nude," [nagaya] but simply "naked" [golaya].

The first epithet is more appropriate to the "lady" in the picture. Separated from all the other subjects, identified, as it were, with Andrei Andreich, "the lady" is best remembered as an ordinary woman.

Chekhov's device of repeating one and the same theme or symbol, in different contexts and variations, bears a marked similarity to Pushkin's prose technique. The often repeated number three in "The Queen of Spades" is an example of such a word-symbol—"three cards," "three villainous acts" (on German's conscience), "three young girls" (the countess' servants), her "three old house maids," "three days" and the "three weeks," separating one event from another, etc.—is the symbol of fate (the three fates).[11] The theme of "impatience," linked with the image of the "animal Terek" in "The Journey to Arzum" provides another example. We find a similar device, incidentally, in Gogol—Chichikov's "chin" and "stomach," which so command his attention. This device is particularly obvious in "The Carriage." Whenever the military are shown in this story a hierarchical order is observed: the general is the first to look over the mare, and he is followed by the colonel, and then the major; "the others clicked their tongues"; the same hierarchy is observed when they ride to Chertokutsky, step out of the carriage and discuss Chertokutsky's behavior and the carriage. The ritualistic solemnity of the general's appearance along with his "gentlemen officers" emphasizes the scandal of Chertokutsky's situation. It is significant that "The Carriage" is purely anecdotal (as are the majority of Chekhov's stories) and that it concludes with a "zero" resolution, an ending equally common in Chekhov: "Having said this, the general immediately slammed the doors, again covered Chertokutsky with the carriage apron and left with his gentlemen officers." It is difficult, therefore, to decide precisely to whom (Pushkin or Gogol) Chekhov was indebted for this device. In any event, we can say that Chekhov employs word-symbols with utmost regularity; they are a major factor in our perception of the unity of his stories. In his brief article about Chekhov,[12] the English critic, Oliver Elton, has correctly noted that Chekhov makes the same use of "theme-symbols" in his plays: Moscow in *The Three Sisters*, the sea gull and the cherry orchard in the plays of the same titles. These symbols

97

are a kind of surrogate to the intrigue from which Chekhov, the dramatist, strives to distance himself (see below).

Chekhov makes extensive use of image-symbols which function thematically in "In the Ravine."[13] The elements of internal rhythm are even more difficult to perceive because they are not given in the *syuzhet*. But we can locate these elements; we have at our disposal materials which, in other writers, might be considered drafts or variant texts. What Khodasevich said about Pushkin's work[14] applies to Chekhov as well; he, too, had his "poetic economy," his storehouse of images, motifs and turns of speech, which he used in different ways in different works. If we compare Chekhov's use of these materials in a variety of contexts, then we can determine their meaning in each separate instance.[15]

It is from this point of view that we should compare "In the Ravine" to "Peasants." The first story is a very remote, but undeniable variant of the second. Indeed, the situations are similar: in both stories one of the sons is a townsman; in "Peasants" he dies, and "In the Ravine" he is sent into exile; the wife leaves her father-in-law's house—in the first case voluntarily, and in the second she is forced out by her sister-in-law. The parallel contrasting images are similar: the dissolute and spiteful wife of one son is contrasted with the two sisters-in-law Marya and Olga in "Peasants" and, "In the Ravine," with the mother-in-law, Varvara, and her daughter-in-law, Lipa. There are also similarities in the relationship between Olga and Fekla and between Lipa and Aksinya. But there is more. We find in "In the Ravine" an episode which is an obvious reworking from "Peasants":

> Praskovya and Lipa began to doze off. When they were awakened by someone's footsteps the moon was brightly shining; Aksinya stood at the entrance to the shed, her bedding in her arms.
> "Maybe it will be a bit cooler here," she said; then she came in and lay down almost in the doorway so that the moonlight fell full upon her. She did not sleep, but sighed heavily, tossing from side to side with the heat, throwing off almost all the bedclothes. And in the magical light of the moon what a beautiful, what a proud animal she was!

Compare in "Peasants":

> Someone rapped gently, ever so gently, at the window. It must have been Fekla, come back. Olga got up, yawning, and whispered a

98

prayer; she unlocked the door, then pulled the bolt of the outer door. But no one came in; only there was a cold draft of air from the street and the entry suddenly grew bright with the moonlight. . . .

"Who's there?" called Olga.

"Me," came the answer, "It's me."

Near the door, hugging the wall stood Fekla, stark naked. She was shivering with cold, her teeth were clattering, and in the bright moonlight she looked very pale, beautiful and strange. The shadows and the glow of moonlight stood out sharply on her skin, and her dark eyebrows and firm, young breasts were defined with peculiar distinctness.

Both concluding episodes are similar as well. In "Peasants" Olga and Sasha leave the village on foot for Moscow:

At noon Olga and Sasha came to a large village. There on the broad street they encountered the little old man who had been General Zhukov's cook. . . . . At first he and Olga failed to recognize each other, then they looked around at the same moment, did recognize each other, and went their separate ways without saying a word. Stopping before a cottage which looked newer and more prosperous than the rest, Olga bowed down and said in a loud, thin, singsong voice:

"Orthodox Christians, give alms, for Christ's sake, as much as you can, and in the Kingdom of Heaven may your parents know peace eternal."

"Orthodox Christians," Sasha echoed her chant, "give alms for Christ's sake, as much as you can, and in the Kingdom of Heaven. . . . "

In "In the Ravine," Lipa and her mother are returning from work by way of the village when they meet the old man Tsybukin, Lipa's father-in-law; he has lost his spirit and is totally dependent on Aksinya:

The old man stopped and, saying nothing, looked at them both; his lips were quivering and his eyes were full of tears. Lipa took a piece of pie stuffed with buckwheat from her mother's sack and gave it to him. He took it and began eating.

The sun had set by now; its glow had died away and it was getting dark and cool on the upper part of the road. Lipa and Praskovya walked on and for some time kept crossing themselves.

99

The material contained in the concluding passage of "Peasants" is used in a new manner here. Clearly, "Peasants" is one of the sources for the later story. The difference between these two works, however, is very significant. Most important, "Peasants" shares many features with the so-called sketch of "everyday life"; the social milieu is in the foreground and the characters, who tend to be everyday, ordinary types, are representative of this milieu. Therefore they are characterized in somewhat general terms and lack the vivid individuality of the figures in "In the Ravine." They are more modest, paler and less significant. If we compare the first parallel passages in the stories, we can see at once how much more demonic Aksinya is than Fekla; she is a beautiful, *proud animal,* and the epithet *magic* attributed to the moonlight strengthens the impression of Aksinya's demonic quality. The relationship between the two sisters-in-law in "Peasants" primarily illustrates the general character of the social milieu; this explains why Marya seems to be Olga's double. By contrast, in "In the Ravine" the social milieu provides the background against which relationships are played out. Here, both the characters are in the foreground, as well as Lipa and Aksinya's relationship to the Tsybukin family.

We may say that in "In the Ravine" the *syuzhet* canvas provides a backdrop for the struggle of the two main themes—Lipa's theme and Aksinya's theme—the eternal feminine principle and the demonic principle in woman. Therefore antagonism between representatives of these two principles is manifest only in the form of petty clashes in the first story, whereas in the second it is fully explored, culminating in the murder of Lipa's baby by Aksinya. Here, as nowhere else, Chekhov achieves Shakespearian tragedy— Shakespearian in the sense that the horror is shown with a simplicity and extreme laconicism which intensifies the overall impression.

Chekhovian tragedy, however, is fundamentally different from Shakespearian. The conflict between the eternal feminine and the woman-demon is neither predestined by the characters of these women nor determined by the intrigue. Aksinya does not despise Lipa because she senses that Lipa is her opposite, but simply because she is an extra person in the house, the wife of her brother-in-law, the convict. Similarly, Fekla despises Olga because she is an outsider; she and her husband are extra mouths to feed. Simple people in Chekhov, as in Tolstoy, resemble Homer's kings and queens. They are simple in the literal sense of the word—*naive*. Once Aksinya has poured scalding water on the child, she parades around with her "old *naive* smile." Such characters lack capacity for reflection and self-awareness, i.e., they lack a conscious attitude to what comprises their "not-I." We cannot say, then, that antagonism between Aksinya and Lipa forms the story's basic theme in the sense in which the term is ordinarily used in literary criticism. I am using the concept of themes here in a musical sense. In the process of reading "In the Ravine" we interpret the conflict depicted and we bring to it a meaning which even the characters themselves do not suspect.

Once we accept this relationship to the stories, then we can see the rationale in Chekhov's form and the close link between form and content. There is no *syuzhet* center in the story. It breaks down into a series of episodes which are not intrinsically connected with the culminating moment in the conflict between Aksinya and Lipa. In all these episodes first one, then the other, or both together, take part. Each woman thus reveals herself and we are then able to form a general impression of both. We are not provided with an introductory, generalized characterization of the "heroines," since this is superfluous. It would only be necessary if the conflict between them were psychologically motivated. (This of course, is not the case; Aksinya would have despised Lipa even had she been like her.) We find, instead, an alternation of images and suggestions which, in terms of structure, approximates a purely musical development of theme and counter-theme, framed by supplementary themes. The repetitions of image-symbols, epithets, indications of movement, sounds and colors which create two complete images, correspond in musical terms to the recurrence of melodies, chords, harmonies, keys and tempos. We can demonstrate this parallel movement of both themes.
I. Aksinya's theme:

a. His [Stepan's] wife Aksinya, a handsome woman with a good figure, who wore a hat and carried a parasol on holidays, got up early and went to bed late, and *ran about* all day long, picking up her skirts and *jingling her keys,* going from the warehouse to the cellar and from there to the shop.... (Ch. I)

b. Aksinya had no sooner married his deaf son than she began to display an extraordinary business sense;... she kept the keys, she

101

rattled away on the abacus, examined the horses' teeth ... and was always *laughing* or *shouting*.... (Ch. I)

c. Before the sun was up Aksinya was *snorting* away as she washed up in the hall, and the samovar boiled in the kitchen with a hum *that boded ill.* [As yet there has still been no mention of anything which bodes "ill."] (Ch. I)

d. Aksinya kept shop, and from the yard could be heard the *clink* of bottles and of money [cf. a.], her *laughter* and *shouting* [cf. b.], and the angry voices of the customers whom she offended.... (Ch. I)

e. On holidays Kostyukov and the Khryminy, Jrs. would go driving. Aksinya, dressed to kill and *rustling* her starched petticoats, used to promenade up and down the street.... (Ch. I)

f. [Preparations for Anisim's and Lipa's wedding]: Aksinya, with her hair curled, in her stays without her dress on, in new, *creaky* boots, *flew* about the yard *like a whirlwind; only* her bare knees and bosom *flashed by.* (Ch. III)

g. [The wedding feast]: In the middle of the quadrille they suddenly crooked their knees and danced in a squatting position; Aksinya, in *green, flashed* by raising a wind with her train.... Aksinya had naive gray eyes [And her eyes seem green to Lipa: "And now I am afraid of Aksinya.... It's not that she does anything, she is always laughing,... and her eyes are so angry and there is a *greenish* gleam in them—like the eyes of the sheep in the pen."], which rarely blinked, and a *naive smile played* continually on her face. And in those unblinking eyes, and in that little head on the *long neck,* and in her slender figure there was something snakelike; all in *green,* with her *yellow* bosom and the smile on her lips, she looked *like a viper* that peers *out of the young rye in the spring* at passers-by, *stretching* itself and lifting its head. [Her relationship with one of the Khrymin brothers only now becomes clear.] (Ch. III)

h. A new project was in the works—a brickyard in Butekino—and Aksinya went there almost every day in the chaise. She drove herself and when she met acquaintances she *stretched out her neck like a snake in the young rye, and smiled naively and enigmatically.* (Ch. VI, cf. f.) [16]

102

i. [After Anisim has been exposed. The quarrel with her father-in-law]: Clothes were hanging on the lines stretched across the yard; she *snatched off* her petticoats and blouses . . . and *flung* them into the deaf man's arms. Then in her fury she dashed about the yard where the linen hung, *tore down* all of it, and what was not hers she *threw* on the ground and trampled upon.

[After she has scalded Nikifor]: And it was suddenly quiet in the yard. Aksinya walked into the house in silence with her former smile. (Ch. VII)

j. People said of Aksinya that she has become a person of great power; and it was true that when she drove to her brickyard in the morning, with the *naive smile,* handsome and happy, and afterwards when she gives orders there, one was aware of her great power. (Ch. IX)

II. Lipa's theme:

a. On all sides, above and below, the larks were singing. . . . As soon as her husband had driven out of the yard, Lipa was transformed and suddenly brightened up. Barefoot, in an old, shabby skirt, her sleeves tucked up to her shoulders, she scrubbed the stairs in the entry and sang in a thin, *silvery little voice,* and when she brought out a big tub of slops and *looked at the sun with her childlike smile* it seemed as though she too were a *lark.* (Ch. IV)

b. [The end of the story]: Peasant women and girls came in a crowd from the station where they had been loading the cars with bricks. . . . They were singing. Ahead of them all was Lipa, and *she was singing in a thin voice, with her eyes turned towards the sky,* as though exalting in the fact that at last the day was over and the time for rest had come. . . . The sun had set by now; its glow died away on the upper part of the road too. . . . (Ch. IV)

I will omit other passages which I have elsewhere cited where the same theme is developed. They all relate to episodes of Lipa's pilgrimages. In contrast to Aksinya, usually shown "rushing about," "flashing across," "dashing about" the courtyard, "snorting," "jingling" (keys), etc., Lipa is sketched in such a way that the reader associates her with the image of wandering pilgrims. Significantly, the sun is constantly mentioned, usually setting and withdrawing in descriptions of Lipa's pilgrimages.

The sun had already set, and its beams filtered through the copse, gleaming on the trunks of the trees. (Ch. IV)

By now the sun had set and a thick mist . . . was rising over the river, in the church yard and in the glades around the mills. (Ch. IV)

The sun went to sleep. . . . (Ch VIII)

The sun had set by now. . . . (Ch. IX)

Similar image-symbols occur in an episode in "Three Years," a description of landscape painting which Laptev's wife sees at an exhibition:

> In the foreground was a small river with a wooden bridge across it, and a path on the opposite bank which disappeared into a dark, grassy meadow; on the right was a small forest, and near it a campfire . . . and the evening sky was smouldering in the distance.

> Yuliya imagined herself walking across the bridge and along the path, farther and farther; it was quiet all around, a few landrails croaked sleepily, and a fire glowed in the distance. And for some reason it suddenly seemed to her that many times before in the past she had seen those very clouds which stretched across the red of the sky, and the forest, and the field. She suddenly felt lonely and felt like walking down the path; and there in the twilight could be seen a reflection of something supernatural and eternal.[17]

This landscape, which so engrosses Yuliya, and her experience while she is looking at it, and likewise, the fusion of Lipa with the lark and the sun into a single poetic image, which completes her characterization, all lead to an understanding of what Chekhov defined as his artistic individuality. This is precisely what Chekhov ascribes to Trigorin when the latter calls himself primarily a "landscape painter." Contrary to the advice he gave others, Chekhov constantly personifies and anthropomorphizes nature. But when he depicts the most significant, most precious and most human aspects of man, he transfers to the human realm what he has perceived in the world of nature; he includes man in nature. Chekhov does not resort to banal simile to achieve this transference. He relies, instead, upon a method of presentation in which there is

no "portraiture" or "framing," no "background" or "foreground."
This fact alone unwittingly leads us to question Chekhov's vision of
the world and life: what is the "content" of his works insofar as it is
revealed in "form?"

Footnotes to Chapter Five

1. See, for example, N.L.Brodskii, "Proza *Zapisok okhotnika.*" In " *Turgenev i ego vremia,* Moskva, 1923, 193ff.

2. Particularly in "The Journey to Arzum." See examples cited in my article, "Puteshestvie v Arzum," in *Belgradskii Pushkinskii sbornik,* 1938.

3. Compare with a letter to Grigorovich: "I am depicting the plains, a lilac distance, shepherds, priests, night storms, inns, wagon trains, birds of the steppe, etc. . . . . I am trying to give each chapter a common smell and common tone. . . . " But he thinks he has not been successful: "Instead of an artistically integrated depiction of the steppe, I present the reader with an encyclopedia of the steppe" (Jan. 12, 1888).

4. This was quoted by another critic, Izmailov, in his critical-biographical study, in volume XXII, *Polnoe sobranie sochinenii A.P. Chekhova,* izd. Marksa, 1911, with the remark that, "Obolensky has sensed, quite correctly, the philosophical synthesis of 'The Steppe'." (!). This "lack of color" and the "lack of grandeur" in the depiction of the steppe, although censured by the critics, were of course, deliberate on Chekhov's part. It revealed his striving for truthfulness and his desire to avoid everything stereotypical and conventional. It is interesting that he evidently had only one predecessor here—an "essayist," the brilliant and gifted Driyansky, forgotten and never judged on his merits. He writes in his "Notes of a Petty Man" ["Zapiski melkotravchatogo"]: "How many poems have been written, how many songs have been sung about this steppe. And it is thought that this is the promised land, where there is light and warmth and space for men; this is how these endless pampas from Buenos Aires are imagined. . . . Wild grain, and tumbleweed and the deep blue sky with the shrill calls of the cranes, flying who knows where. . . . A far cry from the steppe beyond Tambov! We drove into the steppe; on the right is a willow, on the left is a willow, again willow after willow and behind them nothing but willows and willows. It is pale yellow, hilly, full of mud and clods. . . . "

5. Compare the image of the "awakening" of the steppe at dawn: "And suddenly the whole wide steppe *flung off* the twilight of early morning, and was smiling and sparkling with dew."

6. The portraits of Kuzmichev and Father Khristofor, used in reproducing two contrasting images, provide examples of such hints, suggestions, and promptings. The *gauntness* [(sukhost'),* lit. dryness] on Kuzmichev's face is mentioned several times; it contrasts with the "moist" little eyes of Father Khristofor. This *gauntness* imparts to his face an *"inquisitorial* appearance"; he is *fanatic* in his business, his face is *shaven.* All of this is subtly motivated in that Kuzmichev's fellow traveler is an *orthodox priest;* the impression of a person who is both contrasted to him and at the same time close to him should, of course, create an image of a catholic priest.

7. It would be necessary to quote and analyze the story word for word, from beginning to end, to prove absolute musical consistency in the construction of "The Steppe." I will point out details which reveal the unity of the introduction and the final scene. In the introduction: "The boy gazed at the familiar places, while the *hateful* chaise flew by and left everything behind." In the final scene when everything has irrevocably ended, Egorushka's heart is drawn to the cart on which he set out. Leaving the inn with his uncle for his new apartment, he sees

the "familiar" cart: " 'Good-by, cart!' thought Egorushka." Memories of his grandmother, buried in the cemetery which he passes, are connected for Egorushka with a yearning for the life that has passed. "When grandmother died she was put in a long coffin and *two five-copeck coins* were put on her eyes, which would not stay shut." Compare also in the final parting scene when both the uncle and Father Khristofor give Egorushka a ten-copeck piece: "Egorushka kissed his hand, and began crying; something whispered in his heart that he would never see the old man again." And further: "Nastasya Petrovna, I have already applied to the high school," said Ivan Ivanych, in a voice *as though there were a corpse in the house.*"

8. "And in the triumph of its beauty, and in the overflowing of happiness, you feel a tension and anguish, as though the steppe is aware that it is alone, that its wealth and inspiration perish in vain, celebrated by no one and needed by no one, and in the joyful humming you hear her sad, hopeless call: a bard, a bard."

9. "The table was almost alone, for, besides a wide sofa covered with torn oil cloth and three chairs, there was no other furniture in the room. And, indeed, not everyone would have called these chairs chairs. It was a pitiful likeness to furniture...." This purely Gogolian *nature morte* is significant here as an example of literary suggestion.

10. *Op. cit.,* 202ff.

11. About this see my article "Simvolika 'Pikovoi damy': (Zametki o Pushkine)" in *Slavia,* 1932; see also S. Shtein, "Pushkin i German," *Acta et Commentationes Univ. Tartuensis,* 1928, v. 13.

12. Chekhov. *The Taylorian Lecture,* Oxford, 1929.

13. I am deliberately examining those Chekhov works which I consider the best, precisely because they combine these two elements—extreme laconicism and *syuzhet* concentration. I will omit those works where he uses a more ample form of narration, thereby avoiding the rigors of a concentrated style: "Three Years," "A Boring Story" ["Skuchnaya istoriya"], "An Anonymous Story," and "The Duel."

14. Cf. V. Khodasevich, *Poeticheskoe khoziaistvo Pushkina,* Berlin, 1924.

15. As an example of an internal borrowing in Chekhov, we may cite a passage in "The Steppe" about a poplar which is similar to a passage from "Champagne": "A tall poplar covered with hoar frost appeared in the bluish haze. It looked at me sternly and dejectedly, as though, like me, it realized its loneliness. I stood a long while looking at it." Here also the idea of loneliness is connected with the image of a poplar.

16. I have noticed, by the way, a similar image of a woman in Turgenev: "Anna's eyes were simply pinned on the speaker and a face more spiteful, more snake-like, and more beautiful because of that very spitefulness I had certainly never seen." ("King Lear of the Steppes") Kharlov's daughters in the Turgenev story treat him in much the same fashion as Aksinya behaves towards her father-in-law. Might we not detect here traces of Turgenev's influence?

17. Compare to a similar image in "The Black Monk": "A broad field lay before him.... No human dwelling, not a living soul, could be seen in the distance, and it seemed that if one were to walk along the path, it would lead to a most supernatural and mysterious place, where the sun had just set and the twilight glow blazed expansively and majestically."

Chapter Six

Anecdotal Structure

Man, as a phenomenon in the realm of empirical reality, makes his way through life in response to a series of chance accidents. We cannot say the same of the creative life of an artist; in his artistic development he reveals his own pure, intelligible "I." We can speak here of a certain immanent *fatum,* or inner necessity. The words of Goethe are appropriate here: "Ein guter Mensch in seinem dunkeln Drange,/Ist sich des rechtes Weges wohl bewusst." The good man is the creator-man; so says the Creator-God in *Faust.* This, indeed, is Goethe's motto for the second part of *Dichtung und Wahrheit:* "Was man in der Jugend wünscht, hat man im Alter die Fülle."

As if in response to immanent destiny, Chekhov began his artistic career with humorous feuilletons for *Fragments* and *The Dragon-Fly* [*Strekoza*], journals devoted to the anecdotal. Popular anecdotes provided him with the subject matter for his stories:

> Marya Vladimirovna [Kiseleva, his good friend] is well [he writes to his brother Mikhail Pavlovich in 1885]. She sent mother a bottle of jam and in general is kind beyond belief. She supplies me with anecdotes from old French magazines.... (May 10, 1885)

Years of practice writing stories with anecdotal subject matter gave Chekhov his real *Lehrjahre.* The work often oppressed him, but it brought its reward; it enabled Chekhov to find himself.

The traditional *syuzhet* base of the anecdote is *quid pro quo* misunderstanding—error: the theme of misspent energy, and, as a result, the "zero" resolution. All the stories of Antosha Chekhonte are based on this structure as, indeed, are almost all humorous stories, novellas and dramatic works since the beginning of literature. The discrepancy between expectation and realization creates a comic effect, as long as the result is not terrible or sad. Such an effect is most readily achieved by bringing the intrigue—the weaving of the story line—to a "zero" resolution. The anecdote differs from the novella or the drama in that it depicts a self-contained event which begins with a conflict and ends in a resolution of the conflict. In the novella or the drama, by contrast, an event shown is considered a moment within a total process, a moment in the present which assumes both a past and a future. This explains, in part, why elements which critics call *Vor-* and *Nachgeschichte* are particularly prominent in the novella.[1] Turgenev, for example, invariably introduces his characters with a brief, but thorough *curriculum vitae.* Moreover, in the conclusion he usually explains how the events of the story affected their subsequent destiny.

Here Chekhov remains forever faithful to Antosha Chekhonte; his characteristic tendency to overcome literary stereotypes is evident. Perhaps de Maupassant was influential in this regard; his short story is also usually nothing more than an elaborated anecdote transferred to another level, from the level of mere comedy to humor or even tragedy. But there is no doubt that Chekhov's own literary practice played the decisive role.

Be that as it may, we must assert that in this aspect of his work Chekhov the artist acted in complete accord with Chekhov the literary theoretician. "Beginning writers," he told Shchukin,[2] "should often do just this: fold the work in half and tear up the first half." He clarified this point: one should not "lead into a story"; one must write so that "the reader understands without the author's explanation what the story is all about from the course of events, the conversations of the characters and their actions." Even more important is his formulation that a writer should cross out the beginning and the end of a finished story, because these are the most difficult parts and, therefore, the most likely to turn out badly: "Here we writers lie the most."[3] Why are they the most difficult? It is because what relates to the *Vor-* and *Nachgeschichte* can and should be shown only by means of hints and light touches. At least this is how Chekhov consistently approaches the problem.

But again the question arises: why is it necessary to write in this way? It is not difficult to find the answer as long as we are concerned with the short-story/novella, i.e., a narrative directly derived from the anecdote. A detailed exposition of moments preceding and following the central events violates the requirement of artistic unity; it is replaced here by exposition which has more or less the character of "taking minutes."

This, however, does not exhaust the meaning of Chekhov's remarks. To understand the essence of his artistic development we should recall that even during his mature period Chekhov had occasion to write stories by no means humorous, yet on a formal level wholly identical to the anecdote. First, they have no prologue or epilogue; and second, they are structured on a motif of misunderstanding, *quid pro quo*. Such a story is "At a Country House" ["V usad'be"] (1894), where the landowner Rashevich, in conversation with his guest, inveighs against the *petite bourgeoisie* who are currently setting the tone; only later, when his guest tells him about himself, that he, too, is a *petit bourgeois,* does the landowner acknowledge that he has made *une gaffe.* Similarly, in "The Grasshopper," the heroine, who deceives her husband and spends her time with celebrities and geniuses, learns only after her husband's death that he was a prominent scholar and that fame awaited him.

The touching story, "The Letter" ["Pis'mo"], offers a marvelous example on the motif of misspent energy—not due to misunderstanding determined by circumstances, but as a result of an emotional reaction. The deacon, who has requested and obtained a letter of reprimand for his son from the archdeacon, adds the postscript:

> They have sent us a new school supervisor. He is spryer than the old one. He is a dancer, a talker and a jack-of-all-trades, and the Govorovsky girls are wild about him. The army chief Kostyrev, too, will soon be sent packing, they say. High time!

It is amusing that he does not even understand that "his postscript had completely spoiled the stern letter." We shall later speak of another, similar example in the "The Kiss" ["Potselui"].

No less significant are cases where the anecdotal base has been turned, so to speak, inside out; a man makes a decision which he considers trivial, and only later it becomes apparent that this decision determines his entire subsequent destiny: the relationship between the hero and the heroine in "The Lady with a Lapdog" develops precisely in this way. Having started an affair with the woman, the hero does not realize how passionately he loves her; it seems to him that it is nothing more than one of his numerous, brief romances without consequence.

"Neighbors" is another variation on the anecdote. Ivashin sets out to see Vlasich, with whom his sister is living, determined to punish the seducer: "I will strike him with my whip in her presence and say all kinds of rude things to him." The incident concludes with Ivashin only feeling a stronger friendship for Vlasich. There was no need to expend all that energy. The misunderstanding was of an inner character. He does not know himself how he should act; moreover, he does not know whether he was genuinely disturbed by the behavior of his sister and Vlasich. In these latter cases there is *in nuce* another more complicated reworking of the anecdotal *syuzhet*. The "zero" resolution of the story-anecdote corresponds to what we might call a gradual melting, a coming to naught, an evaporating, a fading of relationships among people.

From the perspective of external form, works such as "Ariadne," "Three Years" and "My Life" have nothing in common with the anecdote. Yet their psychological depth represents a reinterpretation of the theme of misunderstanding. Such misunderstandings arise not because the person has been mistaken in himself or his loved one, but because he has imagined himself and his beloved as constants. Not only does the river of life differ from what it was in the preceding moment, but he who was immersed in it also differs from what he was at the moment of immersion.

This is expressed with special subtlety in Chekhov's last story chronologically, "The Betrothed" (1903). Influenced by Sasha, a family friend, Nadya abandons her home and goes to study in Petersburg. Her mother and grandmother forgive her, and she returns for the spring holidays. She stops in Moscow to see Sasha:

> He was just the same as the year before: a beard and unkempt hair, in the same frock coat, with the same large beautiful eyes; but he looked unwell and worried; he had grown both older and thinner and kept coughing. And for some reason he struck Nadya as gray and provincial....

They sat and talked awhile; and now, after Nadya had spent a winter in Petersburg, Sasha—his words, his smile, his whole figure—had for her a suggestion of something out-of-date, old-fashioned, long since done with and perhaps already dead and buried.

Not only has Sasha really grown older and thinner and is already at death's door, but Nadya too is no longer the same as she had been. In his time Sasha gave her all he was capable of giving; he made possible her development and now—at least, in her own mind—she has surpassed him. Sasha represents an earlier stage in her life. Thus, when she receives his letter telling her about his illness,

she knew what it meant, and she was overwhelmed with a foreboding that was like a conviction [that he was dying]. And it vexed her that this foreboding and the thought of Sasha did not distress her as much as before. She had a passionate desire for life, she longed to be in Petersburg, and her friendship with Sasha now seemed a sweet, but far distant past.

The ceaselessness of the psychic process precludes man's ability to understand himself and to account for what happens in his soul:

It seemed to Nadya that she was very anxious, that her heart was heavier than ever before, that she would spend all her time until she went away in misery and agonizing thought; but she had hardly gone upstairs and lain down on her bed when she fell asleep at once. . . .

Actually, once it seems to Nadya that she is very anxious, then, indeed, she really becomes anxious. Her mistake is that she accepts that moment for a continuing present.

Chekhov and Tolstoy have in common a dynamic perception of man and life. The difference between them is that Chekhov is more one-sided than Tolstoy and, therefore, more consistent. Tolstoy refused to depict his people by "portraiture," or to characterize them exhaustively, because he considered man too complicated to be thus depicted. It is simply impossible to say of anyone that he is handsome or ugly, intelligent or stupid, etc., because everyone is intelligent or stupid, evil or good in his own way; moreover, every man is at times intelligent and at times, stupid: sometimes good, and sometimes evil. But despite this, Tolstoy sketched his characters impressionistically, with separate strokes; herein lies his incomparable mastery. Each one of his figures has his *character indelebilis,* although it is impossible to put into words precisely what this essence is. Therefore, each figure also has his own destiny. As a result, the Tolstoyan *roman fleuve,* despite its dynamic character, bears a similarity to classical tragedy with its static character. In Tolstoy, the intrigue concludes either tragically or with a happy ending.

A duality is evident in Chekhov's treatment of people. As in Gogol, they are either comic types whose *character indelebilis* is reduced to a maniacal obsession—like "the man in the case," or "the hereditary nobleman, Chimsha-Gimalaisky" who dreams about owning a country-estate with gooseberries—or they are kind, sympathetic, spiritual people, resembling one another, whose indelible mark is merely a characteristic of their social milieu and not a reflection of their personalities—for example, Laptev's inferiority complex in "Three Years." As noblemen, *raznochintsy,* clergy, peasants and merchants, they are "typical"; as personalities, they differ from one another primarily in their respective attractiveness, sincerity, responsiveness to someone else's happiness or sorrow, and by the degree of their receptivity to life's impulses. Chekhov's man is least of all a monad in the sense that he embodies some idea. He is, if one may so express it, a geometric point where all possible perceptions cross, the object of external influences rather than the subject; his humanity lies in his reacting to these influences with mind and heart.

Here again Chekhov's language attests to this. It is no accident that when Chekhov describes man in the role of "subject," thinking, remembering, desiring, etc., we frequently find that simple declarative sentences are replaced by impersonal phrases such as "he felt like" [*emu zakhotelos'*], "it reminded him" [*emu vspomnilos'*], etc. These phrases convey a state of mind similar to one constantly rendered in Chekhov by the verb "to seem" [*kazat'sya*], or by constructions of the type "something reminded him, her, me" [*chto-to napominalo emu, ei, mne*]:

"Volodya the Big and Volodya the Little":

The peal of the convent bell was very deep, and, *as it seemed* [*kak kazalos'*] to Sofya Lvovna, *something* [*chto-to*] in it *reminded* [*napominalo*] her of Olya and her life.

And for some reason *she was reminded* [*vspominalas' ei*] of her own aunt. . . .

Sofya Lvovna remembered Olya and she *became* [*stanovilos*] terrified. . . .

He *was reminded of* [*vspomnilos'*] those tales of easy conquest. . . and the tempting thought of a swift, fleeting love affair. . . *suddenly* took

"The Lady with a Lapdog":

He *remembered* [*vspomnilis'*] those tales of easy conquest. . . and the tempting thought of a swift, fleeting love affair. . . *suddenly took possession of him* [*vdrug ovladela im*].

(The subject here is the *thought,* whereas the person is the object to which the action is directed.)

When the first snow has fallen, . . . *it is pleasant to see* [*priyatno videt'*] the white ground, the white roofs, *to draw* soft delicious *breath* [*dyshitsya*], and in that season to *recall* [*vspominayutsya*] the days of one's youth.

Now discussions *did not interest him* [*emu bylo ne do*], *he felt* [*on chuvstvoval*] a deep compassion, *the desire arose* [*khotelos'*] to be sincere, tender. . . .

(Here the "I" momentarily becomes the "subject," but only for an instant.[4])

We could cite numerous other examples. These and similar constructions predominate in Chekhov.

Footnotes to Chapter Six

1. M.A. Petrovskii, "Morfologiia novelly," *Ars Poetica,* 73.
2. *Iz vospominanii o Chekhove, Russkaia mysl',* 1911, X, 44.
3. Bunin, *Pamiati Chekhova, op. cit.,* 61.
4. Contemporary philosophers of language have clarified the function of the passive mood as a means of reproducing a specific human character—the ability to suffer, i.e., to respond with feeling to an external influence. K. Vossler ably defines the passive mood as "die Leidensform der Verba. . . . " "Ein Leiden," he says, "gibt es, objectiv genommen, nur im eigenen Gefühl. Ja, alles Leiden ist Gefühl und weiter nichts. Wenn wir sagen, die Erde werde von der Sonne bestrahlt, und wenn wir das so ausdrücken, dass die Erde als Trägerin einer Leidensform des Bestrahlens erscheint, so schreiben wir ihr etwas Menschliches zu." (*Geist und Kultur in der Sprache,* 1925, 61, with reference to the research of H. Schuchardt, *Sprachursprung,* Sitzungsber, d. preuss, Ak. d. Wiss., 1921.)

Chapter Seven

Dramatic Works

Having examined the characteristics of Chekhov's style which enable us to understand his basic artistic idea, we are now able to resolve a certain puzzle in the history of his art, namely that of his dramatic works. The most knowledgeable critic of Chekhov's drama, S. Balukhaty,[1] has convincingly shown the many innovations in Chekhov's drama and has subtly analyzed those devices whereby the playwright renders on stage life as it really is. Already during his lifetime Chekhov was duly credited for the contributions he made to the theater. Chekhov's name, as we know, was linked with the Moscow Art Theater, whose directions shared his aspirations for the drama.

It was primarily the performance of Chekhov's plays at the Art Theater that established a new era in the history of Russian theater. It is puzzling, therefore, that despite Chekhov's close association with Stanislavsky and Nemirovich-Danchenko, and despite their efforts to understand the spirit of Chekhov's art, their production of his last play, *The Cherry Orchard,* in which his dramatic intentions were fully realized, left Chekhov profoundly dissatisfied. He wrote to his wife (quoted in B., II, 225):

Nemirovich and Alekseev (Stanislavsky) positively fail to see what I wrote in my play, and I am ready to wager that neither of them has read it carefully even once.

Compare this to what he said to E.P. Karpov:

Is this really my *Cherry Orchard?* ... Are these really my types? ... With the exception of two or three in the cast, none of this is mine.... I write of life.... It is a gray, everyday life ... but not this tedious whining. ... They make of me either a crybaby or simply a dull writer. (*Ibid.,* 274)

Evidently Chekhov was displeased with Stanislavsky's efforts to emphasize the emotional tone of the play. Stanislavsky strove to realize this tone (as is clear from his director's remarks in the text of *The Seagull* [ibid., 296ff]) by providing elaborate comments on gesticulation, mimicry and details which would add brilliance, clarity and concreteness to the images. This is precisely what Meyerhold criticized.

In Meyerhold's opinion [writes S. Balukhaty (*Ibid.,* 302)] the use of images which are impressionistically scattered onto a canvas makes up the basic characteristic of Chekhov's dramatic style; it provides the director with material suitable for filling out the characters into bright, defined figures (types). Hence, the characteristic enthusiasm of directors for details which distract from the picture as a whole.

He then quotes Meyerhold's letter to Chekhov about the staging of *The Cherry Orchard:*

Your play is abstract, like a Chaikovsky symphony. The director, first of all, ought to sense it with his ear. In the third act, unnoticed by anyone, against the background of stupid patter, Horror enters—it is just this "patter" which should be heard: "The cherry orchard is sold." Dancing. "Sold." And so on until the end. (*Ibid.,* 256)[2]

Meyerhold considered Chekhov a symbolist and thought that his plays should be staged symbolically, not realistically (as in the Art Theater). In a way he was right. He may have understood Chekhov more profoundly than Chekhov himself.

Every work of art, like every person, has petty traits which at first glance may seem insignificant; they are, in fact, very characteristic—like birth marks—and the coincidences to be found are very revealing. In *The Cherry Orchard* we find a twice-repeated stage direction:

They all sit, deep in thought. It is quiet. Only Firs' muttering is audible. Suddenly a distant sound is heard, as if coming from the sky, the sound of a breaking string, mournfully dying away. (Act III)

116

Consider the end of the play:

> A protracted sound is heard, as if coming from the sky, the sound of a breaking string, mournfully dying away.

Evidently Blok found something in this stage direction which had an innate appeal; he used it in "The Song of Destiny" ["Pesnya sud'by"]:

> At this moment a sound is carried from the plain—tender, soft, musical: as if a crow cawed or someone touched a taut string.

I will cite one other parallel, from "Three Years":

> Yartsev drove on farther to his place. . . . He dozed off, swaying in his seat and thinking about the play. Suddenly he thought he heard a fearsome noise, a clanking, and shouting in some strange tongue, which might have been Kalmuck; he saw a village overcome by flames, and neighboring forests, covered with hoar frost, and light pink from the fire could be seen all around in the distance . . . ; some kind of savage people, on horseback and on foot, swept through the village, both men and horses just as crimson as the fire's glow in the sky.
> "The Polovtsy," thought Yartsev.
> One of them—an old man with a fearsome, bloody face, covered with burns—was tying a young girl with a pale, Russian face to his saddle. The old man was shouting wildly about something, and the girl gazed sadly, thoughtfully. . . .

How much this excerpt shares with sections from Blok's cycle, "Homeland" ["Rodina"]! They have in common not only themes, but more importantly, tone and coloring. Symbolists recognized their predecessor in the later Chekhov (see about this B. II, 257). Interestingly, Chekhov himself advised Suvorin to produce Maeterlinck's plays and wrote that "were [he] the director of [Suvorin's] theater, then . . . he would have made it decadent in two years. . . . Perhaps the theater would seem strange, but, nevertheless, it would have its own physiognomy" (quoted in B. I, 103).

A similarity to the Symbolists notwithstanding, there is no doubt that Chekhov was adamant on the subject of truthfulness and naturalness in art—i.e., the correspondence of art with everyday

117

reality. He would have been horrified had *The Cherry Orchard* or *The Seagull* been produced as was the *The Puppet Show* [*Balaganchik*] or *The Unknown Lady* [*Neznakomka*], or produced as Treplev had wanted to stage his "mystery play." And to a degree he would have been right. Chekhov stood midway between realism and symbolism. Only from a pseudo-historical, doctrinaire point of view would it be possible to regard *ipso facto* the phenomena of a transitional period as imperfect. We have seen that in his best works Chekhov developed his own form wholly appropriate to their idea and content. He was able to attain complete artistic perfection by merging "genre" and "landscape" into one; he did not frame characters with setting, but showed both people and setting as a manifestation of a single life.

It is evident that his dramatic works do not succeed in this respect. Otherwise, how can one explain the failure of his plays on the stage? S. Balukhaty is correct in saying that Chekhov the dramatist remained true to himself; in the drama he struggled with various traditions and aspired to overcome all sorts of conventions. We concede that he found new means to express that same vision of life in the drama which is reflected in his narrative works. His plays do not divide characters into "major" and "minor figures"; they lack the traditional "intrigue" which begins with a "conflict" and ends with a "resolution." His task here, as in his stories, is to show in one segment of time—however incidental or trivial it may be—all life as a single process, having neither beginning nor end. But S. Balukhaty has not given sufficient attention to Chekhov's frequent lack of consistency in his struggle with scenic traditions and dramatic conventions. Above all, he has not considered the significance of the many incongruities which Chekhov let slip by; the mere fact of these inconsistencies is extremely important.

I will discuss some of the most significant examples. Let me first consider the final scene of *The Wood Demon* [*Leshii*], (in which there happens to be a "resolution"). More important than the fact of a denouement is that of all the possible resolutions, Chekhov chose the most stereotyped: the "kind old man" "arranges"—moreover quite unexpectedly—the "happiness" of two young couples.[3] In the third act of *Uncle Vanya* [*Dyadya Vanya*] Astrov and Elena Andreevna are embracing and do not notice when Voinitsky appears on stage. S. Balukhaty (B. I, 178) mentions the interesting fact that Chekhov himself seems to parody this banal device in Act Four of the same play. As he is saying good-bye to Elena Andreevna, Astrov tells her: "As long as there is no one here, let me kiss you before Uncle Vanya comes in with his bouquet." The same shortcoming occurs in *The Cherry Orchard.* Anya appears on stage, unnoticed by Gaev and Varya, and overhears what Gaev is saying about her mother; this is a hackneyed device of old-fashioned drama.

The farther Chekhov progressed in this artistic development, the more subtly, the more carefully and the more diversely did he reveal the traits of a given personality, and the qualities which characterized him as a "type"—be he a representative of a certain social milieu, an historical moment, or an expression of some idea or human psychic feature.[4] We find this in *The Three Sisters,* when Soleny continually takes out a bottle of perfume and sprinkles it on himself; this oft-repeated action ultimately becomes boring and irritating. It is nothing more than an unsuccessful method of deprecating this pseudo-Lermontovian character.

There is an analogous example of deprecation in *Uncle Vanya.* I have in mind Astrov. His prototype, Khrushchov in *The Wood Demon,* still fits into the hero mold: he is a positive type. Linked to Khrushchov is Fedor Ivanych who is "dissolute" and abuses the traits of his own "generous nature." Thus, in *Uncle Vanya,* a reworking of *The Wood Demon,* Chekhov has created an amalgam of Khrushchov and Fedor Ivanych. Like Khrushchov, Astrov utters the same noble speeches, imbued with lofty ideas, and without warning he sometimes repeats the cynical verbal pranks of Fedor Ivanych. That, however, does not make him more real or more ordinary. This process of character "fabrication" provides evidence against Chekhov the dramatist; it shows that Chekhov's creativity was on the wane when he began to write for the theater.

I would point out, moreover, that Chekhov is far from being consistent in his attempt to replace stage "types" with real people. Epikhodov in *The Cherry Orchard* and the kind old nurse in *Uncle Vanya* are more clearly pure "types" than people.

My purpose in mentioning such evidence will become apparent if we consider the above relationship to a striking feature common to all Chekhov's plays. Chekhov continually strove for maximum verisimilitude and fought against anything which rang of falseness;

ultimately he accomplished this in his stories. The characters in his plays, however, indulge in melodramatic outpouring of feelings, they argue emotionally about topics from "progressive articles," using a "literary" language full of complex sentences which people would ordinarily never use in conversation. This lack of verisimilitude is even more striking and shocking when his characters suddenly switch to everyday, conversational language. In view of this, one might be convinced that Chekhov was betrayed by his artistic powers when he began writing drama. It prompts one to think that in a certain respect people (like Tolstoy, for example) were correct in thinking that drama was something alien to Chekhov.

How can we explain this? I think it may be that the inner form of the drama was utterly incongruous with his vision of life. Every drama, whether it be "classical," "realistic" or "symbolic," is composed of action which occurs *hic et nunc* in the present, in the literal meaning of the word. Whether the characters are "classical heroes" or "comic types," embodying some human "passion," "virtue" or "vice," or whether, as in "realistic" drama, they represent certain aspects of "everyday reality" or of social mores, or finally, whether they personify certain intelligible quantities as in "symbolic" drama—regardless of the extent to which they are endowed with ordinary human characteristics—they are still pure monads. In drama everyday life is shown statically and not dynamically, from the point of view of being, not of becoming; true, it is shown as a struggle, as a series of external or internal conflicts, but these conflicts are revealed outside of real time. No matter how boldly dramatists of the Augustan Age in England and elsewhere in the nineteenth century violated the principle of "unity of time," which confined the action to a twenty-four hour period (conventionally regarded as "present" time), dramatic action was, nevertheless, perceived as occurring in the "extended present." The reason is that the *dramatis personae*—despite the complexity of their characters, revealed in different ways in different "scenes" ("acts")—are shown statically and not dynamically; the conflict, intrigue and resolution are all separate moments of a comprehensible existence and not of an evolutionary process.

The design of Chekhov's drama is of a wholly different nature. The monads, who reveal themselves as much by their actions as in their speeches, are replaced in the plays by people transplanted from his stories. As in the stories, they are shown "flashing by," emerging from the past and ready at any moment to be submerged into the past. In his stories Chekhov comes to the aid of his characters as well as of his readers; he remembers and reflects along with them and for them; he combines his "genre" with his "landscape" into a single whole, and his characters are no more than symbols, merely elements of one poetic image. On stage they are unwittingly forced to become somewhat independent—and here they prove to be helpless; they remain the same patients, and not agents, not *dramatis personae.*

It is significant that Chekhov went to great lengths, even here, to "help" his characters. I have in mind certain stage directions in *The Cherry Orchard,* which have already been pointed out by S. Balukhaty (1, 157):

> A room *which to this day is called the nursery....* Dawn is breaking, and the sun will soon be up. It is already May..., *but it is cold everywhere,* and there is a morning frost. (Act I)

> An open field. A small tumble-down old church, *long since abandoned...,* large stones that *apparently once were* tombstones.... There is a row of telegraph poles in the distance, and far, far away on the horizon one can make out the faint outlines of a city, *which is only visible in very fine, clear weather.* (Act II)

Or about Anna we read: "Her calm mood returned."

The underscored phrases are clearly intended for a reader, rather than for a director. It is as if Chekhov occasionally forgot that he was writing for the stage. Certain contemporary critics had good cause to remark that his plays were more suited for reading than for staging. If we delete all these stage directions (and there are many), the total effect is diminished. It is simply not possible to show these directions on stage. Such details attest that Chekhov did not achieve complete mastery of the inner form of the drama. It is no accident that his best play in this respect, *The Cherry Orchard,* more closely resembles the short story or novella than any of his other plays. We have already mentioned that Chekhov was particularly dissatisfied with its staging; the Moscow Art Theater was not responsible for this failure, however, but Chekhov himself.

We can best explain Chekhov's theater by contrasting it to Gogol's. The *dramatis personae* in *The Inspector General* [*Revizor*] and *The Marriage* [*Zhenit'ba*] essentially are deprived of character too, but in a completely different sense. Chekhov's *dramatis personae* lack character because they do not possess enough will power to realize their desires. Gogol's figures, by contrast, lack character because in general they have no personal desires. For example, when Khlestakov first appears on stage, basically he wants one thing only—to eat. Gogol's characters have an almost animal relationship to life; they react spontaneously to outside stimuli, especially to anything which might for some reason inspire fear. We find only one such character in Chekhov—"The Man in a Case." Like animals, because of their complete emotional and spiritual void, they easily submit to "training" and can be filled with any content one wishes. Unbeknownst even to himself, Khlestakov suddenly becomes an imposter and an extortionist, automatically playing and then gradually assuming the role which has been imposed on him by the provincial officials. The same thing occurs in *The Marriage;* all the major characters seem possessed by something. They submit to external suggestion: for example, when Kochkarev plays with Agafya Tikhonovna or Podkolesin as if they were puppets; or they submit to a kind of auto-suggestion, as in the case of Kochkarev who does not understand what forces him to try so hard:

> Why the devil . . . am I worrying about him . . . ? Goodness only knows why! You just ask a man sometimes why he does a thing.

They are playthings in the hands of destiny: "It's true enough that you can't escape your destiny," says Agafya Tikhonovna. Even when Podkolesin flees his bride, this still does not reveal his character as one which is totally incapable of an independent decision. He submits to a kind of automatism—like a cat which jumps out of an open window because it it open.

Gogolian comedy is, so to speak, ancient tragedy turned inside out. Its senselessness defines its polar relationship to tragedy. As in Chekhov the "zero" resolution, based on the motif of escape, corresponds to the tragic resolution which gives rise to a feeling of catharsis. The difference between the drama of these two authors is that in Gogol the characters, although drawn by destiny into a "weaving" of circumstances and subject to suggestion, nevertheless act, becoming involved in the most varied comic situations; moreover, they themselves create these situations. Thus, the outer form of Gogol's comedy is consistent with the inner form. Gogol's comedies demand staging, in contrast to Chekhov's, which seem more like a sketch for a story.[5]

The fact is that Chekhov, unlike Gogol, is a realist. He depicted living people, however characterless they were. They are characterless because they are weakwilled, indecisive and lack confidence and not simply because they lack personality as do Gogol's *dramatis personae*. The latter can put on any mask, "mug," and become any *persona*—in the sense in which the term was used in ancient drama. This is precisely the reason why Chekhov's people are unsuited for the theater.

Footnotes to Chapter Seven

1. Cf. his study, *Problemy dramaturgicheskogo analiza Chekhova,* izd. "Akademiia," Leningrad, 1927, and *Chekhov-dramaturg,* Leningrad, 1936. In subsequent references to these books I will refer to them in the text as B. I and B. II.

2. It is interesting that here Gorky, the "realist," is, in some respects, similar to Meyerhold the "symbolist." "Chekhov," wrote Gorky, "has in my opinion created a completely original play, a lyrical comedy. When his elegant plays are performed as dramas, they become heavy and are spoiled" ("O p'esakh," M. Gorkii, *O literature,* Moskva, 1937, 159.)

3. It should be noted that at the insistence of the actors Chekhov completely reworked Act Four of *The Wood Demon.* The original edition has not been published to date. S. Balukhaty, who saw this manuscript, writes about the discrepancy in the two editions, unfortunately too briefly and too generally. Still it is apparent from what he says that the resolution mentioned was also present in the original edition but treated differently.

4. For another definition of "type" and the different functions of "types" in literature, see the subtle and profound remarks in Gerhadt Dietrich's superb book, *Gogol und Dostojewskij in ihrem künstlerischen Verhältnis,* 1941, 39.

5. The brilliant Rozanov displayed a striking lack of understanding of Gogol's theater when he asserted that Gogol's comedies were only the "fruits of leisure" and that Gogol basically was not a dramatist: his plays "were essentially the same *Dead Souls* transferred to the stage.... " "The stage accepted him [Gogol] with gratitude, but has not forgotten that this is more literary art than theatrical art; it is painting rather than action. And a stage without action is like a body without a soul " (*Novoe vremia,* March 19, 1909). Quoted in S. Danilov, *Gogol' i teatr,* Leningrad, 1936, 14ff) Rozanov did not understand that the inner form of *Dead Souls* is nothing more than a classical comedy. S. Danilov's objection *(op. cit.)* to Rozanov's thesis is that Russian officials really did take bribes, and therefore in depicting them Gogol did not err against life's truth; that his theater is realistic; *ergo* it satisfies the demands of dramatic art. It is based on the same misunderstanding—it is but another example of the kind of misunderstanding about which G. Dietrich *(op. cit.)* speaks quite extensively.

Chapter Eight

"An Anonymous Story"

Aldous Huxley, one of the most intelligent people of our time, and an extremely able connoisseur of art, says in *Along the Road* (Albatros, 39), that Chekhov's stories "are wearisome." He explains himself with the remark that Chekhov, unlike his admirer, Katherine Mansfield, does not limit himself to "looking at people through a window," but lives with them. Here Huxley concurs with Tolstoy, who called Chekhov "an artist of real life." Yet Chekhov's people, Huxley would argue, are "gloomy," and in fact, boring. I think that he is mistaken. However meaningless, dismal or boring the lives he depicts—and indeed his characters always complain of them—Chekhov considers the emptiness of life only as his starting point. His most perfect stories cannot "weary," precisely because they are perfect. And, as I have tried to show, they are perfect because their form is wholly appropriate to their content. These "gloomy people" are, after all, not forced upon the reader, because they are shown only by hints and as images of recollection. The same does not apply to his plays where, by necessity, the characters appear before us in the flesh. Form and content do not correspond in his drama.

S. Balukhaty (II, 315) cites an English critic who maintains that since Shakespeare, not a single dramatist has "penetrated the human soul" as well as Chekhov. This is a somewhat exaggerated claim; we need only recall Pushkin's "little tragedies." But it is true that both in his plays and in his stories Chekhov, like Shakespeare—and like Pushkin and Tolstoy—shows man in all his limitless complexity. The difference is that Shakespeare and Tolstoy present their characters positively, so to speak, whereas Chekhov reveals them negatively. In Shakespeare and Tolstoy the character gradually unfolds before us and those manifestations, which at first seemed unexpected, subsequently shed light on those details previously given. We begin to understand the person depicted by the artist, although we may be unable to formulate exactly what we have understood about him.

But when we turn to Chekhov, the complexity of his characters leads us to suspect that there is something we do not understand about them; we sense that they are far from being as simple as they appear. But this "something" which we feel is, nevertheless, hidden from us. This "something" is part of Chekhov's unique appeal, but it is also the reason why his people—i.e., people as he sees them—cannot be theatrical figures. This also explains the disjunctures of form and content in his plays; the stage directions (of the type noted above) intended for the reader, rather than the director, further attest to the hybrid character of Chekhov's plays; they are neither drama nor story.

Of course, I do not wish to imply that all of Chekhov's plays are weak in formal terms. They do contain—especially *The Cherry Orchard*—numerous uniquely Chekhovian means of expression. And if I do not dwell on them it is only because S. Balukhaty has treated the subject so thoroughly. But the positive elements in Chekhov's plays cause the incongruities which I have mentioned to stand out even more prominently—incongruities which are nowhere in evidence in "Peasants," "The Steppe" or "The Bishop." In this sense we can regard Chekhov's dramatic writing as a kind of "error."

To understand the singularity of an author, however, such errors are as significant as his particular achievements. With this in mind we must examine one other instance of an error, one completely different from what we have just discussed in the plays. In "An Anonymous Story" Chekhov has attempted to structure a narrative based on the motif of "misunderstanding" which gives rise to the "weaving" of a series of errors, internal as well as external in nature. The hero misleads those around him by pretending to be someone else. Orlov deceives Zinaida Fedorovna, telling her that he is leaving on a business trip when, in fact, he is temporarily moving in with Pekarsky. The hero deceives himself, attempting to be involved in conspiratorial and revolutionary activity; only at the decisive moment is he convinced that he is emotionally unsuited for this life. Zinaida Fedorovna is deceived both by Orlov and later by the hero.

Such "weaving" determines the form of the story. We find many narrative elements which Chekhov had so carefully removed from all his other works. Once tempted to explain the complexity of specific phenomena of life as a series of errors and misunderstandings based on mutual and personal misunderstanding, Chekhov was thus led in the direction of the "classical novel." "An Anonymous Story" contains a conflict, intrigue and tragic resolution, as well as an epilogue. There is, furthermore, a climactic point—when Orlov is visited by his father after he has run off to Pekarsky's, the decisive moment for the narrator—which ends in an incongruity. This coincides with the narrator's talk with Zinaida Fedorovna, which results in a double exposure; he tells her who he is and at the same time tells her that Orlov is deceiving her. Together they leave Orlov's house.

If we leave aside the motif of *quid pro quo*—quite literally— which forms the *syuzhet,* and these external "linkages," we can observe numerous other clichés in the story characteristic of the "classical" adventure novel (moreover of a type not to be found in "Dubrovsky" or "The Captain's Daughter").

These clichés are purely external in character. Chapter Five begins: "Afterwards I will tell you what happened last Thursday." We certainly do not expect to find in Chekhov this relic of an age-old device, intended to "liven up" the narrative by giving it the quality of oral narration. This device—rather frequent in Turgenev—seems to substitute "dear readers" for a fictitious audience. Alternatively, we find a device intended to foster the illusion of reality. The reader is introduced to a set of circumstances in such a way that the author seems to remain aloof; what the reader needs to know is conveyed by a character in the story. Thus, having moved to Orlov's, Zinaida Fedorovna tells him that "her husband has long suspected her, but has avoided explanations; they frequently quarreled," and so forth. From the preceding it is clear she has had a long-standing relationship with Orlov. Can we assume she told him nothing of her husband's suspicions before this? Her words in the same episode make it apparent that this assumption is false: "You have had time to prepare for my arrival. Every day I have threatened you." This device finds its equivalent in classical drama when the *dramatis personae* draw the spectator into the intrigue; a character meets an "old servant" or "a childhood friend" on stage, and proceeds to tell him what that listener must already know—about himself, his parents, or his romance with the heroine, and so forth.

In the epilogue, two years after the resolution (Zinaida's death), the narrator meets Orlov, who acquaints him with the fate of the secondary characters: "My father, as you know, has left the service and is retired.... Remember Pekarsky? Gruzin died of diphtheria last year...." Here again, as in the classical novel, the author tries to give his "fiction" the illusion of reality and considers that the reader must be concerned with the fate of every character. All these small points are symptomatic. At first glance, it seems incomprehensible that these age-old devices should turn up in Chekhov, a writer so keenly aware of literary clichés and so careful to avoid them.

Here again we must have recourse to *contre-épreuve*. As we have already seen, there is little doubt that Chekhov frequently was influenced by his early artistic career. We find such a passage in the marvelous story, "A Woman's Kingdom": Anna Akimovna, oppressed by everything at her aunt's holiday reception, "went upstairs to her room."

> "Actually there is a great deal of cruelty in these holiday customs," she said a while later, *as if to herself,* looking out of the window at the boys.... "On holidays one wants to rest ... but these poor boys, the teacher and the clerks are obliged for some reason to traipse through the snow, and extend their greetings...."
> Mishenka, who stood by the door and overheard this, said: "It didn't start with us and it won't end with us.... It has been said of the rich: 'Money begets money.' "
> "You always express yourself so tediously and incomprehensibly," said Anna Akimovna, and she walked to the other end of the room.

It would appear that a simple comic device has been set in motion here; a character delivers a monologue which is overheard by another, unnoticed figure. Actually this is not the case: Anna Akimovna clearly saw the footman Misha and only spoke "as if to herself." A symbolic meaning is attached to the comic presentation of this dialogue. Anna Akimovna despises the vulgar Misha, but she must share her impressions with somebody; he is a neutral audience for her. Therefore in the beginning of the scene the author conceals the fact that Anna Akimovna is not alone in the room, alluding to it only with the phrase "as if to herself." Only at the conclusion of her apparent monologue is the situation clarified. This noteworthy device permits a subtle depiction of a character's experiences and lack of insight into these experiences.

"An Anonymous Story" is another matter altogether. Archaic stereotypes are used here, as I have said before, in their primitive form, without the innovative touches which give them new meaning. This suggests the idea that here, too, Chekhov undertook something alien to him. Such a complicated intrigue presumes that the characters be depicted very graphically. They must be shown either as "types" or "masks," the personification of some idea (as in classical drama or the "novel-tragedy" of Dostoevsky), or they should be shown as people living in the "extended present," (as in Cervantes, Fielding, Dickens, Tolstoy and Flaubert). We find neither method in Chekhov. The secondary characters are reminiscent of comic types. Orlov has a dual character; most often he is just such a "type," but occasionally something human seems to flare up within him, and then he no longer resembles himself.[1]

If we turn to Zinaida and the hero, then we must say that we simply do not see them. Although these characters are developed in "the extended present," they are nevertheless shown in a typically Chekhovian manner; they emerge as recollections from the past. Of course the most important and essential aspect of the story— otherwise why would it have been written?—concerns the spiritual crisis of the "anonymous" man; the hero, however, communicates absolutely nothing which might help us to explain how and why this spiritual crisis occurred, what it embodied, how he came to be in this state. (It is not hard to imagine what Dostoevsky would have made of this!) His letter to Orlov, in which he only rambles on about his crisis, is most notable for its naiveté and abundance of platitudes. Its tone is striking as well; it is as if the letter were copied from a second-rate novel of the period of Romanticism and *Weltschmerz*. Equally unconvincing is Zinaida's despair when the narrator tells her that he has abandoned his revolutionary activity. Although she still demands principles from Orlov—"you are a man of principle and you must only serve an idea," she tells him—it is nonetheless clear that these are only words. Actually, she is tormented by his coldness and nothing more.

Having undertaken something which was incompatible with his nature, Chekhov attempted to create a work whose inner form was identical to the classical novel. Since this form was alien to him he unwittingly succumbed to a conventional method of combining predictable events. Unable to cope with the inner form, he became a slave to its outer shape, particularly to clichés unrelated to inner form, because they can exist simply as conventional material long familiar to the average reader.[2]

It would be appropriate here to mention yet another piece of *contre-epréuve*. Tolstoy, a master first and foremost in the large form narrative—where Chekhov failed—was also highly skilled in dramatic writing. He struggled with clichés no less stubbornly nor less rigorously than Chekhov; he consciously and boldly violated literary tradition. In the realm of theater, however, he fully complied with these traditions, with the principles of dramatic writing and the formal properties implied in the genre. Thus, in *The Fruits of Enlightenment* [*Plody prosveshcheniya*] and *The Living Corpse* [*Zhivoi trup*] everything is structured on the motif of *quid pro quo,* to which Chekhov faithfully adhered in his stories during his entire literary career, but which he excluded from his dramatic works. In Tolstoy this motif does not result in clichés which might harm the total effect of the work. In no way does Tolstoy display the kind of formulaic predictability to which Chekhov succumbed in "An Anonymous Story." The fact is that in the drama the element of *quid pro quo* in its pure form has a completely different function than merely to create an illusion of reality or to introduce the reader to the *syuzhet*. This element degenerated into pure cliché in narrative literature, whereas in the drama it is expedient; the misunderstandings, errors, unexpected recognitions, etc. spur the *dramatis personae* into action. It provides them with an opportunity to reveal themselves fully; they react to something unexpected which forces them to disclose the hidden, secret characteristics of their "I." In the novel these characteristics can be shown more simply; life is shown in its totality, "from beginning to end," as continuous present time. Chekhov, however, was incapable of this, as "An Anonymous Story" attests, particularly since this unsuccessful attempt at "the continuous present" contrasts sharply with such successful works as "A Boring Story" or "My Life," where the past or what is passing is shown in the past. It is quite probable that since Chekhov could not apprehend what was immutable in the eternal state of becoming, neither could he understand the inner form of the drama, which is connected with its ethical basis.

The drama is a kind of experiment performed on the human personality. A man becomes involved in an "intrigue," a kind of tangle; by the manner in which he extricates himself, he reveals himself and thereby furnishes the material necessary to pass sentence on him—guilty or innocent. At its extreme, narrative literature, like the drama, is a kind of judicial process; the novel and the short story, therefore, are usually very close to the drama, not merely in their ability to engage interest on an external level, but from the point of view of their inner form as well.

Chekhov is unique in this respect. He refused to judge people.[3] This is not the product of benign indifference, but a reflection of his intuition. He is not so much a story teller, as a poet. He does not close his eyes to evil, but he envisions evil as a kind of cosmic force to which all people—good or bad, kind or evil—are doomed; some are its weapons, others its victims, but more often than not they are victims.

Tolstoy forbade people to judge Anna Karenina: "Vengeance is mine, and I shall repay," says the Supreme Judge in the epigraph to the novel. This means that Anna is, nevertheless, indicted. But can a man who is an agent rather than a victim be judged?

> A nomad lay no farther than a yard from me; behind the walls in the rooms and in the yard, near the wagons among the pilgrims—not a hundredth part of these nomads expected to see morning. . . . As I fell asleep, I imagined to myself how surprised and, perhaps, even overjoyed all these people would be if the reason and the language could be found to prove to *them that their life was as little in need of justification as any other.* ("The Rolling Stone")

Man—every man—above all inspires pity in Chekhov. The student Vasiliev ("A Nervous Breakdown") succumbs to an attack of nerves in a house of prostitution, and his companions take him to a doctor. Neither they nor the doctor seem to want to understand what precipitated the shock. They talk about "forced intellectual work and overexertion." Vasiliev is exasperated by their moral insensitivity; they feel sorry for him and cannot understand why he cannot think calmly about the unfortunate, fallen women. A sudden crisis takes place within him:

> Vasiliev for some reason suddenly felt intolerably sorry for himself, for his companions, for all the people he had seen two days before, and for the doctor; he burst into tears and sank into a chair.

A blizzard forces a court magistrate and doctor, traveling to a village for a post-mortem ("On Official Duty") to spend the night at the estate of a landowner. They are welcomed into his happy, comfortable family:

> The magistrate laughed, danced a quadrille, paid court to the ladies and kept wondering whether it were not all a dream. The wretched rook at the village headquarters, the pile of hay in the corner, the rustle of cockroaches, the disgusting, poverty stricken setting, the voices of the witnesses, the wind, the blizzard, the danger of getting lost on the road, and suddenly these magnificent, bright rooms, the sound of the piano, the beautiful girls, the curly-headed children, the gay, happy laughter—such a transformation seemed to him like a fairy tale; and it seemed incredible that such transformations were possible within a distance of two miles in the course of a single hour. And dismal thoughts prevented him from enjoying himself, ... and he even felt sorry for these girls who were living and would die here in the wilds, in the provinces....

Not only the unfortunates, the failures, but, it would seem, happy people, as well, elicit a feeling of pity in Chekhov. The narrator of "The Beauties" speaks of an Armenian girl whom he saw in a village:

> And the more often she flashed before me with her beauty, the more acute became my sadness. I felt sorry for her and for myself and for the Ukrainian, who mournfully watched her every time she ran ... to the carts. Whether it was envy of her beauty, or that I was regretting that the girl was not mine, ... or whether I vaguely felt that her rare beauty was accidental, unnecessary and, like everything on earth, of short duration; or whether, perhaps, my sadness was that peculiar feeling which arises in many by the contemplation of real beauty, God only knows.

Compare this to the next episode—an encounter with another "beauty" at a railway station:

> "So-o!..." the officer muttered with a sigh.... And what that "So-o" meant I will not undertake to decide.
> Perhaps he was sad, and did not want to leave the beauty and the spring evening for the stuffy train; or perhaps he, as I, was unaccountably sorry for the beauty, for himself, and for me, and for all the passengers....

Thus, the feeling of pity is combined with a cosmic feeling which accompanies the emotion of grief. Here we find a similarity to Lermontov in whose work the theme of grief, as Klyuchevsky has brilliantly shown, dominates. In Chekhov, the feeling of pity is transferred to the entire world, in full accord with his vision of life, as reflected in "The Shepherd's Pipe" ["Svirel' "]:

> Meliton plodded along the river and heard the sounds of the pipe gradually dying away behind him. He still wanted to complain. He looked dejectedly about him, and he felt intolerably sorry for the sky and the earth and the sun and the woods and his Damka.[4]

Footnotes to Chapter Eight

1. This is in sharp contrast to Tolstoy's Karenin. Karenin's moments of emotional awakening are never represented as invented or false; this is so because when he is shown with those features which are most characteristic of him, he, Karenin—who is doubtless a prototype for Orlov in certain respects—is a living person, and not a mask.

2. A letter to Suvorin gives evidence of the extent to which Chekhov succumbed to these predictable events and clichés in working on "An Anonymous Story," and how difficult he found it to cope with these problems because he lacked experience: "You won't like the ending because I've muffed it. It should have been longer. But a longer story would be just as bad, because there are only a few major characters and when you get the same two heroes flashing by in the space of two or three pages, it gets boring and the heroes start to become diffuse" (Feb. 24, 1898). The problem, actually, is not that there are only a few characters, but that they "flash by." *Crime and Punishment* and "The Kreutzer Sonata" ["Kreitserovaya sonata"] also have few "heroes." But they are always present and hold our attention.

3. "I wanted to be original," Chekhov wrote to his brother Aleksandr Pavlovich about the play *Ivanov.* "I have introduced not a single villain, not a single angel (although I could not deny myself buffoons); *I have accused nobody and justified nobody*" (Oct. 24, 1887).

4. Compare in the same story the words of the old shepherd: "What a pity, brother! Lord, what a pity! The earth the forest, the sky...all creation—everything is created after all, it is adapted, there is a rationale to it all. But it is all wasted in vain. But most of all I feel sorry for people."

Chapter Nine

"The Bishop"

No one is master of himself and his wife if only because everything is subject to the law of time. Man strives for happiness, but he has only to attain what he has sought, and it is no longer the same since it has been transformed from expectation into realization; furthermore, he himself is now no longer the same as he had been. This is the tragedy of life. On the other hand, to attempt to overcome this in the realm of empirical reality means to fall into "negative infinity." This is vulgarity [*poshlost*]. Vulgarity is smugness, a state of calm changelessness. Sometimes Chekhov even seems to see vulgarity in "indifferent" nature, "radiant with eternal beauty":

> All those linden trees, shadows, clouds, all those smug and indifferent beauties of nature seemed *vulgar* to him now, as they always do when a man is dissatisfied and unhappy. ("Three Years")

A keen sense of time passing often provides the thematic content of numerous Chekhov stories in which the motif of recollection occurs. One such story, "Verochka," is especially revealing in this respect because of the premise underlying its complex structure. The story begins:

> Ivan Alekseevich Ognev *is remembering* that August evening and how he opened the glass door with a rattle and went out onto the verandah. He was wearing a summer cape and a wide-brimmed straw hat, *the same one* which . . . *is lying forgotten* in the dust under his bed.

The memory is so vivid in Ognev's mind that the past is already referred to in the present by virtue of the fact that the hero is, perforce, displaced by the author; the author picks up the story and relates that upon coming from Kuznetsov's house, Ognev met with his daughter in the garden. What was depicted in the beginning of the story as present time, now becomes transferred to the "past-future":

> When Ognev remembered her *later on, he could not* picture pretty Verochka except in a full blouse....

A return to the "past-present" follows, and the author again speaks for Ognev, not, however, directly in his own voice, but with the voice of his hero:

> Ognev kept glancing at Verochka's bare head and shawl, and *days of spring and summer rose to his mind one after the other* [i.e., a time when he was a constant visitor at the Kuznetsov's].... He *began recalling* aloud how reluctantly he had come [to the place where he had made their acquaintance].... Ognev recalled his expeditions around the district [i.e., Ognev *remembers* what and how he *remembered*]....

Further on Verochka confesses her love for him.

> As a man, suddenly frightened, cannot afterwards remember the succession of sounds accompanying the catastrophe that overwhelmed him, so Ognev cannot *remember* Vera's words and phrases.

Here, as well as in the beginning of the story, the use of the present tense signifies that Ognev has moved from the past to the present, and thereby again assumes the perspective of the author. The same occurs later:

> And Ivan Alekseich *remembers* that he again returned [to the Kuznetsov estate]. *Urging himself on with his memories,* forcing himself to picture Vera, he strode rapidly to the garden.... Ognev *remembers* his cautious steps, the dark windows, the heavy scent of heliotrope and mignonette.

Further on we again encounter a dramatic realization of the past: "His old friend Karo...came up to him and sniffed his hand..." and so forth, right up to the ending of the story: "When Ivan Alekseich reached his room he sank onto the bed...then he tossed his head and began packing." There is no indication that these events belong to the realm of recollection.

Man is subject to time not only because he and those around him grow, age and approach death, but also because the circumstances on which man depends take shape and develop in time; a missed moment can never be recaptured. Moreover, subjugation to circumstances and to milieu exists independent of time. In general, man is not a free agent in the realm of empirical reality; he is bound by something. Chekhov traces this subjugation of man in its different aspects in all his mature works, most frequently by elaborating anecdotal motifs. The motif of the missed and irretrievable moment lies at the center of "Verochka," "Ionych" and "The Story of Mrs. NN" [Rasskaz gospozhi NN"].

In other, related works Chekhov deftly traces the very process by which the present is transformed into the past, or, more precisely, the process by which the future is regenerated through its point of intersection with the past, i.e., the present into the past.

> When the sledge started,...she [Ilovaiskaya] looked back at Likharev with an expression as though she wanted to say something to him. He ran up to her, but she did not say a word to him; she only looked at him through her long eyelashes *with little specks of snow on them*.... It suddenly began to seem to him that with a couple more nice touches or two this girl...would have followed him without question or reason. He stood a while as though rooted to the spot, *gazing at the tracks left by the sledge runners. The snowflakes greedily settled* on his hair, his beard, his shoulders.... *Soon the track of the runners had vanished,* and he himself, covered with snow, began to look like a white rock, but still his eyes kept seeking something in the clouds of snow. ("On the Road")

[Nadya's escape from home on the pretext of accompanying Sasha to the station]:

They sent for a cab. Her coat and hat already on, Nadya went upstairs to look once again at her mother, *at all of her things;* she stood in her room by the bed, *still warm,* looked around, and then went quietly to her mother. Nina Ivanovna was sleeping, and it was quiet in the room. Nadya kissed her mother and *tidied her hair,* and remained a few minutes longer. . . . Then, *taking her time,* she went downstairs. [The cab sets out.] Nadya only now began to cry. Now it was clear to her that she was surely leaving, something she hadn't believed when she said good-bye to her grandmother and looked at her mother. Farewell, city! *And suddenly she recollected everything:* Andrei [her fiance, with whom she had decided to call it off] and his father and the new apartment . . . , and all of this no longer frightened or oppressed her; it was, rather, naive and insignificant and *kept retreating further and further away.* And when the train started, *the whole of the past, so large and serious, contracted into a little ball,* and the vast, expansive future, which until now had been scarcely palpable, began to unfold.

We occasionally find works in Chekhov which seem nothing more than experiments in reproducing the process of experiencing the present as it retreats into the past. "A Visit to Friends," from his late period (1889), is one such story. It begins:

The morning mail brought this note: "Dear Misha! You have forgotten us entirely. Come and see us soon. . . . " [Podgorin goes to visit the Losevs, whom he hasn't seen for a long time.] He loved them dearly, but more, it seemed, as memories than as they really were. The present seemed unreal, incomprehensible and alien to him. . . . He was no longer drawn to Kuzminki as before. It was cheerless there. The laughter, the noise, the bright, carefree faces, the trysts on quiet, moonlit nights—all that was no more; and above all, youth was gone; and it was probably fascinating only in memory.

Upon his arrival he meets Losev's sister, Nadezhda, whom he had once planned to marry. But he is convinced that he does not really love her, and early in the morning he returns to Moscow. The concluding part reads:

When he arrived home the first thing he saw was the note he had received the previous day: "Dear Misha!" he read. "You have forgotten us entirely. Come and see us soon. . . . " And for some reason he recalled how Nina would twirl around as she danced, how her dress would billow, showing her legs in flesh-colored stockings. . . . But ten minutes later he was already sitting at his desk working, without a thought of Kuzminki.

S. Balukhaty (II, 222ff) has noted that this story provided the thematic basis for *The Cherry Orchard*. These works are very different, however. The figures in the play are characterized far more distinctly than in the story, where they are shown as Podgorin sees them. He knows them well and feels very much at home with them; therefore, they have lost their special charm in his eyes. (Nadezhda, particularly, is shown in this way: "She was slender, stately, with golden blonde hair and kindly, caressing eyes; whether she was pretty or not Podgorin could not tell for he had known her since childhood and took her appearance for granted; he noticed in her only what strikes him as 'new' ":

> She wore a white dress, open at the neck, and the sight of her long, white, bare throat was new to him and not entirely pleasant.)

These people have become alien to him, and he has lost interest in them:

> He loved them [Nadezhda, her sister and their friend Varya] dearly, but more, it seemed, as memories than as they really were. The present seemed unreal, incomprehensible and alien to him.

Individual episodes are developed in connection with this basic theme:

> Almost...for the first time in his life...he was completely sincere and said what he wanted to say. A little later he was sorry that he had been so harsh.... Still later he no longer thought of Sergei Sergeich nor of his hundred rubles.

Podgorin himself (in terms of the *syuzhet*—the prototype of Lopakhin) is barely characterized. Basically, only this one experience is shown—the "withering away" in his soul of something which had once been near and dear.

When Chekhov speaks for his characters or from their point of view about their perception of people and life, he renders essentially his own personal perception of life; this is reflected in the composition of his works and in the light, seemingly careless strokes with which he sketches his characters:

He walked along, thinking how frequently one chances to meet good people in life, and what a pity it was that nothing remained of those meetings except memories. At times one catches a glimpse of cranes on the horizon, and a faint gust of wind brings their plaintive, ecstatic cry, but a minute later, however, one eagerly scans the blue distance, yet cannot see a speck or catch a sound. People are just like that; with their faces and words they flit through our lives and drown in our past, leaving nothing more than faint traces. ("Verochka")

Compare "The Story of Mrs. NN"

I was loved, happiness was near at hand...and time went on and on.... And all this, sweet and overwhelming in remembrance, passed quickly by. It happened to me just as with everyone, it left no trace, it was not valued, and it vanished like mist.... Where is it all? My father is dead. I have grown older; everything that delighted me, caressed me, gave me hope—the patter of the rain, the rolling of the thunder, thoughts of happiness, talk of love—all this is nothing but a memory now, and I see before me a flat, deserted distance....

We find a variant of this in "The Rolling Stone":

Because I was climbing, it seemed to me that everything was disappearing into a pit.... Aleksandr Ivanych leaped down, smiled wistfully and looked at me for the last time..., and began his descent and disappeared forever in my mind.... The impressions of Svyatogorsk had already become memories, and I saw something new—*a flat plain* and a brownish-white spot in the *distance*....

This is sufficient to understand the carefully motivated motif of "departure" which repeatedly appears at the conclusion of Chekhov's works. In this connection we have seen that externally he seems to take after Turgenev. In his early works such endings were often determined by the *fabula* itself. A tutor has finished his lesson and asks to be paid; the boy's father promises him the money in two weeks. He has no recourse: "Ziberov agrees and ... goes to his next lesson" ("The Tutor"). A doctor's assistant, instead of pulling a sexton's aching tooth, breaks it and then chases the patient out: "The sexton takes his communion beads from the table and, holding his cheek with his hand, leaves for his in-laws" ("Surgery"), and so forth.

This type of ending has an influence on the resolution. In other instances such an ending, so frequently found in Turgenev, is influenced by the compositional plan, where the narrative is devoted to something which happened on a trip or somewhere on the road, and so forth. This occurs both in the early and later stories: "... The doctor and the magistrate said nothing, got in the sleigh and drove off to Syrnya" ("On Official Duty").

Chekhov's frequent use of precisely this compositional plan is far more than a simple framing device to facilitate beginning or ending a short story. The theme of the road and the trip harmonizes with Chekhov's artistic intuition. Such endings have profound symbolic meaning, as, for example, in "A Nervous Breakdown": "He stood a while in the street thinking,—and then, having parted with his friends, he lazily plodded back to the university." Vasiliev's whole life is projected in two words here, from the moment when he is seized by despair and indignation in the face of man's insensitivity; suddenly he feels the insurmountability of evil, and the impossibility of struggling with it. We find another example in "Dreams" ["Mechty"], when the narrative (about a tramp whom the local police are taking to town) breaks off just at the moment when the rested travelers prepare to go further:

> "Well, it's time to go," says Nikandr, getting to his feet, "We've had a rest." A minute later the wayfarers are marching along the muddy road. The tramp is more hunched over than before, and his hands are thrust deep into his sleeves. Ptakha is silent.

Even more significant are endings of this type which are not imposed by the compositional plan, as in "A Boring Story." This story, an autobiography of a professor, need not have ended with the episode of parting with Katya. Turgenev, in all probability, would have informed the "kind reader" that the professor returned home from Kharkov, and would have described what later happened to Katya and to the professor's daughter who secretly married Gnekker. Chekhov's ending, which breaks off the narration like a series of dots in the middle of a sentence, is determined by what is left unstated in the story. The professor himself fails to realize that it is not science, nor the university, but Katya who is the most precious thing in his life; because he is close to death, his parting with her already signifies the end of life:

Katya gets up, and, with a cold smile, holds out her hand without looking at me.

I want to ask her, "Then you won't be at my funeral?" but she does not look at me; her hand is cold like the hand of a stranger. I escort her to the door in silence. . . . She goes out, walks down the long corridor without looking back. She knows that I am following her with my eyes, and most likely she will look back at the turning. No, she does not look back. I've seen her black dress for the last time; her steps have died away. . . . Farewell, my treasure!

No less characteristic is an analogous ending from "My Life." It is unnecessary for the elaboration of the *syuzhet*. The relationships between the characters in the story, which form its intrigue, have already been resolved. It has been shown earlier that Anyuta Blagova shall continue to love Poloznev secretly, but their relationship is not destined to develop. In any case Chekhov need not have confined himself to the ending he chose:

On holidays, . . . I take my tiny niece by the hand and walk leisurely to the cemetery. . . . Sometimes I find Anyuta Blagova by the graveside. We greet each other and stand in silence, or talk of Kleopatra [Poloznev's dead sister], of her child, of how sad life is in this world. Then, when we leave the cemetery, we walk along in silence and she slackens her pace on purpose to walk beside me a little longer. . . . When we reach town, Anyuta Blagova, agitated and flushed, says good-bye to me and walks on alone, austere and respectable. . . . And no one who met her could look at her and imagine that she had just been walking beside me and even caressing the child.

What have we here? Mechanical self-repetition? Chekhov using his own clichés? Of course not. Here we find a summary statement of the entire theme of the story. The meaning of "My," and of "Life," generally is revealed in a poetic image: eternal wandering, encounters and partings along the way, the constant search for something, all of which leads nowhere and ends only in death. The symbolism of the ending of "My Life" is in complete harmony with the symbolism of its whole; the motif of the pilgrimages of Poloznev, like those of Lipa in "In The Ravine," permeates the entire story— and this creates its second dimension. Were it not for that motif, essentially the story would be deprived of content; there is nothing new or significant in the quixotic Poloznev and his protest against commonplace vulgarity. Certainly Poloznev himself can hardly aspire to the role of "hero" of a novel (to which this novella is close). It is not the commonplace which informs this work; its theme is the same as that of Lermontov's "Clouds" ["Tuchki nebesnye"], "The Sail" ["Parus"], "The Leaf..." ["Dubovyi listok..."], "I Walked Out Alone On The Road" ["Vykhozhu odin ya na dorogu"], in fact all of his lyric poetry.[1]

Once we take into account this double dimension of Chekhov's works, we can solve a puzzle in the development of his art. Three stories, which represent the apogee of his art—"The Man in a Case" ["Chelovek v futlyare"],[2] "Gooseberries" and "About Love"—have a common frame, one even more archaic than Turgenev's *Sportsman's Sketches* and similar to Boccaccio's *Decameron;* at first two, then three friends converse: the teacher Burkin, the veterinary Ivan Ivanych and the landowner Aleksin. Each tells a story. What prompted Chekhov to use this frame? How can we explain this return to an archaic stereotype? Could it be that the incidents narrated and the travel impressions provide the speakers with an opportunity for a philosophical exchange? In part, yes. Speaking of his brother, Ivan Ivanych remarks in "Gooseberries":

> He was a gentle, good-natured fellow, and I was fond of him, but I never sympathized with this desire to shut himself up for his whole life on his own little farm. We say that a man needs no more than six feet of earth. But six feet is what a corpse needs, not a man.... A man needs not six feet of earth or a farm, but the whole globe, all of nature, where he can have room to express all the qualities and traits of his free spirit.

Compare this to the beginning of "The Man in a Case"—the description of the unfolding panorama as the men who are talking climb a hill:

> In the calm weather when all of nature seemed calm and pensive, Ivan Ivanoych and Burkin were filled with love for that plain, and thought of how great and how fine this country was.

But this, however is not the main point. A single theme forms the center of the first two stories, the theme of a vulgar man's happiness, a happiness found in the realm of "negative infinity": a happiness attained by Ivan Ivanovich's brother when he bought a farm with gooseberries; a happiness attained by the teacher Belikov—who all his life feared every manifestation of life, "in case something should happen"—only when he died.

> Now when he was lying in his coffin his expression was gentle, agreeable, even cheerful, as though he were glad that he had at last been put into a case which he would never leave again. Yes, he had attained his ideal!

This third story provides a countertheme to the variations on happiness in the first two stories; here we are dealing with authentic human, and therefore, fleeting happiness. The image of Aleksin contrasts with the images of the teacher Belikov and Ivan Ivanovich's brother, therefore emphasizing the spiritual kinship of the first two, living corpses. The three stories form an unmistakable triptych.

Two other works, "Ward No. 6" ["Palata No. 6"] and "Gusev," are in an analogous relationship to each other. Although they do not have a common frame, they are, nonetheless, two variants of a single theme—the themes of Nekrasov's "Hospital" ["Bol'nitsa"]; the second story, moreover, attempts to expand the theme and provide an answer to the first story. The similarity is primarily one of location: a hospital ward and a ship's infirmary. We find curious details in both stories: there are five sick people (in the first story five people before the doctor, Andrei Efimich, is put in the hospital). In both stories only one of the patients acts independently, protesting the irregularities and generally assuming an active role. Both stories end with the death of the individual to whom the "protestants" address their speeches. The theme is one and the same: the theme of doom. The residents of "Ward No. 6" are doomed to remain there until death, because the authorities have so willed it. The mad are not let out. The passengers in the infirmary are doomed to death, because not one of them, apparently, will be able to endure the prolonged ocean crossing in the unbearable heat. Three of them die in the course of the narrative. There is one other similarity, incidentally, in the episodes which symbolize an attempt at "liberation": in the first story, Andrei Efimych's abortive attempt to escape (the next day he is "captured"); in the second, Gusev's attempt to get some fresh air on deck. Nothing is achieved in either case. In Moscow, Petersburg and Warsaw, Andrei Efimych is even more depressed than at home; and once Gusev is on deck, he is convinced he cannot stay there, and returns to his berth, from which he never again rises. Here, apparently, is the kernel of V. Sirin's [Vladimir Nabokov] astounding allegory, *Invitation to a Beheading* [*Priglashenie na kazn'*]. The allegorical quality is even more apparent in "Gusev" than in "Ward No. 6." In the latter story circumstances which determine people's lives are shown more realistically and concretely.

These people are victims of the indifference, irresponsibility, ignorance and coarseness of those around them. In "Gusev," first of all, no one except Pavel Ivanych is conscious of this enslavement to circumstances, and his protests fall on deaf ears. Gusev, the only one who speaks with Pavel Ivanych, disagrees with him when the latter is disturbed by the social system to which he believes Gusev has fallen prey:

> "Were you an officer's servant?" Pavel Ivanych asked Gusev.
> "Yes, an officer's servant."
> "My God, my God!" said Pavel Ivanych.... "To tear a man from his native home, drag him ten thousand miles away, then wear him out till he gets consumption and... and what is it all for, one wonders?..."
> "It is not hard work, Pavel Ivanych. You get up in the morning and polish the boots, put on the samovar, clean the rooms, and then you have nothing more to do.... God grant everyone such a life."

Secondly, except for Gusev, none of the people is really characterized. They are faceless to the point of being invisible; they are shown as each sees the other—that is, in essence as they do not see. They play cards together, help one another get up and get a drink of water, but each is to the other no more than "every man" and not an individual. In "Ward No. 6" the doctor Andrei Efimych is tormented by the vulgarity and insensitivity of "normal" people and only in the mad Ivan Dmitrich does he find a kindred spirit. Such sensitivity is entirely lacking in "Gusev," and what is worse, no one suffers from its absence; the people do not perceive the extent of their moral isolation. Related to this isolation is their astounding indifference to the death of a fellow inmate, a reaction wholly in keeping with the story's design. The psychology of their response to the fact of death is not explained; what is shown is tantamount to no response at all. One of the soldiers playing cards suddenly lies down on the floor:

> Everybody was amazed. They called him, he did not answer. "Stepan, maybe you are feeling bad, eh?" the soldier with his arm in a sling asked him. "Perhaps we had better bring the priest, eh?"
> "Have a drink of water, Stepan ... " said the sailor.
> "Here, lad, drink."
> "Why are you knocking the jug against his teeth?" said Gusev angrily.
> "Don't you see, turnip head?"
> "What?"
> "What?" Gusev mimicked him. "There is not a breath of life in him, he is dead! That's what! What ignorant people, Lord have mercy on us ... !"

And nothing more. Next is Pavel Ivanych's turn. Not a word is said about how he dies, because this incident is shown as perceived by Gusev. At the time Gusev is in a semiconscious, semidelirious state. Subsequent to his last conversation with Pavel Ivanych, he notices neither the day's passing nor the approach of evening.

> There was a sound as though someone had entered the hospital, and voices were heard, but a few minutes passed, and all was still again.
> "The Kingdom of Heaven and eternal peace," said the soldier with his arm in a sling. "He was a restless man."
> "What?" asked Gusev. "Who?"
> "He is dead; they have just carried him up."
> "Oh, well," muttered Gusev, *yawning,* "the Kingdom of Heaven be his."

Gusev does not even know who died, nor to whom he wished "the Kingdom of Heaven."[3] The soldier asks him whether the deceased will go to heaven. "Who are you talking about?" "About Pavel Ivanych." And then the soldier tells Gusev that it is his turn: "You will not make it to Russia." All this is as it should be, natural and normal. There is no need, therefore, to describe the moment of Gusev's death. Instead it is said only:

He slept for two days, and at noon on the third day two sailors came down and carried him out of the infirmary. He was sewn up in a sailcloth, and to make him heavier, they put in two iron weights.

Far more horrifying is a mechanical observation of the ritualistic behavior of dying; invariably they wish someone "the Kingdom of Heaven," funeral services are held, and they cross themselves: the horror of this is emphasized by the lexicon, which introduces a grotesque element into the description:

The man on watch tilted up the end of the plank, Gusev slid off and flew head first, turned a somersault in the air and—plop!

"Ward No. 6" concludes with a description of the doctor's death— merely a brief reference: "Next day Andrei Efimych was buried. Mikhail Averyanych and Daryushka were the only people at the funeral."

Once again the indifference of the surrounding social milieu is noted. In "Gusev" this lack of concern for the individual and his fate is shown as a manifestation, as it were, of cosmic indifference. The laconic description of Gusev's death and burial contrasts with the detailed account of the game the shark plays with the corpse. Other fish gathered for the feast are ecstatic over this game, a prelude to what the shark will later do with the corpse. The "charming," joyous mystery of the sunset follows. What is the meaning of all this? What is the meaning of the life and death of each separate manifestation of cosmic reality? "The sea [that is, the cosmos] had neither meaning, nor pity."

Does it follow that this nihilistic formula explains Chekhov's world-view? One cannot hold an artist or poet literally to his words. In order to comprehend his philosophy—and without a philosophy one cannot be an artist—one must necessarily experience his art, dwelling on his most perfect works, works which, so to speak, make up the sum total of his artistic odyssey. "Gusev" marks only one stage of this journey. We have seen that this work provides a kind of philosophic commentary—but primarily to *one* Chekhov story, which expresses *one* phase in his spiritual development. This moment was not to be the last phase. The concluding words of the story already suggest the possibility of further development:

The sky turns a soft lilac. Looking at the gorgeous, enchanted sky, at first the ocean scowls, but soon it, too, takes on tender, joyous, passionate colors for which it is hard to find a name in human speech.

The pledge of catharsis is contained in this scene of ineffable beauty, a way out of this doomed condition, a way to overcome merciless fate. And even if, in the words of Tyutchev—"all this is death"—he still faces the question: "What is death?" And why does he love that "mysterious evil, spilled out onto everything?" "What, then, is evil? Wherein lies the meaning of evil and death?" Every artist answers this question in his own way, in his own images which express the inexpressible.

It is with these questions in mind that we shall consider "The Bishop," his penultimate story (1902), and one especially important for an understanding of Chekhov. Following the work he wrote "The Betrothed" (1903), which despite its merit, bears traces of weariness and loss of vitality. Indeed, Chekhov was by then already near death. "The Bishop," together with "In the Ravine," marks the apogee of Chekhov's art. In each story he fully realized what had long comprised the aim of his artistic aspirations: to give a picture "where each part, like the stars in the sky, would fuse into one whole" (see above). I will later try to show the artistic unity of "The Bishop." In the meantime I will only note one characteristic feature: we continually encounter in "The Bishop" examples of that "poetic stock" accumulated during Chekhov's most creative period. Moreover, these are not simply literary formulae, or turns of speech, but images and motifs, which demonstrate that all his preceding works led to this story, a sign of immanent artistic fate. The fact that "The Bishop" bears traces of Chekhov's best works is most significant. I will cite the most important parallels:

["The Bishop"]: In the evening the monks sang.... And [the bishop]...was carried back in thought to the distant past, to his childhood and youth...and now that past rose up before him *lively, beautiful and joyful as in all likelihood it never had been.*

Compare to "Peasants":

They lay down to sleep in silence; the old people...thought how precious youth was, because no matter what it had been like at the time, it left only *lively, joyful, stirring* memories behind....

146

["The Bishop"]: The trees were already awakening, . . . while above them *stretched* the infinite, *fathomless* blue *sky*, God knows whither.

Compare to "In the Cart":

Neither the warmth, nor . . . the transparent forest, . . . nor the marvelous, *fathomless sky*, into which it seemed one would have gone away so joyfully, presented anything new . . . to Marya Vasilevna.

["The Bishop"]: The white walls, the white crosses on the tombs, the white birch trees and black shadows, and the faraway moon in the sky directly above the monastery, now seemed to live their own life, incomprehensible, yet near to man.

Compare to "Ionych":

Startsev went in at the little gate, and the first thing that he saw was the white crosses and monuments on both sides of the broad avenue, and their black shadows and those of the poplars; and it was white and black all around in the distance, and the trees bowed their branches over the white stones. At first Startsev was struck by what he saw . . . ; the world was unlike anything else, a world in which the moonlight was as soft and beautiful, as though slumbering here in its cradle, where there was no life, none whatever, but in every dark poplar, in every tomb, there was felt the presence of a mystery that promised a life, peaceful, beautiful, eternal.

["The Bishop"]: The spring sunshine was streaming . . . in at the window, . . . throwing bright light on . . . Katya's red hair; her hair stood up from under the comb and the velvet *ribbon like a halo*.

Compare to "In the Ravine":

And the scarlet *ribbon shone like a flame* in her [Lipa's] hair.

The image of the bishop, who, by his talents, has risen from the lower ranks of the clergy, and who, before death, regrets his lost past, is already contained in embryo in the image of the deacon in "The Duel." The deacon envisions his future and dreams of his return from a scientific expedition, when he will be made an archimandrite, and then a bishop, and he imagines celebrating mass in the cathedral.[4] But then his thoughts turn elsewhere:

147

As he went back to the fire, the deacon imagined a church procession going along a dusty road on a hot July day: in front the peasants carry banners, and the women and children the icons; then the boys' choir and the sexton...; then in due order he, the deacon, and behind him the priest in his calotte. [...And he thinks how nice it all is.]

Compare in "The Bishop" (his recollections):

In the summer they used to carry the icon from Obnin in procession and ring the bells the whole day long..., and he (in those days his name was Pavlusha) used to follow the icon, bareheaded and barefoot with naive faith, with a naive smile, infinitely happy.

A characteristic feature of "The Bishop" is that Chekhov fully reveals himself, applying his stylistic manner with maximum consistency. We have already witnessed the frequent use of *to seem* in this story.[5] In addition we frequently find other verbs which approximate the function of this verb:

And it *occurred* [*predstavlyalos*] to him that he...was walking in a field...;
One could feel [*chustvovalos*] the breath of spring; Everyone was silent...and *one felt like* [*khotelos*] thinking...;
Footsteps were heard [*slyshalis*]...;
The lay brother *could be heard* [*slyshno bylo*] leaving...;
And immediately *there rose before* [*predstavilis*] him the images of his dead father, his mother, his native village...;
The priest at Lesopole was called to mind [*pripomnilsya*]...;
In Obnin, he remembered [*vspomnilos*] now, there were many people;
Father Sisoi was snoring behind the wall and *something* [*chto-to*] lonely, forlorn and even restless *could be heard* [*slyshalos*] in his aged snoring;
The seminary and the academy slowly, languidly *recalled themselves* [*vspominalas*] to the bishop;
The bishop was *reminded* [*vspominalas*] of the white church...;
He *remembered* [*vspominilsya*] the sound of the warm sea...;
And *he remembered* [*vspomnilos' emu*] how he yearned for his homeland.

To seem and its approximations find a parallel in the frequent use of *as if* [*kak-budto*] and related expressions.

> The crowd kept moving and it *looked as though* [*pokhozhe bylo*] it had no end and there would be no end to it;
> And . . . one could see [*bylo zametno*] she was constrained *as if* [*kak-budto*] she felt more like a deacon's wife than his mother;
> And Katya . . . , gazed at her uncle . . . , *as though* [*kak-by*] trying to discover what sort of a person he was;
> And she kept on saying, "having tea" . . . and *it seemed* [*pokhozhe bylo*] *as if* [*kak-budto*] the only thing she had done in her life was to drink tea;
> But eight years passed and he was called back to Russia, . . . and the past retreated far away into the haze *as though* [*kak-budto*] it had been a dream;
> And *it seemed* [*pokhozhe bylo*] *as though* [*kak-budto*] he [Sisoi] had been born a monk.

"The Bishop" is likewise the epitome of Chekhov's art by virtue of the absence of a *syuzhet*. The entire *fabula* amounts to the illness of Bishop Petr, the arrival of his mother and niece, and of his death. The attempt to simplify the *fabula* element is manifest in all of Chekhov's art. But in the majority of his works the main theme, which can be traced to the anecdote, is the theme of "error," "efforts spent in vain"; all of this, in some way, finds expression in the *fabula*. In "The Bishop," as we shall see, this theme is also present, but less noticeably. It does not determine the *syuzhet*. The whole structure of the story, as well as its rhythm, is controlled by the same motif which forms the "second theme" of "In the Ravine"—Lipa's theme, the motif of pilgrimages and stopping. The bishop rides to church, celebrates mass, returns home, rests, again goes off to church and so forth, and finally returns for the last time to end his earthly journey.

This virtually complete elimination of *fabula* elements in "The Bishop" makes it structurally even closer to a musical composition than "In the Ravine." Here themes only "compete with each other," so to speak, in the musical sense of the word, regardless of any antagonisms determined by the *syuzhet* and the conflicts thus engendered; we find nothing more than the alternation of image-symbols. Nothing, not a single sentence, not a single word stands in isolation; every image prepares for another. The compositional plan is consistent with the principle that if a gun is somewhere mentioned, then it must go off. The story begins with an introduction—mass on Palm Sunday eve:

> In the twilight of the church the crowd seemed to swell like the sea, and it seemed to Bishop Petr that all the faces... were alike, that everyone who came up for a palm had the same expression in his eyes. The doors could not be seen through the haze, the crowd kept moving, and it looked as if there would be no end to it.

The bishop discerns among the worshipers a woman whose face seems familiar to him. It is his mother, but he does not immediately recognize her, and he suspects that he might be mistaken. The motifs which govern the entire story are linked together in the introduction; later, they either appear separately or are combined anew. Thus, the introductory theme returns later in a church service during Holy Week:

> He knew the first gospel... by heart, and as he read he raised his eyes from time to time, and saw on both sides a *perfect sea* of lights and heard the sputter of candles, but as in past years, *the people could not be seen and it seemed as though these were all the same people as before, in his childhood and his youth, that they would always be the same every year* till such time as God only knew.

The themes contained in the introduction are gradually disclosed and more clearly articulated: the impersonality and tedium of the surroundings, the related ritual of repetition, "negative infinity" and recollection and the desire to return to a distant past. These themes recur in different keys, so to speak; they assume first one, and then another, emotional coloring. There are moments in life which one would like to arrest, to stop (this was also Faust's dream):

> And everyone was silent, deep in thought; everything around seemed kindly, youthful, and so near; everything—the trees and sky and even the moon, and one wanted to think that it would always be so.

Elsewhere the bishop recalls his youth: "... And then his life had been so easy, so pleasant, and it had seemed so very, very long, with *no end in sight.*"

150

At the end of the story this theme of "arresting the moment" switches to an ironic mode: the celebration of Easter on the day after the bishop's death:

After midday people began driving up and down the main street. In short, all was merriment, everything was well, just as it had been the year before, and as it would be in all likelihood next year.

The preparation for this variant occurs at the end of the introduction:

Someone nearby began to weep, then someone else farther away, then another and another, and little by little the church was filled with soft weeping. And a *little later,* after about five minutes, the monk's choir sang; there was no longer any weeping, and *everything was as it had been.*

Compare the above to an adjacent passage, lexically even closer to the final part: "There was peace in his heart, *all was well,* yet he kept gazing fixedly towards the left choir. . . and wept."

In all these passages the life cycle is simultaneously shown in two aspects: on the one hand, the repetition of one and the same thing in everyday surroundings; on the other hand, the gradual distancing of the subject from his point of departure and his approach to the final point, accompanied by an ever increasing yearning for the past which is moribund in his memory:

The bishop remembered her [his mother] from early childhood, almost from the age of three. How he had loved her! Sweet, precious, unforgettable childhood. Why did it—that long-past time that could never return—seem brighter, more festive and richer than it had really been?

In the evening the monks sang harmoniously and with inspiration, . . . and the bishop . . . was carried back in thought to the distant past: to his childhood and youth, when they also used to sing of the Bridegroom and of the Heavenly Mansion; and now that past rose up before him—living, beautiful and joyful as in all likelihood it never had been. And perhaps in the other world, in the life to come, we shall recall the distant past and our life here with the same feeling.

151

The rhythm of the story is determined by the opposition of two cycles—life as experienced and life as desired, but unrealized. It is further accentuated by the rhythm of the *syuzhet,* i.e., by the description of the trips to and from church, which we have already mentioned, combined with a repetition of images and set expressions:

> The road from the monastery to the city *was sandy,* and one had to drive slowly; on both sides of the carriage, *in the moonlight,* so bright and peaceful, pilgrims were wending their way in the sand.

And later: "The carriage passed through the gates, *crunching over the sand.* Here and there *in the moonlight* the black figures of monks flashed by." Note the repetition of speech patterns:

> When the bishop got into his carriage to drive home, the entire garden, illuminated by the moon, was filled with the gay, melodious ringing of the heavy, costly bells.

Note also:

> When the service was over and the people were going home, it was sunny, warm, gay; the water gurgled in the gutters, and the unceasing trilling of the larks, tender, telling of peace, rose from the field outside the town.

Consider as well, in the first episode, the mother's entrance:

> How stifling, how hot it was! How long the service went on! Bishop Petr was tired. His breathing was labored and rapid, his throat was parched, his shoulders ached with weariness, his legs were trembling.... *Furthermore,* all of a sudden... it seemed to the bishop as though his own mother... had come up to him out of the crowd.

We find a variation of this moment:

> He looked at his mother and could not understand how she had come by that respectful, timid expression on her face and in her voice. And he did not recognize her. He felt sad and vexed. *Furthermore,* his head ached just as it had the day before; his legs ached terribly, and the fish seemed flavorless and tasteless; he felt thirsty all the time....

152

This episode, which encompasses less than a week, presents his entire life in a condensed form—the perpetual cyclical movement of life and the approach of death. With each day the bishop's condition deteriorates, and finally the agony begins:

> Three doctors *arrived,* consulted together and *then left.* It was a *long,* incredibly long day; *then came the night which passed slowly, slowly,* and towards morning on Saturday the lay brother went to the old mother who was lying on the sofa in the parlor and asked her to go to the bedroom: the bishop *had just passed on.*

The hidden irony of this "to pass on" [*dolgo zhit*] is prepared for by what comes before it—"the long" (day), and "slowly, slowly" (the night passed). Only on the eve of his death does the dying man finally gain insight:

> And it seemed to him . . . , that everything that had been, had retreated far, far away and would never again be repeated and would never continue.

But Bishop Petr's spiritual experience does not end here. Not only is he convinced that the past cannot be returned, but his mother, whom he so loved, already seems different. He is grieved that even she does not recognize in him the former Pavlusha, but treats him as befitting an important person: she is shy in his presence and addresses him formally. The main point is that at the same time that it seems to him "that everything that had been, had retreated," something else also occurs to him: "He is worse and weaker and less significant than anyone." "What sort of bishop am I?" he says. "I should have been a village priest, a sexton . . . or a simple monk. . . . All this is crushing me . . . crushing me . . . " His rebirth at death is revealed to his mother as well. She now feels that he is "less significant than anyone," and this makes possible their former relationship: "And she no longer remembered that he was a bishop, and she kissed him, as though he were a child, someone very near and dear." And the final passage is embued with a conciliatory sadness which purifies the soul:

> A month later a new suffragan bishop was appointed, and no one thought anything more of Bishop Petr. Afterwards he was completely

forgotten. And only the dead man's old mother,... when she would go out at night and meet other women in the pasture, would begin to talk...about her son, the bishop, and this she would say timidly, afraid that many would not believe her. And, in fact, not everyone believed her.

The closing of the cycle, a return to the point of departure, is realized as in Cervantes, when the dying Don Quixote de la Mancha frees himself from his outer trappings and again wants to be what he was before: Alonso the Good. Herein lies the meaning of the Easter service which comes at the moment of the bishop's death: the resurrection in death—spiritual rebirth at the close of life. What had seemed the essence of life, is, in fact, its casing. It retreats in the *haze* ("Everything was as if in a *haze*... "; "In the *haze*... the doors were not visible... "; "But eight years had passed, and the past had retreated far away into the *haze*... ") And the bishop's conscience is illuminated with the light of truth.[6]

Death is a release, a discovery of one's spiritual essence, one's pure "I":

By now he could no longer utter a word, he could understand nothing, and he imagined he was a simple, ordinary man, that he was walking quickly, cheerfully through the fields, tapping with his stick, while above him was the open sky bathed in sunshine, and that he was free now as a bird and could go where he liked!

The departure from life offers a resolution to the conflict, i.e., a weaving of all life circumstances. Such a departure is the only means to correct the "error" of life in its reality. Thus, finally, new meaning is given to the anecdotal canvas. From this it does not follow, of course, that a similar zero resolution indicates merely a transformation of the "I" into nothing, that the discovery of the pure "I" is equivalent to recognition and realization of its lydian nature. The entire symbol system in "The Bishop" and in Chekhov's best works generally contradicts this view. The liberation of the "I" implies a transcendence of its empirical limitations and its isolation, which is tantamount to its enclosure in a "case"; this liberation is a way out of that condition of loneliness, an experience powerfully expressed in "Lights":

And then, when I began to doze, it seemed to me that it was not the sea making sounds, but my thoughts, and the whole world consisted of me alone. Having thus concentrated the whole world inside of me, I forgot about the carts and the city and Kisochka, and submitted to this sensation of terrible isolation, when it seems that in the whole universe, so dark and formless, only you alone exist.

Why is it possible to love this sensation of terrible isolation? Because it is an extreme manifestation of solipsism—a moment which already conceals within itself its ultimate transcendency. The identification of self with the universe, the inclusion of the universe into one's own "I" can lead to the inclusion of the "I" into the universe and to an understanding of the secret of life in death. As Chekhov wrote, "Not one of our concepts of death can be applied to a discussion of non-being, of that which is not man."[7] Consider also, notes from his last years: "Apparently there is something beautiful and eternal, but it is outside of life; one must not live, one must become accustomed to [. . . omission], and then in this state of quiet calm one can look around with equanimity."[8]

For Chekhov, as for Tolstoy (and in all likelihood not without his influence), a prerequisite for this spiritual asceticism, for this "emptying of the soul," using the terms of mystical wisdom, is simplification, the liberation of the "I" from its casing, created by social conditions. It is first of all necessary to become more insignificant and more humble than anyone else; this is the point of departure for St. Francis' spiritual journey. And it is in this respect that "The Bishop" represents the sum total of all Chekhov's art. Previously, and on more than one occasion, Chekhov had approached this problem of simplification: in "My Life," where the main character is a voluntary déclassé, and in "A Woman's Kingdom," where Anna Akimovna dreams of returning to her former life of simplicity and poverty:

Crowds of workers from the neighboring factories . . . walked along the highway and across the nearby fields and headed toward the city lights. Laughter and gay conversation rang out in the frozen air. Anna Akimovna looked at the women and small children, and she suddenly longed for simplicity, coarseness and those crowded conditions. She clearly imagined that distant time when she was called Anyuta and when, as a small child, she would lie under the same blanket with her mother, while nearby in the next room the laundress washed the linen; and from the adjoining rooms could be heard the sound of laughter, scolding, children crying, a harmonica, the buzzing of turners' lathes and sewing machines, and her father... would be soldering something near the stove, or tracing or planing; and she felt like washing, ironing and running to the shop as she had everyday when she lived with her mother. *She would like to be a worker, not a proprietress.*[9]

Simplicity, total simplicity, is a prerequisite of purity for Tolstoy as well as for St. Francis. In contrast to Turgenev's ideal women, whose "falseness" Chekhov could not tolerate,[10] he offers Olga in "Peasants," and Lipa, who introduces herself to the reader with the following words: "I am very fond of jam." And it is precisely to this child-woman and her mother that a revelation is given, something generally hidden from the view of educated, "thinking" people:

Now, when the darkness was swiftly descending, lights were flashing below, and when it seemed that the fog was concealing a bottomless abyss, Lipa and her mother—who had been born paupers and were prepared to live like that to the end, giving to others everything except their frightened, gentle souls—perhaps had a momentary vision that in this vast, mysterious world, among the endless series of lives, they too were strong and superior to somebody; they felt good sitting here high up; they smiled happily and forgot that nonetheless, they had to return home. ("In the Ravine")

The naive experiences of these women are not as profound as the spiritual revelations of St. Francis or Master Eckhart, but, nevertheless, all these experiences have an important quality in common. Prerequisite to spiritual peace is the experience of some "other reality," a reality attested to by the beauty overflowing in nature:

It seemed to them that someone was watching from heaven on high, from that deep blue where the stars are, seeing everything that happened in Ukleevo and keeping guard. And however great the evil, there still was and would be truth in God's world, *just as calm and beautiful,* and everything on earth was only waiting to merge with truth, just as the moonlight merges with the night. ("In the Ravine")

156

The notebooks from Chekhov's late period contain two adjacent remarks:

Faith is the capacity of the spirit. Animals do not have it, and wild beasts and primitive people live in fear and doubt. Faith is accessible only to highly developed organisms.

Death is terrible, but more terrible still would be the realization that you will live forever and never die.

These remarks and those quoted above constitute, it seems to me, the key to an understanding of Chekhov's artistic quests and achievements.

Footnotes to Chapter Nine

1. The function of Chekhov's themes of parting and the road have already been noted by Iu. Aikhenval'd in his article "Chekhov," in the collection *Pamiati Chekhova* (p. 10 ff): "Life for him often takes the shape of motion or a road: trains arrive and leave, people leave..., cities and stations flash by, bells ring."

2. Incidentally is not this title another example in Chekhov which recalls Turgenev's works? I have in mind Latkin (in "The Watch" ["Chasy"]), who, stricken by paralysis, confuses his words: "'Let us go Vasilevna... there are only saints here; don't go there. And *the one over there in the case*,' he pointed at Davyd [the latter is in bed], 'he is also a saint. And you and I, friend, are sinners'." If this supposition is correct—and I am not entirely sure—it may provide a curious example of the psychology of art in general. What is a casual remark in Turgenev, is no way explained, a character's slip of the tongue, is perceived by Chekhov as a symbol from which the story develops, a symbol which permeates the entire story.

3. All of this was already contained in the symbolism of Nekrasov's poem: "...Too bad, he fell asleep or died? Otherwise he certainly would have made fun of you. *Number 17* fell silent."

4. Compare also in "A Boring Story," where the professor tells Katya of his youth: "At times I used to walk about our seminary.... If from some far away tavern the wind carried the squeaking of an accordion, or a sledge with bells dashed by the garden fence, it was quite enough to send a rush of happiness, filling not only my heart, but even my stomach, my legs, my arms.... I would listen to the accordion or the bells dying away in the distance and imagine myself a doctor, and paint pictures, one better than the next."

5. In one passage *to seem* is used three times: "And all this petty and useless business oppressed him by its weight, and it seemed to him that now he understood the diocesan bishop, who had once in his youth written on "The Doctrines of the Freedom of the Will," and now *it seemed* he had become entirely lost in trivialities, forgotten everything, and no longer thought of God. The bishop must have lost touch with Russian life while he was abroad; he did not find it easy; the peasants *seemed* coarse to him...."
Incidentally such repetitions of *to seem* are encountered in his other works.

6. Images of light and radiance abound in "The Bishop": "Why did [his childhood] seem *brighter* . . . then it really had been? . . . "; ". . . The church bell on *bright* summer days . . . "; ". . . The spring sun . . . gaily *glimmered* on the white tablecloth, and in Katya's red hair"; "[her hair] was like a halo"; [her] hair . . . stood up from under the comb *like a halo*"; "The mother smiled and *beamed*."

7. *Zapisnye knizhki A.P. Chekhova*, Moskva, 1927, 92. In S. Balukhatyi (I, 105) there is an important indication that reflections of Marcus Aurelius' *Meditations*, evidently Chekhov's favorite book, are found in Nina's monologue in Treplev's play (in *The Sea Gull*). He indicates that this book was in Chekhov's library and there are notes in the margins in his own hand. The experience of unity, an awareness of the fluidity of life, a compassionate attitude towards people, a reconciliation with reality, a refusal to judge anyone at all—all this links Chekhov to the classical sage. I will leave aside the question of Aurelius' influence on Chekhov. It is more a question of spiritual affinity. To be sure, we can already discern similar moods in A. Chekhonte, that is, most likely before Chekhov knew M. Aurelius.

8. *Ibid.*, 105. Compare also: "Only that which is subject to our five senses dies in man, but that which is outside these senses, which is probably enormous, unfathomable, and lofty . . . lives on." (*Ibid.* 79)

9. Compare in "The Bishop": "What kind of a bishop am I? *I would like to be* a village priest."

10. "Aside from the old lady, i.e., Evgeny's mother [in *Fathers and Sons*] and mothers generally . . . , and simple country types, all of Turgenev's women and young girls are intolerably affected and, quite simply, false. Liza, Elena—these are not Russian young girls, but some kind of pythons, playing the oracle, full of pretension inconsistent with their place in society" (To Suvorin, Feb. 24, 1893).

Chapter Ten

"The Privy Councillor"

Exclusive concentration on one single problem and the presence of a focal point in the artistic quest are indispensable conditions of perfection, i.e., of artistic unity, of the coordination of each part of a work of art—all of which, as we have seen, Chekhov achieved in several of his works. From this point of view we might contrast Chekhov with his talented follower, Kuprin. There are quite a few passages in Kuprin which, when taken in isolation, might easily be attributed to Chekhov.

A fierce hurricane would start blowing from the northwest, from the direction of the steppes; because of it the trees would sway, now bending low, now straightening up, just like waves in a storm; the iron roofs of the cottages would rumble at night, and it seemed as if someone were running over them in hobnailed boots; the window frames rattled, the doors banged and there was a wild howling in the chimney hearths. ("The Bracelet of Garnets") ["Granatovyi braslet"]

The company keeps marching along the muddy road and it seems that there will be no end to this movement, that some kind of monstrous force has seized the thousands of grown, healthy men, has torn them from their home fires, from their familiar, favorite tasks and is driving them—God knows where and why—midst this foul-weather night.... It will soon be dawn, little by little the soldiers' faces are outlined in the darkness—gray, dirty, lustrous from the fog and lack of sleep. They all look alike and look even more severe and submissive in the pale and dim morning twilight. (From the end of "The Campaign") ["Pokhod"]

[A winter storm]: And when I listened to this demonic concert, my thoughts involuntarily stopped at the idea that here I was, sitting in this dilapidated manor house, lost midst the cheerless, snowy plains; I was face to face with a decrepit, sick, old man, far from the city and from familiar society; and it began to seem to me that the howling of the storm and this prolonged yearning and the monotonous movement of the pendulum would never, never end. ("The Breguet") ["Breget"]

In these passages we are presented not only with Chekhovian themes and Chekhovian symbolism but also—and this is the main point—with a Chekhovian speech structure—that is, a system of language which ordinary imitators would overlook. Kuprin is certainly not an imitator; he is not Chekhov's *epigone*. An *epigone* transforms the style of the artist whom he imitates into a mannerism, such that its separate elements stand out; they are perceived in and of themselves, but the style itself is in no way perceived. An *epigone* seems unconsciously to parody his model. Kuprin's relationship to Chekhov is of a wholly different character. His talent for depiction does not seem inferior to Chekhov's and one might say that Kuprin, in this respect, found his own style in Chekhov; in the words of La Fontaine, he took from Chekhov what was his own. It would be difficult to find a better or more obvious example than the relationship between Kuprin and Chekhov to refute those formalist critics who argue that the essence of art is contained in the search for new means of expression and that "form" by itself determines the "content" of an artistic work and provides, as it were, its motivation.

Kuprin achieves maximum expressiveness in "Lieutenant Rybnikov" ["Shtabs-kapitan Rybnikov"] in his description of the prostitute's experiences when the lieutenant, actually a Japanese spy, turns up at her place for the night. The passage creates an astounding impression; indeed, it is in no way inferior to the episode of Emma Bovary's death, or the beginning of *Crime and Punishment,* or to certain passages in *Anna Karenina.* It is also marvelous in and of itself. This episode has no relation to the whole, to the content of the story; it is devoid of symbolic meaning.

Some of Kuprin's works are particularly close to Chekhov's— for example, "Small Fry" ["Melyuzga"]. This story clearly shows the influence of "The Man in a Case," "Teacher of Literature," "Ward

No. 6" and "Gusev." There is a definite unity, a definite correspondence here in the inner form, the idea, and the outer form. Nevertheless, this correspondence is far from complete. Both characters—the teacher and the surgeon—are so vividly characterized that their fate should inevitably have been presented as "immanent"; their deaths ought to have been as internally motivated as the doctor's health in "Ward No. 6." In Kuprin, however, they perish by virtue of external circumstances—as do the depersonalized people in "Gusev." And so it is everywhere in Kuprin. Like Chekhov, he is a multifaceted "painter of life"; but in some respects, possibly, his canvas is too large. Everything holds his attention equally in life, and he cannot concentrate on any one thing. Everything interests him in and of itself, but he does not comprehend the general meaning of the whole of life's manifestations; he does not see life in its totality.

There is an even closer link to Chekhov in Kuprin's "The Night Watch" ["Nochnaya smena"]. Not only is Chekhov's language everywhere in evidence (for example, sentences beginning with "and it seems": "And it seems to Merkulov, that now it is—a warm evening... "; "And it seems to Merkulov that he himself is driving along this black dirty road... "), but we also encounter direct paraphrases of certain passages in Chekhov (for example, compare the letter which Merkulov receives from the village to a similar incident in "At Christmas Time" ["Na Svyatkakh"]). Taken as a whole, had this story been preserved without a signature, it would doubtless have been ascribed to Chekhov. This attribution would have elicited doubt only because the story is marked by a somewhat prolix style. But this is Chekhov of an early period, the period of artistic experimentation, when the true Chekhov had not yet come into his own. Here we find reflected in both writers a sympathetic, loving and compassionate attitude toward man. But here, as everywhere in Kuprin, we do not find any of that Chekhovian comprehension of the whole of life. Kuprin remained forever fixed at the point where Chekhov began.

Russian criticism has declared Chekhov "a writer without a world view"; his critics have asked how it was possible that he could be a writer "without a world view" and yet be a very significant writer. This question is fundamentally immaterial and senseless; it arises from an over-simplified and debased understanding of the

161

term "world view" itself and the concept it implies. If we take the term "world view" out of its literal context and assume it to imply a certain ideology and a program connected with it, then, indeed, Chekhov cannot be said to embrace a world view. Chekhov not only did not make an effort to work out such a world view, he even consciously avoided it—in part because he was sickened by what was so characteristic of people who possess such a world view: their narrow, malicious impatience with those who do not share their beliefs and their blind self-satisfaction.[1] A world view thus understood is at odds with that genuine world view, i.e., with that vision of the world and life which Chekhov held.

A world view, in the accepted sense of the word, assumes an ability and an inclination to extract, isolate and define something, and at the same time, to record it. After all that has been said we need not reemphasize how alien this concept was to Chekhov. His world view cannot be expressed in a system of concepts. It is contained in his symbolism. Something flashes by, enters our field of vision, image after image, and then slides away; these flashes and disappearances, which arouse anxiety and spiritual tension, are followed by a catharsis—a resolution through the fusion "of all this" into something whole which points to ("it seemed") an inexpressible truth, to a fulfillment and completion in another plane of reality. The retreating sun, a church cross reflecting its rays—this is the formula, in a literal sense of this word—for the whole of Chekhov's world view.

I feel it necessary to dwell on the similarities in the world views of Chekhov and Tolstoy. They have in common a Heraclitian-Schopenhauerian feeling for the life process, a striving towards liberation from all kinds of partial manifestations through death, death as a fusion with the universe, a tendency towards simplification as the first stage on the road to liberation.[2] It is precisely this spiritual affinity of these two very great "artists of life" which explain why there are so few straightforward and obvious similarities (in lexicon, structure, etc.) between them, but so many of the kind which are barely discernible but which, on careful reading, prove to be especially significant. Chekhov was in no way a "Tolstoyian" or a "student" of Tolstoy as a writer, precisely because he was inwardly and spiritually so close to him. He exposed his monadic character, so much akin to Tolstoy's, while pursuing his own artistic odyssey, which, as we have seen, radically differed, as a rule, from Tolstoy's. The differences are twofold. The two writers demonstrate that the more outstanding and significant an artistic personality, the more unique it is. Additionally their lives were very different: the one a member of the Russian aristocracy, connected with a living tradition of the epoch of the Napoleonic wars and with the Decembrist movement, who had lived through the great reforms; the other a *raznochinets* who had come up in the world in an epoch of social stagnation, disintegration and moral isolation. Tolstoy, who belonged to a wide social circle, a contemporary of great events, quite naturally revealed his genius in works of the large form, the *roman-fleuve*. Chekhov, the son of the epoch of "small matters" [*malye dela*], moved away from the social milieu with which his childhood and adolescent memories were connected, and joined the Russian intelligentsia at a time when it was experiencing a difficult spiritual crisis; just as naturally, he revealed himself the master of the small form. But it is just as significant that their artistic paths nevertheless crossed at times, and that Chekhov found so much that was *his own* in Tolstoy.

Man as monad, the individual, the indivisible, whole, represents a closed system, in which all elements exist in a state of coordination and interdependence, because they tend to gravitate towards a common center. All manifestations of personality are manifestations of one psychic complex, though not necessarily in the Freudian sense of the word. The basis of this complex in Chekhov, i.e., his general tendency, is to transcend his empirical "I" which comprises his incidental, transitory casing, and to discover his true intelligible "I." If he tried to "squeeze the slave out of himself" in his youth, this was already a sign of this tendency; but it has a far greater significance. In general Chekhov "squeezes out of himself" everything that is close to him, to which he has become accustomed, and what he, in any case, depends upon spiritually and emotionally. He accustoms himself to look at all of these elements as something incidental, transitory, destined to disappear, and he tries to distance himself from it.[3] Both his Heraclitian perception of life and the themes determined by it, as well as his humorous relationship to all data, are deeply rooted in this attitude. We call this type of humor *Pathos der Distanz,* the experience of distance which separates the subject from everything that surrounds him and from himself, from

163

his own "I." Hence, we derive a sympathetically disinterested perception of life, the ability to renounce the accustomed evaluation of objects according to their respective merit, a disregard of their hierarchy; we are able to see something beautiful and touching in what is generally considered insignificant and petty, to see a life principle in something which is generally considered dead. Understandably, the distance between object and subject plays an important role in the quality and process of perception; the greater the distance, the more does the perceiving subject—if he has a sense of humor—single out in objects what is hidden from those who are preoccupied with everyday reality, with its inevitable concerns about utility and pleasure. Conversely, the closer the objects of perception are to the perceiving subject, the stronger is Chekhov's tendency to experience a distance between them and himself; it arouses in him a feeling of estrangement from them. In the first instance the distance is a given condition; in the second, one must create it. That is why Chekhov succeeded as no one else, it seems, to penetrate the soul of a child, a dog, a simple very childlike woman; to show his Egorushka, his "darling" and his Kashtanka as they actually are, without idealization, without ornamentation, without ascribing to them spiritual qualities conventionally regarded as lofty. These characters are shown, however, in such a way that they become profoundly likeable; they move us, and they live in our consciousness. And that is why, when Chekhov portrays people of his own social milieu, of his own culture, he somehow removes them from himself and from us. A tendency towards simplification in his late period notwithstanding, Chekhov does not, like Tolstoy, consciously react negatively to civilization or culture, to contemporary art, or to university learning. (Indeed, how much more attractive, for example, is Chekhov's professor in "A Boring Story" than the professor in *Anna Karenina*.) On the contrary, he staunchly supports the idea of progress, progress which is conditioned by the successes of civilization. But at the same time, Chekhov never abandons the thought of the vanity of all our concerns, interests and efforts. He feels that people consciously or unconsciously deceive themselves in their actions, expecting perfection in the realm of empirical reality, where everything, in fact, is temporal, transitory, unstable and imperfect; they do not see that beyond the world of our realities there is another, higher kind of truth that we can speculate about when we perceive the beauty in the world, but are incapable of consciously articulating.

Art generally does not and cannot exist without the vision of a second plane of reality. In this regard all artists are of one mind. They differ only insofar as they choose to express this dual perception of reality in their art; no matter how much the artist is consumed by the idea of "a second plane" of reality, his art is perforce directed to our life, to empirical data, since this is the reality to which we are bound. Unless we experience this first plane of reality we cannot experience that other reality. In particular, as far as the artist-narrator is concerned, no matter how successfully he may distance himself from everyday reality, verisimilitude is a factor of artistic merit and perfection in his works. The experience of distance is not at all equivalent to coldness, indifference or a nonchalant attitude toward life; it is only an attitude which enables the artist to view life and reveal it from a perspective denied the ordinary person who flounders in the everyday stream of life and is incapable of reaching shore and pausing for even an instant, unless the artist gives him a helping hand. The perspective from which the artist views reality reveals the meaning of life and simultaneously this "second plane" of reality. What then comprises the verisimilitude in Chekhov's works, which are devoted to the life of people of our cultural milieu, people whom he intentionally shows as "lowered," colorless and incompetent? Neither their characters nor their fate would seem to interest us since nothing special, new or significant happens to them. Indeed the majority of Chekhov's works seem to offer us precisely this type of content. I will again mention Tolstoy's remark about Chekhov (as recorded by Sergeenko[4]): "Chekhov is an incomparable *artist ... of life.*" And "the surest sign" of this, Tolstoy considered, was that "one can reread Chekhov several times—with the exclusion of his plays of course, which he had no business tackling." This is quite true, and I think each of us has experienced this personally. The question is, then, why are we so drawn to reread not only "The Steppe," or "In the Ravine," or "The Bishop," or "The Darling," but also "A Boring Story," "Three Years," "Ionych," "Verochka," "The Betrothed," "Ariadne," "The Lady with a Lapdog," "The House with an Attic," "Name-Day," etc.? The magnetic lifelike quality in his works consists in the fact that nothing is expounded or explained in them;

rather, it is *shown*. The psychic element is never isolated from the physical; emotions experienced by a character are concretized, since they are shown together with their associations, which relate to the realm of sensual perception. These emotions are typically shown by hints suggesting these associations, in the manner of Tolstoy, and with the same rigid consistency. It follows, then, that no character is ever delineated as something independent, existing "in and of himself"; he is not defined, but shown—again as in Tolstoy—as he is seen at a given moment and in a given milieu by another person. More accurately stated, he is not seen in and of himself, but as a part of all that is *hic et nunc* given to the viewer. I will not offer examples, since this point is already illustrated by all the excerpts cited above.

In the final analysis, no matter how insignificant Chekhov's characters are, they are in no way nonentities; however similar they may be to one another—this applies especially to the intelligentsia— they are nevertheless individualized, and made to come alive. It is as if they were people resurrected in our minds, people whom we once knew, whose lives had once been a part of our own. We thus identify with the characters—as we do with those of Tolstoy—together with Chekhov, we begin to pity them; we are seized by a sense of anxiety, an agonizing and yet enrapturing experience of life's inexpressible mystery, concealed in all its countless manifestations—so similar to one another and yet unique in their ephemerality and in their apparent uselessness. It is as if we recognize ourselves in these people, who lived somewhere, some place, who rejoiced and grieved; and we sense that what has happened to them could have happened to us as well; and it begins to seem that indeed it has. We are, so to speak, posited within them—precisely because Chekhov shows them vaguely, without underscoring what is singular and unique in every personality; because the episodes in which they appear are the most ordinary and prosaic; and because the narration is limited by the frames of these episodes. We become imbued with an awareness of life's unity, we feel ourselves to be specks in the vortical movement of the universe. At the same time, we are aware that each of these specks is an "I" such as we ourselves are, and has the same right to life and the pursuit of happiness, the same happiness which we ourselves expect in our own lives. Thus we become even more frightened by the thought that so many similar, partial manifestations of all-life have become a part of the past, that so many hopes, expectations, and strivings, have come to nought. This complex experience is already suggested in an early Chekhov story "Another Man's Trouble" ["Chuzhaya beda"][5] (1886). The Kovalevs buy at auction the estate of a ruined landowner. Kovalev's wife finds it difficult to enjoy "another man's trouble," but gives in to her husband's wishes.

> When the Kovalevs moved to the deserted Mikhalkovo, the first thing that Verochka noticed were a few traces left behind by the former occupants: a schedule table of lessons written in a childish hand; a headless doll; a titmouse coming for its customary crumbs; a penciled scribble on the wall: "Natasha is a fool!" and the like. There was much repainting and repapering to be done; there was much to be torn down in order to erase the memory of other people's misfortune.

We find here a striking similarity to Rainer Maria Rilke's "The Notebook of Malte Laurids Brigge." I have in mind a passage in which the author's alter ego speaks of that horror, that anxiety, which seizes him at the sight of a wall of a house that is being torn down, but which still bears the traces of "stubborn life": "It was horrible that *I recognized it. I recognize everything here* [in Paris], and that is why everything immediately becomes part of me." Rilke completes what Chekhov left unsaid, and thereby sheds light on the distinctive dialectic of Chekhov's world view: Chekhov's experience of distance enables him to surmount the bounds which divide the "I" from the "not I"; a humorous attitude towards life makes him "an incomparable artist of life: it is with profound humanity that he treats his superfluous people—in essence all of Chekhov's characters are superfluous—and he refuses to judge them on the basis of their respective usefulness or merit. These qualities enable him to discover that other plane of reality, where nothing is superfluous and where, to use his words (see above), there reigns "quiet and beautiful truth."

To understand the internal make-up of the ideological and artistic quest of each artist—that kernel from which all his art grows—it is often useful to examine examples of his work which provide evidence of experimentation and evolution. These are ordinarily drafts, rough copies. Chekhov, as we have said, has left us almost no material of this type. But some of his completed works may be considered experimental in nature. "The Privy Councillor" is one such example. This story is especially revealing, precisely because it is not a sketch or a rough copy, but a fully finished and artistically irreproachable work. Why it should belong to the category of artistic experimentation will become clear, I hope, from what follows.

The narration is given from a character's point of view as a childhood recollection. There is, therefore, a distance between the storyteller and his former "I"; this determines the densely humorous and ironic coloring of the whole narration, which abounds with elements of caricature. Consider, for example, the description of preparations for the privy councillor's arrival:

> [The tidying of the estate] Only the sky above and the water in the river were spared.... If the sky had been lower and smaller and the river had not flowed so swiftly, they too would have been scoured with pumice stone and rubbed with loofah. [The cat and the dogs are removed.] But *no one* [NB not *"everything"*] was so badly treated as the poor sofas, easy chairs and rugs! Never before had they been so violently beaten as on this occasion, in preparation for the visitor.

Compare this to an episode at the end of the story. The governor has come to visit the uncle, and the uncle asks the narrator's mother to give them "a bite to eat":

> A ferocious slaughter followed. A dozen or so fowl, five turkeys and eight ducks were killed, and in the fluster the old gander, the progenitor of our whole flock of geese and a great favourite of mother's, was beheaded. The coachmen and the cook seemed frenzied, and slaughtered birds at random, without differentiating age or breed.

Nowhere, it seems, not even in his earliest stories, does Chekhov approach this not quite Gogolian, almost Rabelaisian, hyperbole. The entire narration is sustained in this tone. Related to this hyperbole we find in the *syuzhet* a saturation of elements of the vaudeville sketch or the old-fashioned novella. The entire *fabula* is basically an uninterrupted chain of errors, misunderstandings, energy expended in vain, unrealized expectations and sudden disclosures. Furthermore, Chekhov's use of these devices seems designed to approach the limits of caricature. The privy councillor shows an interest in the manager's wife in the presence of her husband, Fedor and the teacher, Pobedimsky, and he asks permission to kiss her hand. Fedor and Pobedimsky create a row, both screaming: "I won't allow it!" and bang their fists on the table. The uncle leaves in confusion, and they all continue screaming and banging their fists. The mother runs in and asks what has happened, why her brother is so disturbed. Having guessed what is going on, she says:

> "I won't have it. No banging on the table!...."
> "Leave off, Fedor! And what are you thumping for, Egor Alekseevich? What have you got to do with it?"

> Pobedimsky was startled and confused. Fedor looked intently at him, then at his wife, and began pacing about the room. When the mother had left the premises, I saw something which long afterwards I still considered a dream. I saw Fedor seize my tutor, lift him up in the air and chuck him out the door.

Fedor's realization that there is something inappropriate in the relationship between his wife and Pobedimsky only *after* the mother's intervention is more than a comic episode; it is also connected, as we shall see, with the general plan of the story. As a rule, all the misunderstandings and errors are focused around the main theme—"main" from the point of view of the narrator's former "I": he had expected a great deal from his uncle, the privy councillor, but none of these expectations materializes.

The Lydian nature of the resolution is boldly emphasized, as in no other Chekhov work, and is exposed through the cyclical nature of the structure. The story begins with the first meeting of the narrator and the uncle. " 'Who's the boy?' asks the uncle upon seeing him." And the story concludes:

> As he said good-bye to Mother he [the uncle] shed tears,... when he got into his carriage his face beamed with childlike pleasure.... Radiant and happy, he made himself comfortable...and all at once he caught sight of me. A look of utmost astonishment came into his face. "Who's the boy?"

At first glance this moment has all the earmarks of extreme improbability and caricature. Indeed, the uncle sees his nephew daily in the course of three weeks. But that is just the point—that he does not notice him, as, apparently, he also does not notice the woman with whom he flirted, as well as all the others:

> Until his very departure he failed to distinguish who among them [Fedor and Pobedimsky] was the tutor, and who was Tatyana Ivanovna's husband, that same Tatyana whom he sometimes called Nastya, Pelageya, and sometimes Evdokiya.

The uncle literally does not recognize his nephew.

From the nephew's point of view, the uncle also remains essentially an unknown quality. The mode of narration reveals this by means of hints. The boy first sees his uncle from the back; nothing is said about how he looks from the front. Their subsequent meetings generally take place in the evening when the boy is fighting sleep, and it is only in this drowsy state that he looks at those around him; during the day he sometimes peeks through the keyhole, to see what his uncle does in his room. The uncle, for his part, "pays no attention whatsoever to him," which distresses the boy.

"The Privy Councillor," like "Gusev" and "The Man in a Case," is an allegory. The interpersonal relationships are essentially shown from the point of view of a naive child. They are based on mutual ignorance, lack of understanding and ineptness, as well as on the absence of any desire to overcome this insensitivity. The distinctive feature of this allegory is that its theme is elaborated by expressions characteristic of the anecdote, novella and vaudeville sketch—that is, expressions Chekhov uses mainly in his comic stories. Moreover, all these expressions are used to their fullest. The theme is concealed in the comedy of the situation and the humorous method of presentation. "The Privy Councillor" may be placed in the category of comic stories. As in Gogol, just this preponderance of humorous and ironic elements intensifies—by virtue of contrast and surprise—the impression of other moods which occasionally surface, especially at the story's end. The row with Fedor is only the last straw, which exhausts the uncle's patience. He usually goes abroad in the summer, and only the lack of funds makes him decide to spend this summer at his sister's. But "he does not like [the sister's] cooking" and she shocks him: she does not extend her hand when greeting the governor! Their relationship cannot be mended, and the sister offers him money to go abroad, which satisfies him completely. The uncle fully reveals himself, so to speak, when he asks in parting: "Who's the boy?"

> The question jarred my mother terribly, for she had assured me that God had sent uncle to us to make me happy. I wasn't in the mood for questions. I looked at my uncle's *happy* face, and *for some reason I felt terribly sorry for him.* I couldn't restrain myself; I jumped into the carriage and fervently embraced this man, so scatter-brained and weak, *like all people.* As I looked into his eyes, I wanted to say something pleasant, so I asked: "Uncle, have you ever been to war?"

Here we find a strengthening of the cyclical structure: once he has found out that his uncle is a privy councillor, the boy imagines him to be "a general, a gentleman with epaulettes, with an embroidered collar that sticks up to his very ears and with a drawn sword in his hand." Having asked his uncle a question, he clearly strives not only "to say something pleasant" to him, but also to attain, in some measure, the realization of his dreams.

I have deliberately postponed a discusssion of this story until the end of my study, because only in light of what has been said above does it become clear that the story is a kind of experiment which Chekhov performed on almost all the components of his art, so varied in their origin and properties. This experiment consists in using these components with maximum boldness, yet, at the same time, fusing them into a single whole, into an expression of the dominant idea. There is not, nor could there be, anything in common between this boy, who is very much like Egorushka in "The Steppe," and the old man who, like most Chekhov heroes (as can be seen from the uncle's short confession to his sister), has let the opportunity to participate in worldly happiness slip by. Now he grasps at whatever comes first, which, according to his words, is "natural" and "vital"; yet when this slips away from him, he immediately forgets about it. Who precisely this privy councillor is, what he writes all the time, we do not know; moreover, we do not need to know. He too is *everyman.* Therefore, he can be best shown as the boy sees him—at a distance, which separates them from one another. But the boy's contact with his uncle was, at that time in his life, a tragic experience. The story, however, is told by the narrator at a time when these experiences have already receded into the distant past. That which was experienced tragically is recast into a comic mode, so as to create a "double distance," as in fact it should be. *Everyman* is pitiful and, at the same time, comic, as is everyday life generally, with its repetition of one and the same phenomenon, that "negative infinity," which forces one to postulate the existence of another plane of reality.

Footnotes to Chapter Ten

1. "If you are politically reliable, then this is enough to be a fully satisfied citizen; the same applies to liberals: it is enough to be unreliable, and all the rest will somehow be unnoticed" (*Zapisnye knizhki*, 84). A "world view" thus understood aroused revulsion in Chekhov. Like all creative personalities, Chekhov was an individualist: "I am afraid of those who look for a tendency between the lines, and who would regard me either as a liberal or as a conservative. I am not a liberal, not a conservative, not a believer in gradual progress, not a monk, not an indifferentist. I should like to be a free artist and nothing more.... My holy of holies is the human body, health, intelligence, talent, inspiration, love and the most absolute freedom— freedom from violence and lying, whatever forms they may take" (To Pleshcheev, Oct. 4, 1888).

2. See I.A. Bunin's remarkable book *Osvobozhdenie Tolstogo,* Paris, 1937,—the most profound book ever written about Tolstoy.

3. His letters are especially revealing in this connection. Many of them were addressed to people to whom he was very close, and doubtless quite candid. But these letters, as well as all the others, are nonetheless written in a humorous or ironic tone. It is as if Chekhov were afraid to speak seriously of what interested and absorbed him, as if he were trying to give the impression that, for example, his artistic work was something petty, insignificant. Generally whatever he touches upon he "lowers." He speaks in the same tone, for example, in letters to his wife which concern their personal relationship. This does not produce an insincere or cold impression, however; his letters convey the same spiritual warmth as his artistic works.

4. *Tolstoi i ego sovremenniki,* 1911, 226.

5. It was not included in his *Collected Works* during his lifetime.

Chapter Eleven

"The Kiss"

The internal necessity which determined the peculiarities of Chekhov's art (his achievements as well as his errors) and the connection between his themes and his means of expression—from the period of his quests, his "exercises," until the moment when he finally found himself—become clear, I think, in the light of everything that has been examined. In conclusion, I will dwell on one other example which, it seems to me, testifies to this with special cogency. We mentioned earlier the story "The Kiss." Among works of Chekhov's mature period, "The Kiss" is, in certain respects, an extreme case of a story based on a reworking of the comic *syuzhet* theme. We find here a similarity to old literary models not only in the *fabula* base, but in the *fabula* itself; moreover, it is significant that this *fabula* is characteristic of works which belong to an early epoch in the history of European literature—to the times of the *Decameron,* and the *facetiae* of the Italian, English and Spanish Renaissance theater. The motif *quid pro quo* is taken here in its primitive, bare form; darkness causes one of the characters to mistake another person for his, or her lover, and he unmasks himself accordingly. In old-fashioned novels or comedies this motif provided the conflict of the *fabula* in as much as it precipitated various scandals, complicated the lovers' relationship and caused the chance appearance of an outsider. Chekhov's originality is that he goes no further than the initial statement of this conflict. What we subsequently see is nothing more than that the victim of the error experiences a psychic shock caused by the unknown woman's mistake. The "recognito," obligatory in such situations in older literature, is absent.[1] The "zero" character of the resolution, inasmuch as it relates to an internal process (what is happening in Ryabovich's soul), is emphasized in the unfolding of the *fabula*. For a long time Ryabovich hopes for the realization of something, of which the kiss was its guarantee; he is drawn to the estate of von-Rabbek, where this misunderstanding occurred. When the opportunity presents itself for his return to the place where he saw glimpses of a promise for some unknown happiness, he experiences something similar to a Heraclitian truth. Having long waited in vain for a second invitation, he returns to the estate—but does not see or hear anything—and leaves:

> He went down to the river.... He looked down into the water.... The river ran rapidly.... The red moon was reflected near the left bank; little ripples ran over the reflection, stretching it out, breaking it into bits, and, it seemed, *tried to carry it away.*
> "How stupid, how stupid," thought Ryabovich, looking at the *running water.* "How unintelligent it all is!"
> Now that he expected nothing, the incident of the kiss, his impatience, his vague hopes and disappointment, presented themselves in a clear light. It no longer seemed strange to him that he had not seen the general's messenger, and that he would never see the girl who had accidentally kissed him instead of someone else; on the contrary, it would have been strange if he had seen her....
>
> *The water was running, he knew not where or why.* It ran just as it had in May. In May it had flowed from the stream into the great river, from the river into the sea, then it had risen in a vapor, turned into rain, and perhaps the very same water was running now before Ryabovich's eyes again.... What for? Why?[2]

True, the Heraclitian image is interpreted as if in disagreement with the Grecian sage: "the very same" water. The accent here is on the contradiction between the "eternal return" in nature and the irreversibility, the irretrievability of what happens in man's life. But the heart of the matter lies precisely in the discovery of this last truth—which is Heraclitian to its very core. Having returned to his lodgings for the night, Ryabovich learns that what he had waited for has come true: the officers have received an invitation to von-Rabbek's home. But it is already too late:

174

For an instant there was a flash of joy in Ryabovich's breast, but he quenched it at once, got into bed, and in vexation at his fate, as though to spite it, he did not go to the general's.

Here Chekhov, like Gogol, uses the comic *syuzhet* base in its purest form and deepens its meaning to realize the hidden possibilities it contains. Incidentally, Gogol's influence on "The Kiss" is not limited to this moment. In an earlier scene at von-Rabbek's, Ryabovich surveys the women sitting with him at dinner and tries to guess who among them had kissed him. But none conforms to the ideal "beauty" that this woman ought to have been.

"It's difficult to guess," he thought, musing. "If one takes only the shoulders and arms of the lilac one, adds the temples of the fair one and the eyes of the one on the left of Lobytko, then...."
He combined these things in his mind and so formed the image of the girl who had kissed him....

Clearly Ryabovich follows Agafya Tikhonovna's line of reasoning in *The Marriage:*

If only Nikanor Ivanovich's lips could be fitted to Ivan Kuzmich's nose, and if one could take some of Baltazar Baltazarovich's easy manners and add perhaps Ivan Pavlovich's sturdiness—then I could decide at once.

The hero of "The Kiss" also has a bit of Akaky Akakievich about him: an awareness of his insignificance and mediocrity:

While some of his comrades assumed a serious expression, and others wore forced smiles, his face, his lynx-like whiskers, and glasses seemed to say: "I am the shyest, most modest and most undistinguished officer in the whole brigade!"

Precisely such people are destined to find their goal in life in the objects of their daydreams.

A work of recent literature offers a striking analogy to "The Kiss." This is the novel *Le grand Meaulnes* by Alain-Fournier. Here, as well, the conflict is structured on a similar elaboration of the "error" motif. The hero of the novel, having lost his way at night,

175

happens upon an estate where a masquerade ball is in progress. He manages to change from his school uniform into a ballroom costume which had been discarded in the dark, and is taken for an invited guest. He meets a young girl, becomes enraptured by her and tells her so. She reveals her identity to him; her name is Yvonne de Galais, the daughter of the owner of the estate. On the way back to school he is unable to make out the road that had led to the estate. From that time on, he is preoccupied with but one thought: to find the mysterious castle and to see once again the girl with whom he has fallen in love.

I note only those elements of the conflict which reveal a similarity in *syuzhet* in the two works. With regard to other aspects of these works, we should note the following: in distinction to Chekhov, Alain-Fournier employs a variety of devices which complicate the "weaving" of events; moreover, all these devices are borrowed from an older literature—from the adventure novel, the drama of the time of Calderón, Lope de Vega and Shakespeare: a change of clothes, a search for a beloved women or lost friends, a tragic end to a relationship, "recognitions," changing "roles," etc. The complex weaving of life's threads into one knot is commensurate with the complexity of the resolution: for some it is a happy ending, for others a catastrophe.

It is striking that as far as the sad aspect of the resolution is concerned, Alain-Fournier's novel is closer in its *syuzhet* to "An Anonymous Story," than its beginning is to "The Kiss." Both in Fournier and in Chekhov a change of roles occurs at the end: the confidant is almost transformed into "the first lover"; Fournier's heroine dies in childbirth, whereas Chekhov's heroine poisons herself during childbirth. In both stories, the child, a baby girl, remains with the confidant, the one thing which binds the latter to life. But this is not meant to last: in Fournier the child must be returned to the father, who has been found; in Chekhov, the hero, foreseeing his own imminent death, asks the father to take back the child.

How can these coincidences be explained? True, in older novels, instances of the "friend" who finds the child's parents are not infrequent; but the development of this theme in Chekhov and in Fournier shows a considerable departure—and it is precisely this that is important—from the theme's traditional treatment. I have not been able to establish whether Fournier was familiar with Chekhov. His marvelous correspondence with Jacques Rivière attests how profoundly affected they both were by Russian culture, but Chekhov's name is not specifically mentioned. Be that as it may, with regard to the subject of the present work, I must dwell on the following point: Fournier's novel in its outer form is fully "contemporary" with the works of the XVI-XVII centuries. It contains the most diverse variations of the themes of *quid pro quo* characteristic of that era and is more polished than Chekhov's "An Anonymous Story": we do not notice even a hint of stylization or imitation. In it Fournier achieved what Chekhov achieved when he gave new meaning to and transposed onto another plane the motif of "misunderstanding," reversal of anticipation and the like.

Wherein lies the secret of the fascination with this work, which stands formally by itself in recent literature? The secret is that Fournier was able to observe utmost consistency in working out his archaic theme. In contrast to the Chekhov of "An Anonymous Story," but in complete accord with Chekhov, the author of "Gusev," Fournier did not individualize his characters. Each one of them is *everyman* and they all resemble one another, inasmuch as they are characterized by one common feature—a youthful striving for something, a striving for an unattainable happiness, for themselves and those close to them. Moreover they are characterized by a conviction purchased at the price of failure and misfortune; what was once allowed to escape cannot be returned, what had been will not be again, everything melts and recedes into the past. This is why they replace each other so easily, and change their appearance; in this manner the motif *quid pro quo* acquires its profound meaning and the outer form is fully and perfectly suited to the inner form.

The human personality is a monad, unique and unrepeatable, but its uniqueness is apparent only to itself. In the plane of human intercourse its uniqueness almost never plays any role; at its extreme, the realm of intercourse of pure souls is *civitas Dei,* and not *civitas terrena.* This is also the reason why as soon as man begins to ponder the problem of his own "I," he is horrified by the awareness of his own loneliness.

All these themes—the themes of the replaceability of one personality by another, hence also the theme of superfluity of each separate personality and the related theme of life's fragility and instability, the retreating of the past, the theme of loneliness—all of these especially "human themes"—permeate Fournier's novel. It is not surprising, therefore, how purely Chekhovian some of the passages in *Le grand Meaulnes* sound—for example, the episode of the hero's departure from the Galais estate. A party given in honor of François de Galais' engagement is interrupted when it becomes known that his fiancee has run away from him.

> Il passa près du vivier où le matin même il s'était miré. Comme tout paraissait changé déja.... [and further on, the moment of departure]: Sous les fenêtres, dans la cour aux voitures, un remue-ménage avait commencé.... De temps en temps un homme grimpait sur le siège d'une charrette, sur la bâche d'une grande carriole et faisait tourner sa lanterne. La lueur du falot venait frapper la fenêtre: un instant, autour de Meaulnes, la chambre maintenant familière, où toutes choses avalent été pour lui si amicales, palpitait, revivait.... Et c'est ainsi qu'il quitta, refermant soigneusement la porte, ce mystérieux endroit qi'il ne devait sans doute jamais revoir.

When he reaches the road leading to the school, the hero leaves the carriage, which has brought him.

> Vacillant comme un homme ivre, le grand garçon...s'en alla lentement sur le chemin de Sainte-Agathe, tandis que, dernier vestige de la fête mysterieuse, la vieille berline quittait le gravier de la route et s'eloignait, cahotant en silence.... On ne voyait plus que le chapeau du conducteur, dansant au-dessus des clôtures....

Meaulnes moves from school, where he lived with the narrator, François Seurel, to Paris. The parting. François' mother tidies up the dining room where they had just been together.

> Quant à moi, je me trouvai, pour je premiêre fois depuis de longs mois, seul en face d'une longue soirée de jeudi—avec l'impression que, dans cette vieille voiture, mon adolescence venait de s'en aller pour toujours.

But soon the recent past becomes the distant past. Languishing in loneliness without his friend, François befriends schoolmates, whom Meaulnes and he had earlier disliked.

Le cours de ma vie a changé tout d'un coup. Il me semble que Meaulnes est parti depuis très long temps et que son aventure est une vieille histoire triste, mais finie.

There is an inner necessity which determines the "weaving" of fates of Augustin Meaulnes, Yvonne de Galais, her brother, his betrothed and François Seurel; this "weaving" begins with a conflict similar to the incident narrated in Chekhov's "The Kiss" and leads to a Chekhovian resolution. It is characteristic for the man, from whom everything slips away and who is always alone, to attach himself, finally, to a child. Indeed, a child is a being, in whom—in the words of the "anonymous man"—he finds what he needs:

> I loved the child madly. In her I saw the continuation of my life, and it wasn't just that it seemed so, but I felt that when I would finally cast off my long, bony, bearded frame, I would go on living in those little blue eyes, that silky flaxen hair, those dimpled pink hands which so lovingly stroked my face and were clasped around my neck.

In its boldly provocative and consistent use of seemingly outdated literary genres, Fournier's work sheds light on still another aspect of Chekhov's art, and clarifies the function of yet another of Chekhov's constants. The theme expressed in the ending of "An Anonymous Story" is not an isolated example in Chekhov. The image of an orphan child, in whose love man seeks his spiritual solace, appears in several other stories: the child Katya who is taken in by the professor's family after her father's death, and is dearer to the professor than anyone in his family ("A Boring Story"); the daughter of Poloznev's sister (who dies in childbirth) becomes the sole being precious to him after his wife leaves him ("My Life"). In "Three Years," similar relationships appear in a more subdued manner (Laptev, who has grown cold towards his wife, becomes attached to his dead sister's children, abandoned by their father). This theme already appears in a marvelous story of the transitional period (1886), "Day in the Country" ["Den' za gorodom"] (which Chekhov for some reason did not include in his *Collected Works*[3]), which describes a friendship between the old shoemaker Terenty and the two poor orphans, the six-year old Fekla and her brother Danilka:

Terenty bends down to Fekla, and a smile spreads on his grim, drunken face, found only in those who see before themselves something little, foolish and absurd, but dearly loved.

Compare that passage to the ending when the children fall asleep in a deserted barn:

And Terenty comes to them at night, makes a sign of the cross over them and puts bread under their heads. And no one sees his love. It is seen only by the moon which floats in the sky and glances caressingly through the chinks in the wall of the deserted barn.

I do not, I repeat, have data available to explain the coincidences in Fournier and Chekhov; the latter's influence on Fournier could be direct, or, what is more likely, by virtue of their spiritual affinity, they turned to similar models and made similar artistic discoveries. In any case, it is important to state that Fournier in one work has combined in a single whole what we find scattered in different works of Chekhov. Moving from a conflict similar to the conflict in "The Kiss," Fournier arrives at the resolution of "An Anonymous Story" and in such a manner, moreover, that we sense the inner necessity of his resolution, as if it were already given in the conflict. Fournier's unconscious experiment with Chekhov's works confirms what we said earlier about the presence of immanent fate in the history of Chekhov's art. All his works, both the successful and the unsuccessful, are "moments" of one internally inevitable process and consequently all other such moments are potentially stored in each of them—with the exception, of course, of a number of feuilletons written for *Fragments* and *The Dragon Fly,* which could have been written by any other feuilletonist and which are significant to the history of Chekhov's art only as exercises, intended to help Chekhov find his own artistic path.

The more significant the artistic personality, the more immanent is its *fatum;* the more vivid its singularity—its "monadic character"—the more profound is its connection with its time and spirit. Here we can isolate the value of individuality, because it experiences itself in relation to the whole. Therefore, the creative genius creates history as much as he is created by it.

The average man slavishly submits to a multitude of

conventions of his age and his surroundings, to tastes, ideologies, party programs and so on; however, the man who stands above his epoch and, as it were, outside it, is imbued with what is concealed in all its external phenomena, themselves often merely coarse distortions of the spirit of the age. His battle with the present—and this is the root of any art—is essentially nothing more than the search for a more perfect expression of the essence of its spiritual tendencies, which amounts to its *pathos*. Thus at the same time that we can identify the inner necessity in Chekhov's art, we must also consider that he was a man of the nineteenth century. No other age was so permeated with the spirit of historicism, with the experience of *real time;* it found expression in the philosophy of Schopenhauer and Bergson and in music, a "time art," just then becoming the leading, fundamental art, to which all other arts gravitated. As we know, Tolstoy, the greatest nineteenth-century writer of "real" life, was quite taken with the teachings of Schopenhauer; moreover, all of Bergson's philosophy is contained *in nuce* in his discourses on the historical process scattered throughout *War and Peace.* Chekhov goes further than Tolstoy here. The latter is still unable to part with the idea of a tragic or happy resolution of the life process, whereas in Chekhov we have seen that the concept of a resolution—completion, attainment of a goal—simply does not exist.

Here Chekhov comes close in spirit to a writer in whose art we find an expression of the ultimate conclusions of an idea basic to the nineteenth century, a writer "in search (by necessity so futile!) of time lost." We noted above certain similarities between Chekhov and Proust; at first sight, perhaps, they seem insignificant, but in fact they are far from incidental. These coincidences are all the more characteristic since generally they are so far apart from one another. Indeed, what is the basis—not for Proust's worldview in the accepted sense of the word—but for his life experience? The idea of ceaseless becoming. What has been realized, what has become, by virtue of this alone, is no longer the same as what was expected, and not at all because it was realized in some other way than was expected, but because having "become"—at the moment of its realization—it has already moved into the past. True, Chekhov does not go quite this far. It is characteristic of his works that understanding already contains the potential of its own disillusionment, because it either has been realized contrary to one's

181

expectations, or it has come too late; understanding comes at a time when the person who awaited this realization is no longer the same as he was. However, we have seen how intensely Chekhov's attention was directed to what attracted Proust—namely, to the ceaselessness of the life process, and if it may be so expressed, to the unreality of the present.

Besides Proust we ought to mention one other prominent novelist of the same period who has much in common with Chekhov: Thomas Mann. The widespread use of recurring image-symbols (*leitmotifs*[4] as Mann himself called them) is especially characteristic for Mann as well as for Chekhov; in Mann, according to his own words, they perform a musical function (his art was mainly influenced by Schopenhauer and Wagner): the repetition of one and the same images, and the repeated mention of distinguishing, yet trivial features of his characters in different contexts and in different combinations strengthens the general impression—the impression of "that same thing" which, in fact, never is "the same thing." Mann wrote a novella, *Enttaüschung*—actually it is not a novella, but a monologue about an eccentric whom the narrator meets in Venice—which begins with a question he addresses to the latter: is it not true that all that they see here is not what they expected? That is how everything in life is. It is all a continuous chain of disillusionment and disappointment. Essentially this is the basic theme of Mann's major work, *Buddenbrooks*, with its subtitle, *Verfall eines Familie*. The representatives of this family belong to the city patriarchy; for a number of generations they have had but one concern—their prosperity and prestige. And it all ends in "nothing"; the Buddenbrook clan gradually degenerates, falls apart and dies out.

Having begun with an attempt to comprehend the uniqueness of Chekhov's art, we have arrived, *nolens volens,* at a definition of his role in history—not his place in the history of literature, but his place in history as a whole. Chekhov is one of the most brilliant spokesmen for the spiritual values of his age and, thereby, like all great artists, he belongs to eternity because each "eon" reveals in itself everything that was hidden in all those moments that preceded it and conceals in itself everything that is destined to be revealed in those that follow. That is why not only Rilke, Proust, Alain-Fournier and Thomas Mann "echo" Chekhov, but also why Chekhov himself so often "echos" the classical sage.

182

Footnotes to Chapter Eleven

1. Compare the difference between the resolution on the motif of "recognito" in "The Kiss" and in Chekhov's comic stories: "The Mask" ["Maska"], "In the Steam Bath," and "At the Barber's," ["V tsiryul'ne].

2. Again, we must turn to Turgenev; he, as well, has a similar "Heraclitian" symbol: "Two, three... and then six years passed.... Life had retreated, flowed by..., and I only watched as it flowed by. So in childhood you would build a little pond on the bank of a river and put up a dam and try in every way to prevent the water from getting it wet and breaking it up. But it finally breaks and you give up trying and gaily begin to watch as everything you've piled up runs away to the last drop ("The Unhappy Girl") ["Neschastnaya"].

3. It is included in the posthumous edition of Marks, 1911. XXI.

4. See H.A. Peter, *Thomas Mann und seine epische Charakterisie rungskunst,* Bern 1929, (in the series *Sprache und Dichtung),* for a detailed study of the genesis and fundamentals of Mann's art. It contains, incidentally, an exhaustive analysis of his image-symbols.

Appendix to Page 53

To understand the fate of the two lexemes *otvechat'/otvetit'*, "to answer," it is essential to keep in mind that forms of the verbal "aspects"[1] have only gradually supplanted tense forms in the Russian language, and to this day they have not yet completely stabilized. Even now some lexemes are used with both perfective and imperfective meanings, for instance "to bequeath," *zaveshchat'*[2] and "to glean" or "draw," *pocherpat'*. In this regard, insufficient differentiation of verbal morphemes causes the presence of a number of homonymous lexemes: for example, *provodit'*, meaning *conduire* in the perfective and *tracer* in the imperfective; *pokhodit'* meaning *faire quelques pas* in the perfective and "to be like" in the imperfective. Hence, the persistence of *otvechat'* and *otvetit'* in undifferentiated aspectual meanings in the works of all Russian writers, with the exception of Chekhov, from the time the latter form became legitimate in the literary language. For example:

[In Dostoevsky]: "Because he is a scoundrel," she answered [*otvetila*] me strangely." And: "I don't care," she answered [*otvechala*] quietly and calmly. *(The Gambler) [Igrok]*

[In Sleptsov]: "I won't," answered [*otvechala*] the lady of the house. *(The Foster Child)* [Pitomka]

[In Pomyalovsky]: "There's no change at all," she answered [*otvechala*]. But: "Why are you bored?" "I don't know," answered [*otvetila*] Lenochka. *(Bourgeois Happiness)*

[In Herzen]: "You will see," answered [*otvechal*] the policeman cleverly and civily. But: "Yes, sir, I am entering into matrimony," he answered [*otvechal*] shyly. *(My Past and Thoughts) [Byloe i dumy]*

184

[In Mamin-Sibiryak]: "Oh, no, I've had a marvelous sleep," answered [*otvetil*] Egor Fomich casually. But: "Yes, I saw, sir . . ." the old man answered [*otvechal*] meekly. *(The Soldiers)* [*Boitsy*]

[In Garshin]: "He has left me, he has gone," I answered [*otvetil*] in a voice full of desperation. But: "Second cousin," I answered [*otvechal*]. *(Nadezhda Nikolaevna)*

To illustrate how widespread this tendency is I have deliberately chosen examples from writers of diverse social strata and varying artistic merit. True, one might note another tendency as well—towards a distinction in semantic nuances of both lexemes. Thus, Gorbunov, a writer keenly aware of language, apparently uses *otvetit'* to indicate a brief, decisive utterance, whereas *otvechat'* indicates an utterance of more prolonged duration:

"Don't judge," she answered [*otvetila*]. . . . *(The Fisherman)* [*Rybolov*] "Yes, the lady is ashamed of me!" answered [*otvetil*] Burges curtly. *(Jean Burges)*

Compare:

"Son, are you a clever person or not?" began . . . the keeper of the archives. "Whatever you want me to do, I shall," answered [*otvechal*] the son meekly. *(Elizaveta Petrovna)*

Even Gorbunov, however, is not always consistent:

"Can you understand what words will be sung tomorrow?" "You understand a lot," answered [*otvechala*] the cook. *(Jean Burges)*

One does not find here an obvious motivation for the use of *otvechat'* rather than *otvetit'*.

In contexts which are structurally identical to those above, Leskov, an equally fine master in the various "elements" of the spoken language, generally uses *otvechat'*; he uses *otvetit'* where the lexeme designating the act of answering does not follow the answer itself:

"Is this your basket?" "No," answered [*otvechal*] the nihilist. *(Journey with a Nihilist)* "What are these things here?" "I don't know,"

185

answered [*otvechal*] the nihilist. *(Ibid.)* "I haven't met you for some time. . . . " "There's no place to meet," he answered [*otvechal*]. *(The Spirit of Madame Genlis)* [*Dukh g-zhi Zhanlis*]

Compare:

The nihilist looked at him and didn't answer [*otvetil*]. *(Journey with a Nihilist)* I answered [*otvetil*] that I had already seen his wheat. *(Choice Grain)* [Otbornoe zerno]

But this only demonstrates that for Leskov, as well, semantic nuances between *otvechat'* and *otvetit'* did not exist. For him both lexemes were conventionally used signs, one in one contextual category, the other in another, their use distinguished only with respect to structure rather than in an emotional or semantic sense.

The persistence of the tendency not to distinguish both lexemes, their propensity to complete synonymity, is revealed in the fact that even today they are used in the same non-individualized meaning. We find this, for example, in the work of the prose master, V. Sirin:

"Have you ever been there?" "I guess not," answered [*otvetil*] Rodrig Ivanovich. *(Invitation to a Beheading)*

But:

"What are these hopes, and who is this savior?" "The imagination," answered [*otvechal*] Cincinnatus. *(Ibid.)*

Chekhov's reform, however, did not pass unnoticed. Among his closest contemporaries, the prose writers who were influenced by him—Gorky, Kuprin, and Bunin—accepted it unconditionally. Gorky always used *otvetit'* in its non-iterative meaning, and restricted *otvechat'* to iterative actions. For example: " 'Perhaps you are not well. Pavlusha,' she would sometimes ask him. 'No, I am well,' he would answer [*otvechal*]" *(Mother)* [*Mat*]. In Bunin *otvetit'* generally speaking superceded *otvechat'*. Moreover in Bunin and in Chekhov as well, we find yet another tendency: in the large majority of cases *otvetit'* appears with a descriptive modifier—how an answer was made. Without such a modifier it is less frequently used, and in this latter case it is replaced by the more neutral *skazat'*, or it is simply omitted. The same applies to Kuprin.

Footnotes to Appendix

1. "At that time," observes V. Vinogradov about language in the eighteenth century, "just as in high styles of the Slavic language, bookish-archaic forms of the past tense were being cultivated, ... but aspectual categories were only dimly sensed in the artificial differentiation of quantitative nuances of different forms of time; the living, spoken language already clearly distinguished verbal aspects (perfective and imperfective) and these differed not only quantitatively, but qualitatively. And aspectual differentiation compensated for loss of earlier diversity of tense forms." *Ocherki po istorii russkogo literaturnogo iazyka XVII-XIX VV.*, 1938, 66.

2. See *Slovar' russkogo iazyka, Akademii nauk,* 1907, s.v.

INDEX OF CHEKHOV'S WORKS

191

INDEX OF PERSONAL NAMES